Enterprise Networking

Working Together Apart

Ray Grenier

George Metes

Digital Press

9 8 7 6 5 4 3 2 1

Printed in the United States of America.

Order number EY-H878E-DP

The Digital logo is a trademark of Digital Equipment Corporation.

Text design: Janis Owens
Production coordination: Nancy Benjamin
Illustrations: Publication Services, Inc.
Composition: Modern Graphics, Inc.
Printer: The Maple Vail Book Manufacturing Group

Library of Congress Cataloging-in-Publication Data

Grenier, Ray.
  Enterprise networking : working together apart / Ray Grenier, George Metes.
    p.   cm.
  Includes bibliographical references and index.
  ISBN 1–55558–074–2
  1. Communication in management.   2. Information networks.   3. Organizational effectiveness.   I. Metes, George.   II. Title.
HD30.3.G76   1992
658.4'5—dc20   91–23160
                                                           CIP

Contents

Preface

In recent years we have witnessed unparalleled innovations in work processes and organizational forms. Here and there we've seen glimmers of a new structure that reveals the combined value of many of these innovations. This book is an expression of that structure and value—the description of a new holistic work environment that responds to the realities of today's business challenges, technologies, and work attitudes. We call this *enterprise networking*, based on the capabilities inherent in the availability and use of electronic information.

We all know that electronic information has become central to most of our work. But the commitment to open access to networked information as the architectural foundation for value-generating work is new, although we already have evidence that suggests its exciting and dramatic possibilities.

For example, on June 22, 1990, a team of engineers from Northrop and McDonnell Douglas rolled out the prototype of the YF-23 Advanced Tactical Fighter, the result of state-of-the-art aircraft design and manufacturing technologies. This event was made possible by the innovative use of an integrated computer data base that linked the two collaborating partners, their key suppliers, and their customer—the U.S. Air Force. This interactive network connected all elements of the development process, including engineering, tooling, manufacturing, quality assurance, and logistical support. (1)

What interests us most in this effort is the underlying work process, the use of electronic information, high-performance networks and networking techniques, and the cultural adaptations that allowed independent, often competitive, entities to form distributed teams focused on common goals.

This is not an isolated case. Other innovators are rapidly setting the pace toward higher levels of capability, putting themselves and their organizations ahead of the pack.

In this book we argue for the *capability-based environment* (CBE), an appropriate organizing principle for work today. Here teams of knowledge workers use enterprise networking to reduce the time it takes to produce value-generating output, while simultaneously increasing the long-term work capabilities of the organization. Such an organization learns as it works, and builds knowledge in products and processes that continually increase to address exponential growth in work complexity.

We address ourselves to the "work mechanics" of the world: individuals who design work and provide direct or indirect value to the organization's products at every level, from the CEO to the last worker in the distribution chain. Product and organizational designers, information systems and network professionals, human resources representatives, manufacturing planners, and service delivery experts can all be work mechanics.

We differentiate work mechanics from organizational straphangers—those individuals who fill organizational slots, maybe even work long and hard hours, but don't contribute to the organization's process or progress. Work mechanics are skilled in using tools; in innovating and implementing plans, strategies, and designs; and in evolving and maintaining work processes. They are committed to the advancement and well-being of their colleagues, their organization, and their enterprise. Information is both their raw material and primary instrument: just as airplane mechanics learn to use their tools, so must information work mechanics learn to use all the available tools and resources.

Work mechanics have direct responsibility for productive input to the value-added chain, that continuum of work activities that results in the success of the organization's product in the marketplace. *Product* here is broadly defined to include all valued output along the entire chain, from the first refinement of materials—be they stone, steel, or information—to the final output of the organization or enterprise.

A final note on style. We believe that literary fiction contains as much illustrative truth as does the alleged reality we get from headlines and airwaves. We look at fiction as a way of emphasizing truth and will occasionally tap parable and fable, as well as industry observation, to make points. We echo the words of Chief Broom, the narrator in Ken Kesey's *One Flew Over the Cuckoo's Nest:*

All this is true, even if it never happened. (2)

Another device we use early on, with some degree of risk, is to set up a foundation of assumptions. These are facts and expectations that have become manifest either through general experience, scholarly investigation, or, in some cases, personal belief. For example, we're not setting out to prove that networks—technologies whose primary function is to transport information—exist. They are here and growing. We accept that as fact and turn our energies to focus on how *work* relates to networks. You must decide for yourselves if these work models are appropriate. Having recognized the opportunity, many organizations already are making the transition to the new model. With many of the people, technologies, and techniques already in place, work mechanics in these organizations may be encouraged as they see their early efforts reflected here.

We'll offer how-to guidance as much as possible. For example, we've included a chapter (Chapter 14) to help you determine where your organization is on the spectrum of enterprise networking, and how you can design your own work processes along the principles of the enterprise networking paradigm.

Reading this book will not qualify a work mechanic to assume the responsibilities of a network manager or a design engineering manager. But we hope to develop a clear vision, introduce a common language, and leave a well-marked trail for individuals, regardless of their position in the organization, to follow. And we do urge you to get started. The train has left the station, and it's building up speed.

Acknowledgments

Writing this book has been a collaborative, distributed, and, on occasion, simultaneous effort: an extended authorship supported by many interested parties before, during, and after the authors actually put words to paper. The limitations of memory and space prevent us from thanking individually all those who have helped us create, formulate, and express the ideas and experiences that form the basis of this book. But we do wish to acknowledge here some partners-in-mind who taught and learned with us over the past few years in offices, airplanes, and factories; through orderly and chaotic seminars; via paper, electronic correspondence, books, napkin-sketches, and software. Experience inspired us to write *Enterprise Networking*. We have had the opportunity to work with such visionaries as Doug Engelbart, who, over the years, has never flagged in his efforts to demonstrate the value of "action learning" in the evolution of distributed knowledge working capabilities. With John Dutton, Dave Carter, and Tom Rochow at McDonnell Douglas Corporation we learned about distributed work initiatives; Dave and Tom also provided us with valuable perspectives in their careful reviews of the manuscript.

Special thanks is due our management, whose commitment and support allowed us to get the job done: Bill Johnson and Bob Murray sponsored the book and gave us a home while we wrote it. Dawn Rohrbacher managed the authoring process and us, keeping our eye on what had to be done, not what was finished. For helping us plan the book, then editing the earliest drafts, we thank Rajini Srikanth.

Our Digital champions have been Ulf Fagerquist, Scott Huchingson, and Dick Davies, who continue to widen the circle of what we know (and what we know we don't know) about today's exciting new organizational processes and potential. Other longtime supporters include Jeffrey Stamps and Jessica Lipnack of the Networking Institute; and Skip Walter, Charles Savage, and David Stone.

Providing honest, sometimes painful, sometimes exhilarating review guidance were Rod Sutherland, Cliff Clarke, Jim Trant, Bill Johnson, David Stone, John McNamara, C. W. Goldsmith, Joan Mokray, Joe Leben, and Russ Johnston.

We are grateful to Ed Schein for framing the objective of the book in his foreword. And we thank the folks at Digital Press: Mike Meehan, executive editor; Jan Svendsen, project coordinator; Chase Duffy, production manager. In addition, we acknowledge the patience of Nancy Benjamin, who managed the book through production. Also, we appreciate the gracious support given to us by staffs of the Digital Libraries and the Baker Libraries at Dartmouth College. We also thank our readers, and hope that *Enterprise Networking* will inspire ideas that will help you understand and anticipate "work that works" in the coming decade.

NOTES

1. Thomas J. Rohan, "Designer/Builder Teamwork Pays Off," *Industry Week* (October 7, 1989): 45–46. See also William B. Scott, "YF-23A Previews Design Features of Future Fighters," *Aviation Week & Space Technology* (July 2, 1990): 16–21.
2. Ken Kesey, *One Flew Over the Cuckoo's Nest* (New York: Penguin, 1976), p. 8.

Ray Grenier
George Metes

Foreword

Readers will find this a remarkable book. It juxtaposes and largely integrates a number of issues that have plagued organizations throughout history and that have been treated separately to the dismay of managers whose life must be more integrated in running a business.

For example, most of the models of the introduction of Information Technology into organizations pay lipservice to the need for truly "sociotechnical" systems, but then proceed to work either on technology or on people. This book makes a genuine effort to give the reader full information both on the technological issues involved in utilizing IT and the cultural, social, and psychological issues involved in using IT to improve the capability of organizations.

Another polarity typically found in books like these is the theory vs. practical action orientation. This book does a fine job of illustrating the theoretical issue and then showing with many practical examples and cases how things can work, do work, and should work. In many ways, the book thereby shows managers how to make their organizations more capable. Making organizations more capable is a central theme and very relevant in these times of rapid and turbulent change. One of the most important aspects of dealing with change that the authors describe is how to maintain a permanent state of change—how to "achieve the flexibility to remain flexible."

A third dimension that is well-articulated is the individual vs. group polarity. We know a lot about how IT can help the individual decision maker and how IT can help groups, but not a lot about the role of IT at all levels of work where physically separated individuals and groups have to coordinate at the same time. The models and examples presented make it clear what the potential of networking in the broad sense really is, and, more important, how organizations can begin to develop capability in using IT.

I found this book full of new ideas that provided insights and practical suggestions. It is extensive and intensive in its treatment and is, therefore, relevant both for the practitioner and the more academically oriented. I

believe it will make a big contribution in a field that is increasingly important—the potential and actual impact of information technology on organizations and the process of managing work.

Edgar H. Schein
Professor of Management,
MIT Sloan School of Management
January 1991

Part I | Introduction

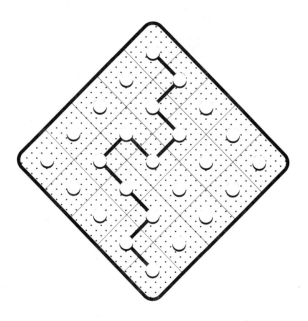

Chapter 1 | Overview

Introduction

A new perspective on organizations and work is rapidly gaining currency across industry, forged from the realities of the information revolution. Challenges and opportunities will, in the coming decades, spring from the emergence of information-based work and information technology; of multinational presences and worldwide distribution of resources; of global market demands for higher quality, faster availability, and competitive pricing of products. Taking the classical advice to "make a virtue of necessity," leading-edge enterprises are beginning to turn these challenges to value.

Consider, for example, the nature of work in the seemingly divergent domains of fast-track, high-rise construction and high-tech aerospace systems development. Beyond the differences in product, both undertakings are highly time sensitive, information intensive, and dependent on the contributions and cooperation of resources located far from the site of the visible action.

A high-rise construction project involves continuous participation from a variety of widely distributed constituencies: architects, materials suppliers, financiers, community representatives, official standards agencies, and potential tenants.

In avionics, key players in the aerospace industry are also facing up to new challenges. In the YF-23 ATF project, teaming members at Northrop and McDonnell Douglas:

- Reduced by 50 percent the normal time from engineering design to release of tooling information.
- Made design and analysis processes concurrent, cutting the time from initial concept to production release.
- Developed a three-dimensional simulation capability that allowed computer-directed machining of parts and tools, reducing time and improving accuracy.

3

○ Reduced complexity and improved production time by using computer simulations to optimize designs. While the older F/A-18 fighter contains about 750 parts in one subassembly, the YF-23 supports the same functions with approximately 350 parts. Fewer parts means significant cost reductions in areas such as procurement, inventory control, maintenance, and support.

These and many other innovations based on electronic information access enabled the distributed design and manufacturing teams to make their design more reliable and easier to maintain. This translated to lower cost of ownership for the customer—the aircraft will require less than half the maintenance of current fighters, yet will be more than twice as reliable.

The high-rise construction and aerospace examples show certain common characteristics:

○ Extreme schedule pressures.
○ Complex work performed simultaneously by different organizations in different places.
○ Dependence on constant, rapid communication of information across different organizations by managers and contributors separated by thousands of miles.

The cost of not succeeding today can be measured in hundreds of thousands of dollars in rework and financing costs, and perhaps millions in lost revenue. Finishing isn't enough; the goal is to finish on time, and that means quickly.

Such complex, time-compressed distributed work wasn't possible a decade or two ago. What has changed is the emergence of information-based work, due largely to the availability of technology that can electronically represent and move data and information thousands of miles almost instantaneously. In fact, many observers now recognize that electronic networks have helped evolve computers from their early applications as numerical computing devices into systems now used largely for moving data and information: into communications and information-sharing devices. (1)

Geographically dispersed—distributed—electronic information work brings with it many difficulties, but it promises value that far exceeds the cost: the simultaneous performance of traditionally serial tasks. In this work mode, organizations with worldwide resources can build information-based products, processes, or services through simultaneous design and realization activities, leading to higher quality in a fraction of the time.

Specification writers, designers, engineers, and analysts can use technology to work cooperatively and concurrently with flexible electronic information objects to develop, exchange, and merge information into single, multiauthored documents, designs, or spreadsheets. They can communicate information in the form of text, graphics, sound, or full-motion digitized video, and receive instant feedback in the same forms. This rate of information exchange collapses the amount of time normally consumed in projects and brings with it the ability to perform sequential tasks simultaneously.

Simultaneity is exactly the capability needed by industry to respond to the forces of time compression current in business environments. Today's markets change more rapidly, windows of opportunity are narrower and products obsolesce more quickly. On the supply side, the high cost of money, of resources, and of missing market opportunities is forcing organizations to reduce the length of product cycles. This holds true whether the product is an automobile, a hotel room, a financial instrument, a health-care delivery system, or an educational service.

The success of simultaneous distributed work (SDW) hinges on the ability of people to work together in teams committed to contributing and accessing information, building shared information-based products, and communicating continuously with each other within pressing time frames. Individual contributors and managers in these teams are often separated by thousands of miles and multiple time zones, and by what we call culture: differences in professional perspectives, work preferences, national culture, and personal outlook.

While modern voice and electronic data and information networks can connect teams, successful teaming with predictable results depends on effective communication and information sharing. Such communication must be designed and maintained through the total commitment of management and team leadership. In high-performing distributed organizations, communications cannot be left to chance. When distributed organizations take communication and information sharing for granted, the results can be disruptive and costly.

For example, recently a new forty-five-story office tower was designed and constructed at Worldwide Plaza in New York City. (2) Four thousand people worked simultaneously on site, with hundreds more toiling worldwide preparing materials like Italian marble and Pennsylvania brick; simulating stresses on building models at wind tunnels in Canada; and redesigning drawings and calculating financial projections in other New York high-rise suites. Time was of the essence; revenue would not begin to flow to the developers until clients occupied the space. Early in the project, designers had decided to change the use of the area under the pyramid-shaped copper roof from dead space to the housing for heavy elevator machinery. However, no one involved in the decision thought to tell the people building the floor under the pyramid of the changes until after the floor was finished. Because of the heavier weight, the floor had to be rebuilt, at a cost running to six figures.

Later in that same project, in accord with the approved design, light fixtures were placed along the base of the roof. The lights would show off the roof as a glowing copper crown, enhancing the nocturnal appearance of the tower. However, there had been insufficient communication with building maintenance experts during the design phase. As a result the lights were methodically ranged on the parapets, then sealed off from internal access by permanent windows, leaving the lights inaccessible for maintenance or replacement.

The problem was noted as soon as the windows were finished; not so the solution. After some discussion, the *best* suggestions for getting access to the lights were to:

1. Smash the permanent windows to gain access from within.
2. Get at the lights from the outside by hauling electricians up forty-five stories on window-washing gantries.

After considering the expense of the first alternative and the impracticality of the second (it was unlikely that union electricians would entertain such a novel way of getting to the job), the situation was left unresolved. In reference to these problems, the "familiar grumble" on the site was "Nobody talks to anybody." (3)

The challenge is one of effective communication—people reaching other people who need access to the latest information. Communicating effectively requires an appreciation of other perspectives. At Worldwide Plaza, designers needed to understand the requirements of those charged with maintenance of the structure; they needed to communicate information that impacted maintenance in ways that maintenance people could understand. In fact, the maintenance point of view should have been part of the redesign process, so that communication could take place in real time, as opposed to being a reactive response to a serious problem.

Clearly, failure to communicate continuously and proactively can have long-lasting and expensive results.

Teams of aerospace prime contractors face an extreme case of such cross-cultural communication. To optimize resources, reduce costs and time, and lower risk, the U.S. Department of Defense ("The Customer," to the U.S. defense industry) has directed the contractors to begin working together, "teaming," on complex defense system contracts. Even hardened competitors, like McDonnell Douglas and Northrop in the YF-23 example, must cooperate—communicate at every level of the enterprise to get the job done.

Such teamwork cannot be accomplished by the stroke of a pen. Most key players in the industry are burning brain cells to figure out how to build the complex communications environments they will need to sustain teamwork.

As one aerospace executive put it:

> Here we are with General Dynamics, Lockheed, McDonnell Douglas and others, all kinds of engine, airframe, and electronics makers and suppliers, spread all over the country—trying to design this Advanced Tactical Fighter together. Simultaneously, we're getting ready to compete with each other on the manufacturing contracts. Not to mention that we have a few lawsuits floating around between us because of previous projects.
>
> We are trying to learn how to work together under these conditions: to share design and management information, to develop and sustain parallel engineering efforts across distances and between organizations.
>
> We need to figure out how to manage our functional, philosophical, and cultural differences—to share just enough of our design and manufacturing processes to get the work done faster without giving away the store. (4)

The importance of communication to organizational success is not new; ideally, organizations are communications paths, built on hierarchical, networked, or other function-and-role relationships. Access to information and communication among workers has always been key to the success of a project, be it an election campaign, war, bridge construction, or bridge game. There is no substitute for getting the word (or the code, or the signal) out. What's different today is that the complexity of work, the rate at which new information develops, and the time constraints on getting that complex work done have put enormous pressures on work-

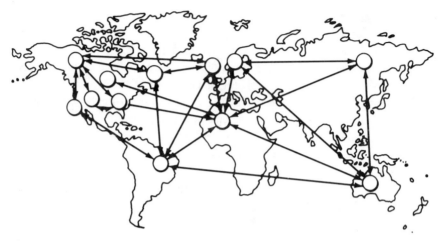

Figure 1-1 Working Together Apart

ers to communicate in new ways, with new technologies, under new constraints.

The challenge of sustained, continuous cross-organizational communication is daunting largely because of communication barriers. These are primarily human, not technological, barriers arising from understandable resistance from within the organization. As cross-organizational dependencies and trust develop, the comfortable insularity of the organizational hierarchy begins to disappear. "Position authority" begins to be superseded by "knowledge authority" as answers come less often from "bosses" and more often from specialists, whatever their position. Naturally, vertical management—the traditional power and authority chain—can view this as a threat; and any evolution toward the horizontal, or networked knowledge, model must expect and address this perception. (5)

The Capability-Based Model

We propose a perspective for addressing this complex, challenging, and constantly changing world. This is not a call to transform reality; rather, we offer a new paradigm, an organizing principle that can systemically relate the elements of that reality to support innovative, successful work forms, rather than threatening organizational success. And we offer guidance on how to evaluate options, measure progress, and remove the barriers that thwart progress.

We call ours a *capability-based* perspective: a shifting of focus from the reactive organization to the extended organizational environment that builds capability to meet new challenges. This capability-based environment (CBE) comprises the set of "stakeholder" constituencies related by common business goals: for example, the builder and the contractors and suppliers; and the multienterprise team of aerospace contractors and their suppliers and customers. The extended enterprise, generating value out of work, is defined not by functional or organizational (cultural) boundaries, but by the combined efforts of its stakeholders. (6) The optimal potential demonstrated in *simultaneous distributed work* (SDW), a designed process that addresses complex, time-critical distributed work in new and exciting ways.

Now we'll look more closely at this environment and work process. As Figure 1-2 illustrates, there are three interdependent aspects of the capability model.

1. Recognition and understanding of the complex realities of the workplace—the work environment.
2. Commitment to the capability perspective on that reality—the capability-based environment.
3. Initiation of simultaneous distributed work processes.

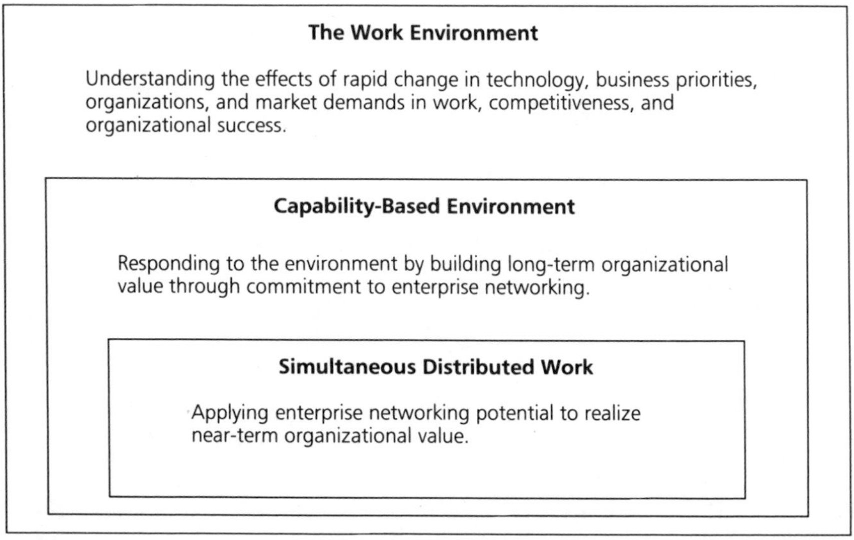

The Work Environment

Understanding the effects of rapid change in technology, business priorities, organizations, and market demands in work, competitiveness, and organizational success.

Capability-Based Environment

Responding to the environment by building long-term organizational value through commitment to enterprise networking.

Simultaneous Distributed Work

Applying enterprise networking potential to realize near-term organizational value.

Figure 1-2 The Capability-Based Model

The Work Environment

In the film *Angel Heart,* Louis Cypher, the enigmatic CEO of the Underworld (Louis Cypher—Lucifer—get it?), aptly sums up one widely shared attitude toward organizational life today: "The future isn't what it used to be." (7)

We all know Louis is right. The future has changed; we might even argue that the future is here, or else we couldn't talk about it! The future is different because high rates of change in demand for products and services; competition models; technology; and business goals have affected the capability of organizations to work toward stable visions. In the past, we could work toward a clearly articulated vision for months or years: we could objectify our goals in building the washing machine that ran forever; producing the most steel or hamburgers or buildings; or providing the fastest claims service in the nation. Now that clarity of vision is gone.

It's gone because fixed goals and strategies have a rapidly diminishing half-life. Organizations are measured more on how they can shift their strategies to accommodate change than on how well they can hold to them. Organizations must work in a new, volatile environment that demands flexibility of purpose, task, and product, within new business constraints that cannot be ignored. The successful organization—environment—will understand these phenomena and shape its strategies to use them to value-generating ends. A short list of these new realities includes:

○ Constant change: social, technological, market, political, economic
○ Global marketplace
○ Increasing demands for:
    quality
    accelerated time-to-market
    cost reduction
○ Overstressed organizational and technological systems:
    obsolescence
    instability
    transition

Organizations can prevail despite these conditions by continuously building long-term capabilities to proactively address opportunities and challenges. We posit a new organizational logic for this environment, a way of working that accepts people, business, and technology as they are, but understands and relates these elements in the *capability-based environment.*

The Capability-Based Environment

The capability-based environment (CBE) is a multiorganizational, cross-functional community that uses electronic information to design, sustain, and manage work and to evolve its own capabilities to learn and to perform over time. This is not a physical, or even formal, organizational entity, but a network of stakeholders defined by interrelated value-generating activities toward common goals. (8)

Stakeholders can include many organizations within a single enterprise; their suppliers, customers, regulatory agencies, and research affiliates—all the constituencies involved in and related to the process of adding value to produce a product or service. The environment is a rich amalgam ideally consisting of a system of commitments, capabilities, technological artifacts, work processes, and strategies.

Networks and Networking

Two related but clearly differentiated foundations of this infrastructure are the artifacts of electronic network technology and the social phenomenon of interpersonal electronic networking.

Networks and networking are at the heart of the model. In the capability-based environment, networks constitute the technological infrastruc-

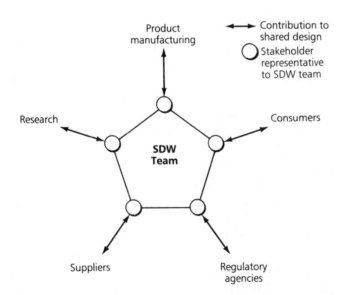

Figure 1-3 The Stakeholder Model for Simultaneous Distributed Work

ture. They incorporate high performance, openness, connectivity, flexibility, interoperability, and manageability. Networks enable the quick and easy movement of information in all electronic forms—data and text, image, voice, and video—to all stakeholders.

Through networking, geographically distributed individuals and teams use electronic networks to build, share, and act upon information and knowledge. Networking success depends not only on electronic connectivity and networking applications, such as computer mail systems and audio teleconferencing, but also on an understanding of and support for the psychological and social frameworks of human communication. (9)

We will emphasize networks and networking both for the role they play in the capability-based environment and as symbols of the balance and interplay required of people and their information tools as we strive to keep our work models current with rapidly evolving technology.

Teaming

The real power of the capability-based environment comes from more than tools and people's ability to use them. The catalyst is commitment, at all levels, to accomplishing work through electronic teaming, an interpersonal work process built on:

○ Access to distributed information and knowledge.
○ Interpersonal electronic communication.
○ Proactive building of capability to meet future needs.
○ Use of enterprise-wide networks and networking application.

Team members can be distributed worldwide or across the room; they can have different professions, functions, and cultures. But they share both their information and the contexts in which they interpret that information to achieve specific team goals. And their success is measured against team goals rather than individual goals.

Capability-based environments are developing today in many industries, including heavy manufacturing, retail, and financial services. Here, enterprises are beginning to meet the challenges of changing markets and constrained resources—people, time, and money. They use electronic information, networks, and networking applications to have open and continual access to customer demand trends, design expertise, economies in supply and manufacturing and responsive sales, marketing, and customer support. Such enterprises have begun to redesign work to exploit their capabilities, particularly by bringing traditional serial work processes into parallel in order to compress time; and by using geographically dispersed teams to electronically build products and services through information. We'll now introduce this emerging work model, *simultaneous distributed work*.

Simultaneous Distributed Work

The capability-based environment provides the "potential" for organizational success over a strategic time span of, say, three to ten years. Simultaneous distributed work processes, on the other hand, enable organizations to use their networking capabilities to reduce the time it takes to complete projects, with nearer-term—say, six-month to two-year—product or service delivery schedules.

Capability growth in this environment does not happen in a vacuum; capability is a major product of simultaneous work. High-performance distributed teams quickly build experience, skill, and knowledge. They feed these capabilities back into the extended enterprise. This constant leveraging of generic capability through specific work provides the quantum improvements enterprise stakeholders need to meet rapidly increasing work demands.

Simultaneous distributed work is characterized by:

○ A vision of exponential improvement in time, quality, and cost performance.
○ Simultaneous task performance in a capability-based, distributed teaming environment.
○ Simultaneous, comprehensive product/process design.

The need for such processes is obvious: given the emphasis on using time-to-market as a competitive advantage, we'd expect organizations to look for ways to reduce the time they take to turn out their products and services. And here we use *organization* to describe groups united by a common goal, ranging in size and scope from a branch recruiting group within a manufacturing plant to a multicorporate team building a new aircraft.

Also, we define "product" in its widest sense, to include spreadsheets, production forecasts, shipping authorizations, specifications, and service promotions. All are products within the value-added chain—in which value is successively, or simultaneously, added to resources through work. (10)

From the market perspective, products include manufactured goods, services, information—even hotel rooms, called "lodging products" in the industry.

Logically, the most effective way to reduce the time it takes to complete complex, information-based work is to move as many work tasks and subtasks out of serial and into simultaneous performance. The network and networking structure in the capability-based environment enables teams to maintain the rapid rate of information exchange required in parallel work. If you are going to redefine the use of a floor while someone else builds the floor, you'd better keep the wires humming with blueprints, schedules, proposals and decisions. In this way you finish together in one try, and the finished products work; the floor easily accommodates the new use.

The subtle but important distinction between parallel and simultaneous distributed work is that the latter requires all stakeholder activities to begin at Day 1 or Time 0—the point at which management initially commits to investing organizational resources in a project. From Day 1 on, all stakeholders remain connected—in constant communication, or the potential for communication, with each other—and with constant access to project information. Project leadership and specific circumstances determine the frequency and nature of actual interactions among these stakeholders.

Simultaneous distributed work can help increase revenues by ensuring that production is in phase with the consumer demand curve. Cost is reduced as borrowing occurs over a shorter period, and project consumption of resources is more efficient. Other paybacks of the simultaneous distributed work model are less obvious, but perhaps even more significant: improvement of product quality, reduction of waste, and reduction of manufacturing cost.

In our model, work is always distributed, involving resources in the next office with specialists across the globe. With electronic information as the key resource and with network information technology tools, it doesn't physically matter where the workers are, as long as they can enter the electronic system. In simultaneous distributed work, partners can cooperate toward common goals even though they are physically, functionally, or organizationally separated.

To summarize, the key attributes of simultaneous distributed work are:

○ Products and services are designed, developed, delivered, and supported primarily in the form of electronic information.
○ Products and subassemblies are tested by electronic simulator.

○ Final fabrication can be driven by electronic data and information built by distributed teams.

○ Work is performed by distributed stakeholders acting together simultaneously from Day 1 to evolve the product or service as a shared electronic-information object: a continuously integrated design.

○ The responsibilities of leadership and management are acknowledged at all levels of the enterprise. These include responsibility for:

clarity

articulation of purpose

support, motivation, and reward

issue resolution

effectiveness of communication

creation and maintenance of commitment to the CBE model and SDW processes.

One simultaneous distributed work application that has gained visibility is concurrent engineering and manufacturing. Efforts at implementing concurrent engineering started in the aerospace and high-technology manufacturing industries. With encouragement from the U.S. Government, these industries began addressing information-intensive product development, simultaneous distributed work, and the potential for moving serial process into parallel to reduce product cycle time. An unclassified government manual describes concurrent engineering in this way:

> Concurrent engineering is a systematic approach to the integrated design of products and their related processes, including manufacturing and support. This approach is intended to cause the developers, from the outset, to consider all elements of the product life-cycle from conception through disposal, including quality, schedule, and user requirements. (11)

"Conception through disposal"—that is the key phrase. All functional groups involved in the product life-cycle work simultaneously, not serially.

The principles of simultaneous distributed work are, however, applicable to any complex, distributed, information-based work environment. For example, in a capability-based environment, design and marketing, communications tasks, sales and sales support, all can be approached as simultaneous rather than serial tasks. Whatever the end product or service, the value of simultaneous distributed work will be apparent in savings of time and money, and in improvement of product quality.

SUMMARY

We've sketched out in general terms an environment, an organizational structure, and a work process responsive to today's and tomorrow's business challenges. In the next chapter we examine that environment more closely. We propose a set of assumptions that will ground our approach in some relatively noncontroversial observations on the nature of today's competitive work world. From this shared set of assumptions, we'll move in Parts II and III to look at organizational capability and the innovative work processes that ultimately create organizational value.

NOTES

1. See Shoshana Zuboff, *In the Age of the Smart Machine* (New York: Basic Books, 1988.) Zuboff examines the implications of the new potential that computers bring to work. See also Paul Strassman, *Information Payoff* (New York: The Free Press, 1985). Strassman characterizes information work as that which involves information and not tangible objects. This work is largely "unstructured and unpredictable," and is not limited to a cadre of "information workers," but is becoming a greater part of everyone's modus operandi.

2. Karl Sabbagh, *Skyscraper* (New York: Viking, 1990). These references to the Worldwide Plaza effort are based on Sabbagh's account. In spite of all the glass and concrete, from some perspectives this building was an "information" product; as one executive put it, "What it comes down to is pieces of paper, numbers, internal rate of return, the net present value, discounted cash flows—that's what it's all about. . . . So we can cut through all the philosophical stuff of the architects, the planners, the sociological statements that some of the partners have made about how we're saving or enhancing the community life and all sorts of stuff. . . . What it boils down to is whether it's financeable and whether there is a return to the partnership." (pp. 377–378)

3. Sabbagh, pp. 336, 345.

4. From a conversation at the Bootstrap Institute, Stanford University, January 1990.

5. Zuboff, Chapter 8.

6. Russell Ackoff describes the stakeholder concept in *Creating the Corporate Future: Plan or Be Planned For* (New York: John Wiley, 1981), pp. 30–34.

7. *Angel Heart*, an Alan Parker Film, a Winkast-Union Production, 1987. See also Stanley Davis, *Future Perfect* (Reading, MA: Addison-Wesley, 1988) p. 8, in which Davis calls for managerial skills in "beforemath": understanding the consequences of events that have not yet occurred.

8. We define the capability-based environment in the context of networks, networking, and distributed knowledge work teams. In *Managing Across Borders: The*

Transnational Solution (Boston: Harvard Business School Press, 1989), Chris Bartlett and Sumantra Ghoshal approach organizational capability from the business/management perspective. In their opening chapter, "Organizational Capability: The Next Battleground," the authors argue convincingly that the successful organizations will be those that can simultaneously develop capabilities of competitiveness, flexibility, and worldwide learning. (p. 16)

9. The concept of the extended enterprise, or corporate network, has become synonymous with a style of managing. See Fred Guterl, "Goodbye, Old Matrix," *Business Month* (February 1989). Guterl writes, "This theory holds that a multinational corporation should be managed not through a vertical chain of command but as a vast network of employees who are linked together by an extensive communications system and united by a clearly articulated corporate vision." (p. 32) We will keep returning to communications and clarity as linchpins of all networked and networking organizations. In *Future Perfect*, Davis defines networking as ". . . hooking people together who are geographically and hierarchically separated so that they may communicate with each other quickly and directly." (p. 86)

10. For a definition and examples of the value-added chain at a global level, see Michael Porter, *The Competitive Advantage of Nations* (New York: The Free Press, 1990), pp. 40–45; and Bruce Kogut, "Designing Global Strategies," *Sloan Management Review* (Summer 1985): 15–28.

11. See Robert I. Winner, James P. Pennell, et al., *The Role of Concurrent Engineering in Weapons System Acquisition* (Alexandria, VA: Institute for Defense Analysis, December 1988), p. 77.

Chapter 2 | Realities and Assumptions

To focus on a particular segment of a scene, visual artists use a viewfinder. A viewfinder can be a device on a camera that shows the area of the subject to be included in the picture, or it can be a card with a rectangle cut out of the middle. You look through the hole at the scene you're considering photographing or rendering in oil, charcoal, pencil, or stone. Then you move the rectangle to frame the part you want to capture or communicate. This lets you focus on the visual components and relationships that you consider important.

We can do the same thing conceptually by framing our perspective using assumptions that define the environment and the conditions that influence our ability to be successful. These assumptions are fairly nondebatable, but need to be articulated to anchor our world. We accept that a new paradigm is in place that requires new rules and tactics. This helps us recognize and understand the activities of early adapters and distinguish what has worked for them, and what barriers still need to be overcome.

For example, we can assume that accelerating change is causing pain to many of our organizations. Change is confusing and destabilizing; it causes anxiety. Change won't go away. The issue is, what do we do about it?

So, beginning with "change," we'll posit this set of assumptions.

○ Change is constant.
○ All work is distributed.
○ Knowledge is the critical resource.
○ There will never be enough time.

Change Is Constant

In the 1980s, the business community recognized exponential change as the dominant force in the environment. Observers began churn-

18

ing out definitions and attributes of change: change as threat, change as opportunity; gradual change, sudden change, accelerating change; technological change, social change; internal change, environmental change; change as the norm, change as threat to the norm.

Of course, change is not new; cycles have been with us since cave dwellers first experienced the seasons of the year. Back in the Middle Ages, a favorite subject of artists was the wheel of fortune, often depicted as a sort of water wheel that raised people (especially kings, since commoners had pretty much all "downs") up to the heights. As time passed it would bring them down into a bath of water or fire, depending on the mood of the artist. So, in a way it was predictable that there would be change, and along certain traditional parameters: wealth, power, love, health.

Today, thanks to the rate of innovation in technological, economic, political, and social evolution, we are assaulted by change coming at us from unpredictable directions. Instead of an inexorable wheel of fortune slowly revolving, we roll about like spheres on a randomly undulating curved plan: a roller coaster without tracks.

People and their organizations seem confused and threatened by change. Enterprises, often whole industries, struggle to compete successfully in markets that erode and shift. They struggle to achieve the micromargins and fast times-to-market that will enable them to gain and hold the edge. The skilled work force—the real strength of the enterprises—exhibits new and challenging social, economic, and professional expectations. The mass of information that increasingly forms the content and context of work has become larger and more complex; innovation in the technology that we use to move and process information hurtles on.

Change also drives progress. Charles Dickens captured the diversity and chaos of an earlier revolution with the familiar phrase: "It was the best of times, it was the worst of times." (1) Ours, too, is a mixed world, as promising as it is difficult. Change is neither good nor bad, it just *is*. Technological change is neutral, yielding benefits or causing problems. But technology will continue to drive sweeping changes, like those that followed the introduction of the printing press, the internal combustion engine, and the microprocessor.

In this new reality, we need to use flexibility and innovation to protect ourselves against the threatening aspects of change, while learning to use its benefits to guide our organizations toward their goals.

We don't realize how rapidly technology changes until one day we are struck by the irony of finding, side by side on our desk, the invoice for the most recent information systems purchase and the proposal for its replacement. In research and development there's often no time even to publish or specify, let alone manufacture, an innovative product before the need has vanished or a new technology has appeared, rendering it obsolete. By the time research in rapidly changing domains such as superconductors, semiconductors, and materials manufacturing gets to paper publication, it is overtaken by more recent knowledge and innovation.

Demand curves change more rapidly today than ever before; new technology and new work processes give us the potential of responding quickly to these demands. Rapid satisfaction of those demands, in turn, hastens the emergence of newer demands, accelerating the process. Whatever enlightenments will grace the world of the 1990s, it is unlikely that the need for instant gratification in commerce will disappear.

Information systems users don't find it amusing that technology is often a solution that causes bigger problems than it solved. The stakes are too high. No matter how low the price, the wrong systems are no bargain. Buyers now keep an eye on the value of their purchases, not just the cost. Recently, a vice president in a financial services organization responded to the "business as usual" information technology sales pitch with these words:

> Wait just a minute. I hear the price of this system you're trying to sell
> me; what I want to hear is its value to my business.
> What does the system deliver to my value chain? What's the life-cycle
> cost? How do I measure the return on this investment? We've bought a
> pile of technology over the years and we're still deciding whether to
> consider it as valuable capital equipment or just sunk costs.
> You know, you keep telling me how this stuff will solve all my prob-
> lems, but I'm beginning to think it's causing my problems. Come back
> when you have answers to the right questions.

Change happens. Once we accept that, we are ready to move and evolve the work model that will help us control that change.

All Work Is Distributed

Conventional wisdom holds that the level of communication and collaboration required for a work group to function as an integrated entity can best be achieved by collocating workers in the group—putting everyone under one roof. Intuitively, bringing people together physically so they can share common facilities will enable them to work better together.

This tradition has led to the practice of clustering individuals with similar functions in the same building or area. There's the engineering building, the marketing department, the sales office, and the branch bank. Once collocation is complete, however, it is never permanent. When change sets in, plans obsolesce and the dreaded relocation phase begins. As new groups are formed, old groups are disbanded and reorganizations take hold. A revealing window into the frequency and cost of change for any collocated organization can be seen in records of telephone and terminal service adds, drops, and moves maintained by harried telecommunications managers.

The limits to physical collocation and the availability of electronic communication have significant implications in today's "no growth" environment. Many companies are consolidating space by moving people from small facilities into larger ones. The purpose isn't collocation for communication, but to reduce the overhead generated by a lot of small buildings. Consolidation may actually disperse, or distribute, organizations as central facilities are closed and people move to available space in other buildings. Electronic communications can provide a cost-effective way of linking these dispersed organizations within and across larger facilities, so that they can maintain the level of communication required for cohesiveness.

New data suggests that collocation does not necessarily foster teamwork, including communication. In a study of five hundred Ph.D.- and M.S.- level scientists and engineers in a large industrial research and development complex, researchers found that people on the same corridor did communicate and collaborate intensively—five times as often as people more widely separated on the same floor. However, communication and collaboration dropped off sharply when workers were situated on different floors. Ironically, the study found that people in different buildings collaborated slightly more often than people on different floors in the same building. (2)

The study went on to verify the intuitive belief that communication logarithmically declines as distance increases.

A similar study found that 25 percent of technical workers whose offices were next door to one another (less than 5 meters) were likely to talk to each other at least once a week. At 10 meters' separation, fewer than 10 percent were likely to communicate weekly. At 30 meters or more, they needed to reintroduce themselves prior to communications. From this data it appears that only very small groups that can effectively collocate within a few feet of each other will communicate as a natural function of their proximity. Beyond 30 meters, they remain essentially strangers and will find it difficult, if not impossible, to overcome their physical separation. Unless given a long-distance communications medium at their disposal, they simply will not communicate. (3)

Collocation makes sense when tools and resources consist of shared 80-ton presses and stockpiles of steel. When tools are computers and telephones and the resource is information (the infinitely distributable resource), the decision to collocate returns far less value and can inhibit the commitment to share information with the distributed stakeholder community.

This is not to deny the importance of face-to-face contact in group work. Collocation does have the advantage of stimulating real-time, face-to-face deliberation and feedback. But there are drawbacks as well, and we'll speak about those later. With the capability to communicate electronically—through electronic mail, computer conferencing, image transmission—comes the capability to distribute work, to leave people close to the source of their information, while contributing to organizational goals far beyond their line of sight.

In fact, it is difficult to imagine that any work process is not a function of individuals teaming—communicating—to build the critical information that defines a particular process, product, or service. The point is important, because information and communication systems designed to support work processes must incorporate the special needs of distributed teams. There are different types of teams, with different group dynamics, and different rules for working together. Without an awareness of the nature of team effort, technology can just as easily create an infrastructure counter to organizational goals. We might end up in a situation akin to the party game "Telephone," in which a statement is passed from person to person only to end up unrecognizable at the end of the line, or as it returns to the individual who generated the message.

Accepting that all work is distributed and that communication is the catalyst that enables individuals to operate effectively as teams, we need to look at alternative forms of communication. Consider the automobile assembly-line worker assigned the task of tightening the bolts on the bumper assembly. This person could be considered an individual contributor, but in fact is a member of a team; a long serial team, but nevertheless one that has been organized to complete the job of assembling a car.

On automobile assembly lines, process designers stage each position to accomplish sequential tasks as the assembly moves from worker to worker: connect part A to basic frame assembly, connect component B to part A, and install part C. At the end of the line a worker steps inside an automobile, turns the ignition key, and drives off the line. These workers do not communicate verbally, but rather by completing their individual tasks, each in its proper sequence. The assembly line is a form of communications network: information is embodied and shared in the moving assembly.

In administrative and service organizations, work follows essentially the same distributed process model as on the assembly line. In these environments, paper is the communication medium, and each worker changes, approves, or otherwise adds to the work process as it moves through the organization.

Knowledge Is the Critical Resource

Only skilled, knowledgeable people know what to do with an organization's information, how to apply it to the value-added chain. Today's leading-edge organizations have learned that their competitive edge lies with these people. They are asking themselves and their technology suppliers what impact new technology will have on their people and work processes as they convert their knowledge into value.

A case in point: The CEO of a large hospital complex had this response to an unsolicited proposal from a major information system vendor:

> Wonderful. I love it. This system you're proposing will help us build the information-access capability we're after.
>
> I can see how it all will fit together. But, just one thing: Tell me how the new technology and new work processes will affect our people. How do we know they'll use the new technology? What will it do to make their work lives better?
>
> You've got to understand that our strength is in the expertise of our people. Unless your company is prepared to help us understand the impact of this new technology on our people and operations, we can't take the risk. Come back when you can address the whole situation, not just the technology.

Smart organizations want suppliers to help them cope with the changes that new systems will introduce even as these investments improve their competitive positions. They demand that information-system suppliers share their risk by accepting their input into specifications and provide state-of-the-art training. This includes classes, on-line information, videos, and manuals that really tell a user of the system how to do work, rather than merely describe the product features.

Work has always had an information content: How much? How many?

How to ship? When we all worked by the sweat of our brow and individually turned raw material into finished products, the information content was support data. Now, as we shall see, information itself has become the raw material. But for information to have real value, it must be available to workers where and when they need it, and it must be in a form that complements the use they will make of it. Information must support, not hamper or detract from, the operational purpose.

We can go further with this and assume that all information is in digital form, or could be: processes, maps, X-rays, conversations, 1940s westerns. Irrespective of content or function, information is increasingly represented and exercised in electronic—digital—form. Digital information is flexible and universally interpretable: it is accessible to knowledge workers over electronic networks and can be displayed in forms comprehensible to them and consistent with the work they do. What isn't in digital form today can be scanned into the system tomorrow.

Nothing will stop the current trend toward greater and more creative applications for information. Our tools are increasingly more sophisticated and complex, and we face the constant compression of reaction and development time. The expectations of workers are changing as they become more familiar with automated information-based work processes.

An effective work force doesn't come without a price; people must learn new technologies, processes, and products. In this environment of change, they must continuously learn in order to keep pace, and to ensure that they continue to process data and information into knowledge and value.

There Will Never Be Enough Time

Work is always done under time pressures. But in today's paradigm, the need to manage time has become the critical priority. Any random browse through the business literature, through the agendas of meetings and seminars, or through the transcripts of lectures and speeches will reveal how consumed we are with doing more in less time. *Time-to-market, time-to-manufacture, just in time,* and dozens of similar time-based banners make it very clear how important control of time has become.

Time is the ultimate metric with which to measure the effectiveness of any model, process, or activity. We argue that managing time provides the framework for designing the technical, social, and managerial infrastructure we need in today's organizations. At a high level, time management is the goal of all the tools and technologies, all the information-based techniques used by knowledge workers as they combine to produce value. The litmus test for organizational tools and processes is a simple reflection on whether the tool, the idea, or the process saves time. Clearly, the best targets for time savings are those activities that have significant time overheads: travel time to bring knowledge and knowledgeable people together, start-up time to bring new resources up to speed, time to reach decisions, and, of course, time consumed by serial tasks that can be made parallel.

Stepping Back

We've spent some time looking at aspects of the work environment: metaphorically, the trees that populate the forest of today's reality. Most of us spend time dealing with trees such as discrete, recognizable issues, problems, and challenges that need attention sometime during the long workday. When beset by too many trees we take refuge in abstracting the mess to some categorical level of forest—get it all into a box with a label. But we know that we can't really work with forests: we can't plant or cut down a forest, only trees. So we return to the more comfortable level of smaller objects and work the trees some more.

Occasionally something happens that gets us to shift our focus to the broader view. Such is the situation of the CEO, executive, or manager, the work mechanic, who suddenly realizes that individual instances of pain and threat and the struggle to respond to them have become the norm and occupy all our time, masking the greater changes that are overtaking the organization. This epiphany reveals that all our responses tend to deal with symptoms, with objects, and not with the greater context.

As one executive, who preferred to remain anonymous, expressed it:

> We realize that the system's broken, but we keep it working . . . with great expenditure of people's time and the organization's money. We succeed not because the system, . . . the technology, the people, the work . . . is what it should be, but because of the interventions we make to keep it all going.

At this point the creative leader begins to consider re-engineering the forest—not just pruning, spraying, and propping up trees. What follows is a fictional account—invention based on fact—of such a shift in focus from the micro to the macro level. In this fictional account, the CEO of a major financial services enterprise delivers a closing presentation at the annual state-of-the-company meeting. He recognizes the realities of the moment, the future that is here, and challenges his senior management to focus beyond yesterday's measurements of success and look at the bigger picture: how the enterprise is poised to succeed in tomorrow's environment. Like Louis Cypher, he knows the future has changed.

Ladies and gentlemen, I'd like to sum up my feelings about what I've heard today, and I must tell you, they are mixed—pride and comfort, frustration and anxiety, excitement and eagerness, and a few others that I still can't pin down.

On the one hand I feel like shouting "Full speed ahead!"; and on the other I sense the need for caution and careful reassessment. But my intent here is to stimulate you with some questions—questions that I have been formulating for some time as I struggle to make sense of our "now and future" business situation. Sure, we need answers, but for now we'll do well just to recognize the questions.

For the past couple of hours, I've been listening to remarks on how good our people are, how good our technology is, how our work meets the demand, how well our markets are holding up. And I'm worried.

I'm worried because it brings to mind an old story I heard about an ice skater, a lad driven by the ambition to spend his life skating across larger and larger ponds. By the time he was nineteen, he had worked himself up to skating the Big Lake, a trackless expanse that seemed his logical next conquest. Over time he had learned the most effective, economical moves, found the best clothing and supplies and the finest skating blades. One winter day he stood on the east bank of the lake and began his trip; he skated due west.

For days, then weeks, he progressed steadily, often moving faster than the eye could track. But then, imperceptibly, he began to slow down. He wasn't tired or hungry, and his skates hadn't dulled. He performed as well or better than ever. But he continued to lose momentum.

The ice was softening, turning mushy and dragging at his once clean blades. He continued to slow down.

There was nothing wrong with his skates, his style, or his logistics. But there was no way he would cross that lake. You can imagine his sad end.

Think about it. I'll say only that my vision for this company does not include cold baths.

To the promised questions: I want no answers today, but I do want thinking . . . if possible, shared understanding. When we agree on the questions, there'll be time to look for the answers.

First of all, do we have a clear sense of what is really going on in our business? How much time do we spend talking *at* each other, as opposed to talking *with* customers?

What are our real goals? Do we understand them? Do they make sense? Do we communicate them? Do we understand what our problems are, try to fix them? Or have we become so familiar with them that we've accepted what doesn't work as well as what does?

We've invested huge amounts of resources in technology intended to improve our work processes. Do we know which of these investments have been successful? Which are no longer contributing, only absorbing resources to keep them going?

We're considered information workers. Do we really work with our information, or defend ourselves against it? Why do we consume so much time deciding what to use and what to ignore? Information has become our medium. Information, and the skill to use it effectively, provides the bridge to connect our distributed resources. It is the key to productive relationships with our customers, our suppliers, the world community, and even our competitors.

Do we use our information properly, to contribute to our value-added chain? Do we even know what our value-added chain is? Do the people who need the information have access to it when it will be useful to them? Can they get it in a form that they can use? Can people team with counterparts in other organizations, with other project stakeholders—whether they are customers, suppliers, or competitors—to get complex work done?

Do we have a value chain at all, or do we now depend on a value network that embraces our customers, our researchers, our suppliers, perhaps our competitors?

What about our networks? Everywhere I turn I see indications that we are rapidly reaching network gridlock. I'm constantly asked to approve programs to expand existing network systems, to improve the performance and capacity of various network segments, to add network management staff, or contract for outside support services. At the same time I hear our workers from various functional units complain that information they need from other units is not accessible where and when needed because our network segments are not technically compatible. Doesn't this imply that our business segments aren't compatible either? How can we be an enterprise, let alone an extended enterprise, under these constraints?

Are we committed to improving our ability to use information to communicate among ourselves, with our suppliers and our customers, or are we driven only to process more data that we can't effectively use?

Do we have a plan to help our people understand how to use these new tools? Network and information-processing systems are critical to our business, but I'm concerned about falling behind in developing the skills needed by our workers to use these tools, to network with each other—to communicate.

Are our people secure enough in this environment to continue to innovate? Does fear of failure shroud any impulses people might have to take creative risks? Does our environment encourage playing it safe, staying with proven technology and methods? Will we be selling trolley cars when the market wants helicopters? Using slide rules instead of workstations? Ice skates instead of. . . ?

You pick that one.

Suppose we do all the right things; how are we going to measure results? How will we reward success and build from failure? What will be our metrics, and how will we be sure that our new metrics are consistent and relevant?

You may have a question for me now: "Why ask us all these questions?"

The answer to that one is easy. You are our work mechanics, the individuals who can and do influence the way we work, and through that work, generate the value that sustains this enterprise. The reports I've heard today clearly indicate that we have adjusted effectively to meeting current daily demands. But my sense is that the future success of our company, our industry, and our people requires that we step back from our business and carefully plan a deliberate strategy. A designed approach, not a tinkering with the status quo.

I see an exciting and challenging future. I see people, technology, and process coming together to release capabilities beyond anything we have imagined to date. We're good, no question, but we need to use what we have to be great; to get to that future.

For that to happen, we need to think about how our people, the processes that support our business, and our information technologies interact to create value. We need a strategy, flexible yet with clear direction. And we need to manage to that strategy. We need clear criteria and process to make our choices, guide our commitments, our responses to change—both opportunity and threat.

This is a very complex system we are charged with. The key is people—capable and empowered to do their jobs through access to information, when and where they need it. We must design work processes that optimize the ability we have to move information throughout our extended enterprise. We need to communicate these concepts to our people, train them so that they will be comfortable with these tools, and demonstrate our commitment by action and reward. We need to

energize our organization to be flexible, innovative, and capable.
Let's get to work.

In this interlude offered by our contemplative CEO, we see the recurring motifs: change, people, technology, and work processes. How do we work with the hand we've been dealt under constantly changing rules? How to we manage all the complexity in the environment? How do we assess where we are, where we want to go, and how we can get there?

SUMMARY

Looking at the totality of our assumptions in this chapter, we see where we are and where we can be. These are the characteristics of our new paradigm:

- We will be working in a constantly changing environment that brings both threat and opportunity.
- We can manage the risk and seize the opportunity to work in change by evolving to a simultaneous distributed work model based on electronic information and information technology.
- Electronic networks and networking techniques that support teams using those networks to move information will form the infrastructure of an environment that will provide long-term value to the enterprise.

This is our point of departure in developing a model for simultaneous distributed work and the organizational form that will support it, the capability-based environment.

NOTES

1. Charles Dickens, *A Tale of Two Cities* (New York: New American Library, 1980), p. 13.
2. Robert Kraut and Carmen Egido, "Patterns of Contact and Communication in Scientific Research Collaboration," *Proceedings of the Conference on Computer-Supported Cooperative Work, 1988* (New York: ACM, 1988), pp. 1–12.
3. Thomas Allen, *Managing the Flow of Technology* (Cambridge, MA: MIT Press, 1977).

Part II | The Capability-Based Environment

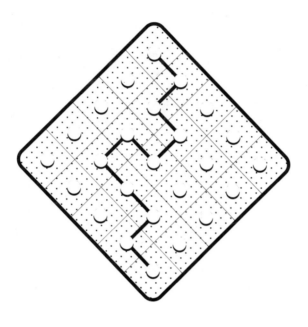

Chapter 3 | The Capability-Based Environment

We've defined an organizational form, the capability-based environment, as a distributed stakeholder community working simultaneously toward both unique and shared goals. This environment is structured on strong yet flexible relationships, nourished by information moving through electronic networks, and facilitated by mutual trust and a commitment to distributed information.

In Part II we'll look at several facets of the capability-based environment:

○ Capability as an organizational option for dealing with change.
○ How information and knowledge contribute to value.
○ The barriers to information sharing and how they can be overcome.
○ Enterprise networking: building and sustaining distributed teams.
○ Enterprise networking applications.
○ Enterprise networks: anatomy, physiology, psychology.
○ A prototype architecture and process for creating and evolving into the capability-based environment.

We'll begin in this chapter by discussing why organizations now more than ever need to build their capability to learn and work, to augment their collective intelligence through information and knowledge sharing. Along the way we'll look at the challenges posed by increasingly complex products, technology, work processes, and work environments, and we'll define and contrast what we call the traditional reaction-based approach to solving problems with the proactive capability-based approach.

Why Capability?

Put simply, the rapid rate of change in all dimensions of work, aggravated by increasing time pressures, makes it impossible for organizations to continue following traditional, reactive models for dealing with challenges, issues, or problems: with work. In the past, we were able to work in and manage change because we could predict cycles, extrapolate trends, and hedge our bets with multiple work efforts "in case something changes." Situations usually were clear enough, remained static, or developed slowly enough to allow us to observe phenomena, frame problems, and begin developing solutions.

We don't have that luxury today. Cycles are obscure, "mutant," or discontinuous. Evolutionary changes obviate trend planning; multiple efforts consume too much time and money.

An example before us today is the evolution of military aircraft survival techniques. From a generation of supersonic, high-flying aircraft like the SR-7 Blackbird, the state of the art has shifted to the Stealth paradigm—surviving by proceeding secretly or imperceptibly. And the next generation will see perceived advantages that are a quantum leap forward over the value of the Stealth. These leaps are happening not in the twenty- to thirty-year spans that used to mark plateaus in military aircraft development, but in a few short years. This is an example from just one leading-edge industry; organizational capability in other sectors will be needing to evolve—if that's the word—at these accelerated rates.

In a way, change reflects the time dimension of complexity, the rate at which we must deal with complex objects and relationships. With the rate of change so high, there is difficulty even in gaining an entry point into the stream of events, let alone framing problem-solving sequences. Today, shifts in market demand occur in hours instead of years. By the time a new line starts up, the target product and even the development process may be obsolete.

There are other difficulties with the reactive problem-solving approach. A problem statement is not an objective, wholly rational analysis; it is a perspective. Even in the simplest cases the appropriateness of a solution depends on how the problem is defined. For example, there's the story about the pharaoh, who, being 199 years old with no plans in place for the afterlife, gave an action item to his chief strategist.

"Fix it so I will live forever," he directed. The wise vizir, with advanced degrees in strategic planning and pyramidology, responded in accordance with the First Law of Problem Solving: Frame the problem in terms of the solution you know how to deliver. "The problem is," said the vizir (and note the language), "you need a pyramid."

Since the vizir had considerable people, stone, and tool resources at his disposal, and no one was tactless enough to bring up questions of feasibility or return on investment, the pyramid was built. And the pharaoh felt relieved, until one day, as they still say in Transylvania, "He ate well; he slept well; he woke up dead."

So the pharaoh was off to the pyramid forevermore, and the vizir and his cohorts were pleased with the success, although there was never any feedback from the end-user on how appropriately the problem was solved.

But the effects of solving a problem from the point of view of the problem-solver as opposed to that of the user can be painfully inappropriate. Consider bridge building. Early stone bridges were built like other stone structures such as obelisks and temples, with the basic problems being thrust and strength under load. Later, new materials such as iron and steel enabled innovation in bridge building (cantilever beams, suspension wires) leading to large increases in span.

At first, iron and steel bridges were built on the same principle as were the stone: thrust and strength of materials remained the focus. In the 1930s, when major suspension bridges began to sway and even collapse, engineers realized that they'd been focusing on the wrong problems, or at least not on all the right ones. Long, high suspension bridges behave like wings, not floors. The problem of stability wasn't structural, it was aerodynamic. Future bridges were to be designed with lift in mind. (1)

Even framing the problem appropriately isn't always enough. At the turn of the century, the canal-building effort in Panama was plagued by disease, mudslides, and mutiny. Excavation led the thirty-five years of effort to link the seas. Then, in 1905, Theodore Roosevelt hired John Stevens as chief engineer of the project. Stevens, a railroad builder, surveyed the panorama of mud and wreckage and observed: "The digging is the least thing of all." (2)

Stevens went on to redefine the immediate problem in terms of *transportation* (of course) rather than *excavation*. But Stevens went further than framing the problem in terms of the solution he knew. First, he took steps to create an infrastructure to support the work he envisioned. He built homes and stores and drained swamps to eliminate disease. He hired motivated workers into the now livable environment. Then he built a railroad. Now the work force had the *capability* to work through rain, through the uncertainty of mud slides and disease, through threat and change.

And nine years later the canal was completed.

So what do these agricultural- and industrial-age anecdotes have to do with networking organizations in our information age? For starters, we still produce and build: not only in deserts, windy river valleys, and muddy hills, but in space, under oceans, under microscopes, and in darkened, people-less factories. We encounter new levels of complexity because our primary material is information, which is expanding, combining, regenerating, arriving, disappearing, and changing at the speed of light. We've strayed beyond the traditional range of visible change to having to cope with rivers of information that change invisibly, in subtle and profound ways.

Figure 3-1 illustrates the exponential relationship between the increasing complexity of work and decreasing availability of time in which to do that work.

To prevail in this new environment—this maelstrom of complexity—we must aim beyond the mark. We can't just plot the trend, frame the problem in familiar terms, then design and deliver the solution. We'll never be able to react to the next level of complexity demanded of us. We need to work at ever increasing capability, continually increasing our knowledge to deal with the expected but unknown complexity that will surely follow.

The Proactive Approach

We can see the evolution toward capability-based work models in the aerospace industry today. Leading defense contractors have been instructed by the Department of Defense to deliver future products within these constraints:

○ 50 percent reduction in linear time-to-develop.
○ 20 percent reduction in costs.
○ Payment upon acceptance of product by customer: the Government buys the plane *after* they see it fly, not on the promise that it will be built.
○ A single point of contact for all the prime contractors, subcontractors, and suppliers.

Management is justly alarmed by these requirements ("gone ballistic" is a term heard in the hallways). Complexity already strains the system—

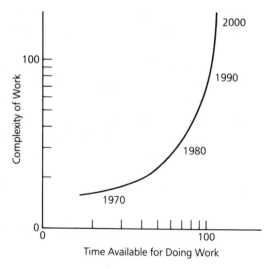

Figure 3-1 Complexity and Time for Work

the materials, the technology, the processes, the people. Traditional planning cannot anticipate the changes that will affect the development cycle. The current design, mock-up, testing, and building processes cannot handle the new complexity or time constraints. Yesterday it looked like "build another airplane": today it's still that, but by the way:

○ Get up-to-date knowledge and information to a distributed, cross-functional, cross-cultural work force so they can work simultaneously to decrease the length of product cycles.
○ Develop a stakeholder work model that enables cooperation with suppliers and competitors.
○ Develop new investment/financial models.
○ Organize for faster response.

These are not just problems to be solved, but criteria for a new work environment that systemically addresses increasing complexity.

In this context, capability is a function of how well organizations use their knowledge, or intelligence, to adapt their work processes to ever-changing waves in the work environment. Adaptation must occur at several levels. Enterprises must fit to the external world of changing market demands, technological capabilities, economic factors, and work force factors. Within enterprises visions, strategies, culture, and shop-floor work designs must be maintained in harmony to manage conflicting goals, charters, and beliefs. (3)

The kind of fit we're talking about is illustrated in Figure 3-2.

The External Environment curve represents an undulating wave, with ever-shortening periods, driven by change. In this rapid change, succeeding levels of the organization—represented by the other curves—try to reshape to fit the waves of their environments. Naturally, the potential for congruence falls away the further you get from the most independent wave: the external environment.

How, then, do you get the capability to:

○ Sense the environment (vision).
○ Understand how to change (strategy).
○ Make those changes at all levels (plan).
○ Sustain new work processes while preparing for the next wave (work).

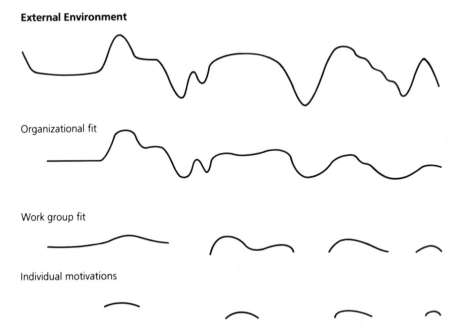

External Environment

Organizational fit

Work group fit

Individual motivations

Figure 3-2 Organizational Fit Over Time

The consensus, especially in large organizations, is that this kind of flexibility can be achieved only with the "flat" (autonomic) management model. If each stimulus or pattern of stimuli or expectation of change requires central analysis, processing, and decision making, the quality and timeliness of the response will suffer. Time is too short and challenges too complex for managers to make unilateral decisions. "Span of complexity" constraints require that autonomic or networked response capabilities must exist at the working nodes of the environment, where the knowledge resides.

Some observers have compared the organization's ability to turn in response to external pressure to the innate abilities schools of fish demonstrate when they turn in unison in reaction to threats or opportunities. Doug Engelbart, who has pioneered exploration of capability-based organizations, chooses (with some irony) the image of "catlike" responses. He contrasts this almost real-time capability with the extremely slow processes of the ill-fated dinosaurs. "Probably," writes Engelbart, "it took these central-nervous-system-dominated beasts several minutes to know they were dead." (4) No organization sets extinction as a goal.

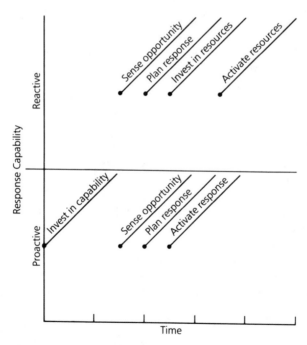

Figure 3-3 Reactive and Proactive Approaches

SUMMARY

There are no silver bullets; neither science nor philosophy will constrain the burgeoning complexity around us. Reactive problem solving will not cope with accelerating rates of change. Success in this environment depends on organizations evolving their abilities to sense threats and opportunities, make critical decisions based on input from all stakeholders, and quickly respond at the scene of the action. These capabilities must continue to evolve over time, as a natural function of the organization, not as adjunct or parallel learning. Organizational knowledge must be built by and be accessible to the entire environment.

In the following chapters we'll look at the attributes of the capability-based environment and at how organizations, through pilots and designed evolution, can continuously develop their future work capabilities: skills, knowledge, technology, and processes.

NOTES

1. Henry Petroski, *To Engineer Is Human* (New York: St. Martin's Press, 1982), p. 158. See also Gordon L. Glegg, *The Design of Design* (London: Cambridge University Press, 1971). Glegg shows how obsolete or wrong-paradigm design caused problems in the transportation industry. For example, early automobiles were designed like carts, which needed little flexibility because they were either pushed or pulled. But automobiles were different. Their engines and brakes produced torque, and those twisting forces caused the vehicles to tumble under stress. (pp. 26, 58)

2. David McCullough, *The Path Between the Seas* (New York: Simon & Schuster, 1977), p. 465.

3. Richard T. Pascale, *Managing on the Edge* (New York: Simon & Schuster, 1990). Pascale rightly advises that the inherent conflict in complex organization must be managed to advantage, not crushed; complacency leads to failure more often than does "functional conflict." (p. 24) In "Make Decisions Like a Fighter Pilot," *The New York Times* (November 15, 1987): III: 3, Thomas M. Hout and Mark F. Blaxill suggest that decision capabilities of fighter pilots are worthy of emulation by managers who seek success in our rapidly-changing environment. Air Force data show that pilots successful in dogfights had faster "observation, orientation, decision, and action" (O.O.D.A.) loops. Managers, by honing their capabilities on those attributes of the business processes, can lead their organizations to higher levels of performance.

4. Douglas C. Engelbart, "Intellectual Implications of Multi-Access Computer Networks." (Available from author)

Chapter 4 | Valuing Information and Knowledge

Data, Information, and Knowledge

We've discussed information, almost as if it were like any other commodity in the marketplace. But information is different. Its meaning is not intrinsic, but depends on the context of its consumers. Therefore, it is by definition ambiguous; and it is persistent. The more you share information, the more of it there is. There always seems to be either too much or too little to suit anyone's need. Either situation can prevent you from doing your work.

We usually value information on a scale somewhere between data at the bottom and knowledge at the top. Data, information, and knowledge don't have intrinsic value; they are valuable only if they are:

○ Accessible.
○ Related to other data, information, and knowledge.

Let's look more closely at the distinctions and relationships between data, information, and knowledge. Our purpose is to build an argument for organizational learning as a primary function of the capability-based environment. That is, the business of the stakeholder environment is to build, access, share, and apply data, information, and knowledge to its work. Value returns to the stakeholders largely through products and services that are composites of that knowledge. An organization's ability to deliver products and services depends on how well it continues to build its knowledge, and on the data and information upon which that knowledge is based.

Technological evolution has been both a cause and a result of the increasing dominance of knowledge-based products and services. The focus of computing has moved through the generations of data processing to word and graphics processing, to textual and image processing, and most recently to artificial intelligence, or knowledge processing. (Wisdom processing's not in sight yet.)

We'll set the stage for the capability-based environment with a quick look at the concepts of data, information, and knowledge.

Data represents real-world observations: 63 oysters, a boulder, 212 degrees Fahrenheit. Data can be recorded in or on any medium: stone, paper, or magnetic tape. Usually the context of data—the system that gives the representation a value—is simple, generally accepted, and unambiguous. For example, the decimal or binary numbering systems have the unambiguous base 10 and base 2 contexts, respectively. The Fahrenheit temperature scale assures that 212 is data that represent the boiling point of water at sea level: no argument. Languages have data too. Letters— O-Y-S-T-E-R-S—are defined in relation to the 26-letter alphabet.

Information relates, or "in-forms," data to particular contexts. In this sense, information is more specific than data:

"We can't sell any more oyster dinners; the last 63 oysters rotted."

"A boulder rolled over the car we were going to use for vacation."

"The sauna shot up to 212 degrees again."

Information, too, can be stored in various media, but the contexts are more complex. Relationships are established not only between the base data and its context system, but between those relationships and the more specific contexts—like the intention of eating the oysters or taking a vacation. These contexts give a sharper meaning to the original data items.

We can see why "information sharing" can be extremely complicated. Clearly, we can share data with almost complete success: everyone knows the context, the system that it relates to—the decimal system or the alphabet. With information, we must ensure that the more specific contexts are shared as well, or else the sharers will come away with different meanings.

Knowledge is the third order of relationships and describes the capability of an individual to relate complex structures of information to new contexts. *New contexts* implies change—action, dynamics. Knowledge involves being able to effectively address the present in terms of past data, information, or knowledge. Knowledge of the effects of falling boulders and excessive heat can be useful in assessing future risk. Knowledge is a capability—it can't be shared, although its techniques and information components can be shared. In the networking environment, value derives from the capability to build organizational knowledge and to access the ever-growing knowledge store as new situations arise.

The interplay of data, information, and knowledge, and their attendant value to the user, is illustrated nicely in the fine French detective film *Diva*. *Diva* has a complex plot that turns on multiple instances of blackmail, police corruption, pirating of audio tapes, and violent death, all of marginal relevance to us here. But there is an instructive side to the film: it provides some insight into the distinctions between data, information, and knowledge.

In a climactic moment of the film, the swinishly corrupt, murderous, pistol-toting police inspector, Saporta, stalks unarmed good guys in a factory loft. Suddenly the lights go off; the only thing visible is a red light indicating the light switch, which is attached to a cable, beside an open elevator shaft. The inspector knows this, having already used the switch a few minutes earlier. What he doesn't know is that his chief adversary, Gorodish, has sneaked in by the stairs, turned out the light, and is holding the light switch over the open shaft.

Saporta silently heads toward the switch, with the intent of turning on the lights to illuminate his quarry. He gropes his way closer and closer to the red light, but instead of reaching it, steps through the open shaft gate, and with the requisite diminishing wail, plummets to his death. (1)

First, let's look at the generically shared data: the red light indicates "pay attention"; a binary switch turns the light on and off. That's pretty unambiguous data, because it's generally accepted context. Both interpret that data correctly.

The information level gets more complex. The antagonists share the following information:

○ The red indicator is part of the light switch.
○ Turning on the light switch will be good for the bad guy, but bad for the good guy.

On the basis of this information, both know that bad guy Saporta will head for the red light.

Saporta, having used the light before, has information that tells him where the switch is: on (related to) the wall next to the elevator shaft. But Gorodish has better information: he has changed the situation, lifting the switch from the wall and holding it out over the open elevator shaft. Saporta's knowledge construct, with the key piece of wrong (old) information, is inferior to Gorodish's. Gorodish knows about a change in the set of information—the relationship of the switch to the wall. He uses his superior knowledge to win the battle of wits.

Knowledge, not information, should precipitate action. But knowledge must be based on all the most recent, relevant, and correct information. We can see information and knowledge at work in another domain. Take, for example, the respected skills of London taxi drivers. In one sense, these cabbies are knowledge workers. That they can drive the tight-turning cabs is taken for granted: their real value lies in their ability to get passengers where they want to go within a reasonable time.

Any respectable road map of London will list all eight thousand miles of streets. That's information. What the drivers must know goes beyond that information. They must know more than just the names of the streets and the location of the destination. They must relate the request to a variety of variables that determine how to get there: the starting location, relationships of roads to each other, current road works, time of day, passenger's sense or urgency, and so forth.

Knowing the street names—the information—is a requirement, but the real value to customers resides in the drivers' abilities to relate that information to all the other current variables and construct the mental map of a timely, accurate journey: the cabbies' product.

The point here has been to illustrate the relative complexities and ambiguities of data, information, and knowledge, and to suggest that they cannot be viewed as objective entities, but only in relation to contexts, including other data, information, and knowledge. We need to keep this complexity in mind when we talk about things like "knowledge work" and "information sharing." We've seen here how the information about the light switch meant different things to the inspector's intended victims (danger), to the inspector (capability to kill his prey), and to the hero (way to knock off the inspector.) Same switch, different values. We must keep in mind that the interpretation of information is a function of the user's knowledge.

The *Diva* and taxi driver examples illustrate in a fairly straightforward manner how people build knowledge by relating information to developing contexts. Our focus is on the much more complex world of people working individually and together to share information and contexts, building group knowledge that can be evidenced in a process, product, or service. Recalling the exponential growth of links between people, and between people and information as the entities themselves increase, we can see formidable levels of complexity.

For example, in the Airbus A320 project, tens of thousands of people worldwide teamed to build the first conventional jet with "fly-by-wire" (computer-directed primary flight) controls. In Europe alone, 28,000 workers at 60 plants were involved with Airbus projects; additional components came from the United States and Australia. The information shared across these sites "related" precisely to the whole design: everything fit, no matter where it came from. Only 5 percent of the total construction process was final assembly. The completed aircraft represents the state of the consortium's knowledge. (2)

Electronic Information

Representing information electronically creates new opportunities for aggregating that information into useful knowledge constructs. Electronic information is easily revisable in form or content. It can be transmitted worldwide at the speed of light, and instantaneously shared across wide geographic areas. Perhaps most important, electronic information— unlike physical representations such as writing, films, audio recordings, or blueprints—is flexible. That is, electronic information can be associated with other relevant electronic information without the constraints of being on a different page, film roll, or record. If, as we've argued, associating (relating information to other information) is what builds knowledge, then indeed electronic information is much more appropriate as the raw material for knowledge-working teams. (3)

In Part III we'll address the value of using electronic information as the basis of work. This value is evident, for example, in time saved by using electronic information. Below is a table representing the comparison of time consumed in transmitting a (semi-) electronic document and in a physical delivery cycle. The scenario is a bid on a contract that involves contribution, review, and approval by distributed engineering, sales, marketing, and legal stakeholders. (4)

The results look like this.

Document preparation cycle	Transmission cost	Work time	Elapsed time
Traditional physical delivery cycle	$450	20 hours	9 days
Electronic scan/FAX delivery cycle	$135	20 hours	3 days

This still involves a paper-based document; as we will see, fully electronic information transmission provides even higher orders of value. (5)

In response to the need to associate electronic information, the concept of hypertext has emerged. (6) First conceived shortly after World War II, hypertext technologies enable knowledge workers to relate information in ways that are significant to themselves and their groups. *Hyper* denotes structure as well as behavior. Information can be "linked," or associated in new dimensions, allowing richer associative access by people who need comprehensive information constructs.

For example, an electronic library may hold many business management books, economic reviews, corporate annual reports, and articles on executive salaries. Hypertext links within these text pieces would point to related information in other texts. The information, like the teams using them, would be networked—associated in a dimension beyond the context of the article or book or presentation that contained each piece.

You could structure links that connected anecdotal information on a highly successful project, with industry's and the corporation's financial performance, with the key executives' compensation. An interested person could access the entire linked trail of information, gaining a fuller information context that communicated not just an event, but its causes and effects.

More recently the hypertext concept has been extended to include other representational modes: video, sound, and still image. Your information could include charts plotting the rise and fall of stock, photographs of the cars key executives drove before and after their notable achievement, or animated videos demonstrating key points dramatically.

The enormous popularity of word processing is largely due to the new flexibility it provides writers, freeing them from the "change-a-word/change-the-page" constraints of the typewriter. At the high end of electronic information work, computer-aided design programs enable designers to modify the wing of a plane—or of a house—to accommodate new requirements, without tearing up prototypes or tearing down walls.

Leading-edge manufacturing processes now use data and information in electronic form not only to design products, but to design and build the molds to cast the components. In some cases, the casting process itself is based on and controlled by electronic information-driven robots that cast the metal or plastic. (7)

A final note on electronic information. To optimize its value, information should be kept in electronic form as long as possible in the value-adding process. Being electronic, the information remains highly communicable and flexible, making it shareable and neutralizing the impact of change on people working in the information environment.

Staying electronic helps postpone large investments in physical prototyping. Experience tells us that state change—for example, turning electronic information into physically represented information, such as paper or wood or metal—is costly and time consuming. Rekeying information and rolling all the data up into a paper spec are predictable time killers. In the aerospace industry, the traditional process for designing a wing involved:

○ Creating a design blueprint.
○ Fabricating a wood or metal prototype.
○ Testing the prototype in a wind tunnel.
○ Observing, recording, and analyzing data.
○ Changing the design as required.
○ Repeating the process until results are satisfactory.

These serial processes required multiple state changes, consuming valuable time and resources.

New processes allow design and manufacturing engineers to work together simultaneously, using electronic simulations. They communicate the information (simulation models) across the network to where they are needed; share and discuss the analytical results electronically; and electronically move the product as information right to the fabrication point.

Finally, state change points provide an opportunity for the introduction of error. Worse, these points tend to fuel the rise of bureaucracies that further inhibit the work flow. The act of transforming the information from one "acceptable" state to another becomes a major task, and breeds a "stovepiped" mentality. We all have had information returned to us because it wasn't on the right form or format. Ideally, from start to finish, information will ride the value-added path in electronic form, available to be associated or presented in whatever form or combination a particular constituency desires, without being frozen into physical representation. These processes have been developed through, and embody, the knowledge of the stakeholder organizations—machinists, product designers, composites suppliers, process controllers, and information systems vendors—that developed them. Knowledge makes it possible to use the data and information to generate value.

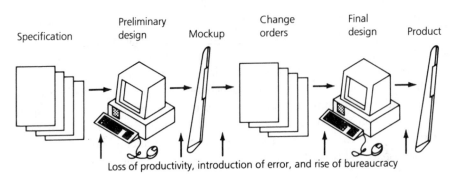

Figure 4-1 State Changes

SUMMARY

Information is not intrinsically valuable; value accrues as information relates to individual or organizational needs. Networks provide storage, access, and communication paths for purposeful information sharing, bringing along the advantages inherent in electronic information. But equally important is the capability of networks to support and make visible the contexts in which information work is done. In the following section, we'll look at the networks supporting interpersonal as well as informational relationships.

NOTES

1. *Diva,* a film by Jean-Jacques Beineix (Les Filmes Galaxies and Greenwich Films, 1981).
2. Len Morgan, "New Age Airbus," *Flying* (May 1990): 42–45.
3. See Jacques Vallée, *Messengers of Deception* (Reading, MA: Addison-Wesley, 1981). Vallée, a pioneer in conceptualizing electronic group work and in implementing networking applications, comments: "If we had invented the digital computer before inventing graph paper we might have a very different theory of information today."
4. Paul Strassman asserts that in the future, paper will be used for reading, and electronic information for everything else. Quoted in Robert Johansen, *Teleconferencing and Beyond* (New York: McGraw-Hill, 1984), p. 139. See also Zuboff, *In the Age of the Smart Machine,* Chapter 5.
5. Stephen A. Caswell, *E-Mail* (Toronto: Gage Educational Publishing, 1988), p. 2. Caswell draws this example from *Electronic Mail and Micro Systems Newsletter* (November 1, 1986). The newsletter is published by International Resource Development, New Canaan, CT.

6. See N. Dean Meyer and Mary E. Boone, *The Information Edge* (Homewood, IL: Dow Jones-Irwin, 1989), for convincing data in support of electronic information and communication on both the cost and value sides.

7. In Chapter 7 we will treat hypertext and hypermedia in the context of "groupware."

8. We'll look at a specific instance of this in Chapter 11.

Chapter 5 | Barriers to Information and Knowledge Sharing

> "The Gods of the Mountain are not the Gods of the Valley"
> —Unattributed commentary on almost everything, ca. 1960s

We've more than implied that there's organizational value in sharing information for a purpose: performing distributed work. One might ask, then, "If information sharing is so good for us, why aren't we all doing it?" The problem, of course, lies in the "we." Each of us differs from other individuals. Groups of us are different from other groups: team A from team B from team C; widget designers from widget engineers from widget financial controllers; nation A from nation B. When we try to share information, these differences are manifest as differences in contexts—intentions, reference systems, and values. Differences become barriers; when we encounter barriers to understanding, we usually react in inappropriate ways.

One way we respond to communication barriers is with force: we turn up the volume. When shouting, pleading, or threatening doesn't get the message through, we become frustrated and assume that the failure to communicate is due to the listener's stubbornness or stupidity. Ultimately, we put up our own barrier and end the communication ("I'll take my ball and go home.").

We once heard an engineer bellow at a group of uncomprehending marketing people: "Why can't you understand this! It's intuitive! If you guys won't do it this way, we'll do it ourselves." Clearly, an unproductive communication event.

We need to discuss barriers because awareness of the different kinds of barriers is the first step toward overcoming them, and toward reaching an effective level of distributed information work. In this chapter we'll examine some significant barriers to communication, especially electronic communication, including:

50

○ Natural complexity of networks.
○ Human differences.
○ Media differences.
○ Cultural "infolects."

Complexity

Paradoxically, electronic sharing of digital information across networks breeds communication barriers, if for no other reason than the large number of communication paths, "links" or "nodes" between people. Networks linking tens of thousands of people are in place today, and networks that serve larger groups are technically feasible. As with any system, as the complexity grows, so does the probability of failure. In the case of people trying to communicate in such networks, each link is an opportunity for a barrier. The potential for cognitive and cultural barriers is almost exponential to the number of people. Since links in a peer-to-peer network grow at a rate of $n \times (n-1)/2$, where n equals the number of people, the number of links in a network of 10,000 people would approach 50 million. Moderating the differences between people and groups in a large network, then, is not trivial. As with everything else in the network, the ability to make the links connect instead of separate must be designed into the organization's work system.

The exponential link-growth phenomenon goes a long way toward explaining Brooks' law: Adding more [personnel] to a late software project makes it later. (1) When large projects fail it is usually due to a failure to communicate rather than a lack of competence or technology. Communication—sharing information—can account for up to 90 percent of project activity. Add ten people to a ten-person project and you have only increased the number of people—the nodes—by ten. However, the significant metric is that you have increased the information-sharing potential from 45 (10 × 9/2) links to 190 (20 × 19/2) links. The 149 new links must be designed, managed, and maintained for project information sharing to be successful. Thus, complexity-as-change as well as complexity-as-size can inhibit networking communications.

Human Differences

Objectively, difference should indicate contrast, not trigger judgments about which entity is better or worse than the other. Languages—computer and natural—use objective differences as the basis of meaning: *shot* and *show* have different meanings because one key sound differs. A computer command-line interpreter will usually be satisfied with a unique character in the command string, and execute the right command.

Unfortunately, people and groups are not always objective and tend to fix upon differences in other individuals or groups as indicative of qualitative difference. We all know intuitively that our way of marketing new products is not just different, it's better. Unattended, this tendency leads to prejudices, such as the ubiquitous and frequently denied Not Invented Here syndrome. These barriers restrain effective cooperation and limit the abilities of organizations to capitalize on their most significant resource, the unique potential of skilled and knowledgeable people.

Enlightened organizations try to redirect the human fixation on differences to positive ends. They ask their people to discover what contributions can result from the dynamic of differences. These "valuing differences" programs are making important headway in breaking down barriers to productivity; they create environments in which our first response to noticing a difference is not judgment, but appraisal; instead of focusing on why the "other" appears to create a threat, we consider how alternative ideas can contribute to joint value. (2)

At the outset such programs were aimed at conventional and obvious distinctions: sex, race, language, and belief systems (religious, professional, and philosophical). But many other attributes of individuals and groups create barriers to communication, cooperation, and information sharing.

Some of these barriers to information sharing spring from the nature of information and the ways in which people interpret information. As we have seen, information has content and is understood in context. The marks on this page don't change from reader to reader. But the informational messages here are received only by readers of English; others find no meaning in the writing. This problem of interpretation extends to all codes that we use to represent information: Morse code, musical notes, and computer languages.

For example, color has long been used to convey information: traffic lights, the different-colored jerseys on flight deck teams, litmus tests. And one recently introduced use of sound has been the beep of the bar-code reader, indicating a successful reading. Different media can be used simultaneously to convey information at more levels than is possible through one medium. We can talk on the phone, wave instructions to an associate, and scribble notes simultaneously; but we can speak, signal, or write only one message at a time. (An exception might be Major League baseball coaches, who seem to be able to simultaneously broadcast hundreds of body signals.)

In distributed work, the problem of mutual understanding and interpretation of information across individual or group boundaries is heightened by the absence of visual feedback. Face-to-face communication can occur between people with no common language: nodding, arm waving, and, often, shouting can result in the successful exchange of basic messages: directions, restaurant orders, and ticket purchases. But when people and groups are working out of sight, these aids are unavailable.

Media Differences

Some media are more appropriate than others for certain kinds of information sharing. We know from the works of Marshall McLuhan that the major communications media—print, television, film, and radio— each have qualities that make them uniquely suited to particular content and intentions. (3) Neil Postman has shown what distortions occur when the medium is at cross purposes to the message: as more and more news coverage occurs through television, the concept of news has changed from information sharing to entertainment. This is signaled at the very start of a news program, by the musical introduction. Music creates a context of entertainment, not serious information sharing. (4)

We also have to ensure that the medium used for information sharing is appropriate to the "receptor context" of the people involved. Communication is "receiver driven"; nothing is shared unless the message is received. To say "I told her but she didn't hear me," "I sent it but he didn't get it," or worst of all, "I taught them but they didn't learn" all sadly miss the point. There is no information sharing if no one but the creator gets the message.

Infolects

Groups of people who, because of role, profession, or other affinity have similar interpretations of specific information, form what we call infolects, which are analogous to language dialects. Problems arise, not within infolects, but between them: the information is not totally incomprehensible to another infolect, but is perceived differently. For example, consider a New England town meeting, where a zoning plan is introduced.

That plan will be interpreted differently by developers, environmentalists, residents, and tax assessors. All have different—and, for them, correct—interpretations of the information presented.

Ironically, fewer problems arise if there is total lack of communication, as between different language groups.

This is a barrier linguists call semicommunication. It can have more severe communications implications than noncommunication. Dialects, by definition, are fraught with semicommunication problems. In some places in the United States, people ask if you want your groceries put "in a sack." In other places your groceries would end up "in a bag." New Yorkers ordering egg creams at home get milk, syrup, and seltzer in a glass. In Nebraska they may get weird looks; or worse, some concoction of egg and cream. Had they asked in Icelandic or Urdu, there would be no partial results based on semicommunication, just the weird looks. (5)

Many of us have experienced semicommunication in that artifact of the 1980s, the "natural-language" software user interface. Here command lines in computer languages were close enough to English (in our case) to make users think they knew what the proper command should be. More often than not, however, the software had some pretty strange notions about English syntax:

Get all rows average size of wheel equals 15.

This almost-English is far more difficult to understand than the old-fashioned, context-free computer languages, like Assembler, where users didn't try to interpret the code with the English context forever resident in their own memory. (6) In a nutshell, that is the information-sharing problem: getting common or at least predictable meaning across the barrier between infolects. In the remainder of this chapter we'll look at barriers to sharing across the spectrum, from the individual level to the global. Some barriers are unique to a particular level, and some are common to all. They are found in:

○ Individuals.
○ Roles.
○ Functional organizations.
○ Cross-functional teams.
○ Multiple enterprises, global initiatives.

In general, infolects have inheritance: barriers found in individuals will be found everywhere, and will need to be addressed at all levels.

Individuals

Besides the obvious language differences, personal likes and dislikes, ideologies, prejudices, and traditions that separate people, certain emotional as well as cognitive traits are particularly inhibiting to productive information sharing in distributed environments. Suspicion, protection of territory (conceptual and physical ownership), conventional beliefs in the supremacy of one's own creativity, vision, methods, and tools create key psychological and social barriers. Again, these are aggravated in the distributed work model, because the "other" is often unseen and unknown, and therefore more threatening.

The phenomenon of interpersonal noncommunication (or ineffective information sharing) has not escaped attention. Several years ago interpersonal communications specialists began to convince us that in business meetings, what is said isn't necessarily what is heard. That is, just because you know what you mean, there's no guarantee that everyone or anyone else does. Teachers and drill sergeants have known this for some time.

As is often the case when new insights are unwrapped, we went overboard to make sure that there was agreement in the interpretation of what was said and what was heard. We clarified to ridiculous lengths:

LISTENER I: Let me play back what I think I heard you say. . . .

LISTENER II: Let me say what I think she said that she thought she heard you say. . . .

SPEAKER: What I meant to say is . . .

Although some illumination may have resulted from this process, it drove business meeting communication overhead to unacceptable levels, while addressing only the symptoms of the problem.

People absorb concepts (learn) differently; they perceive information differently; and they see significance in different places. Some people learn sequentially; order and predictability is essential for them to "receive" information messages. They become frustrated and angered when they need to interact via information with random learners—who are "all over the place"—connecting not by sequence, but by association. While a numbered electronic mail folder might satisfy message storage requirements for a sequential person (receiving messages by selecting numbers in a sequence), a random person prefers content links between messages and between points in messages (associating the information within the messages without concern for the "ordering" of the messages)—the kind of index and access to information that hypertext applications provide.

People differ, too, in how they prefer to perceive information and in how they judge the validity of information. Some people are spatially oriented, or right-brained: a graph, organization chart, or sketch will quickly convey information to them that twelve pages of text will never communicate. To the spatial person, that's too long a linear trail to grasp as a whole. It might make perfect sense to a more sequential, linear, left-brained person.

Use of the mouse as an input device, and of windows in operating systems and user interface for personal computers, has been especially valuable to legions of right-brained people. Left-brained people prefer keyboards and command lines, with their discrete linearity.

Similarly, words are great for describing concepts: *What* and *why* and *how*. And they carry procedural messages well: *do this, next that,* finally *this* again. But information relating place A to place B is best conveyed in pictures.

Spatially oriented people are frustrated by newspaper descriptions of car chases, redistricting, or new tunnels through neighborhoods that are described in paragraph after paragraph of sequential prose: "two blocks east from the old courthouse, then north .5 mile to the six-way intersection that causes tie-ups that run back to turnpike exit 12." Of course, conversations between linear and spatial people can be exercises in noncommunication. (7)

Finally, individuals value different kinds of evidence. Some want data and statistics; others judge wholly by the reputation of the person making the assertion. Some want logic, not numbers. When sharing information, it's important to be sensitive to these differences, to share beliefs in a way that crosses the barrier to the other individual's contexts.

Roles

There's a saying in organizations that "where you stand depends on where you sit"; that your perspective on the right thing to do depends on the goals you recognize in your organizational role. Roles carry not only unique goals, but differing contexts and often languages that make information sharing difficult.

A case in point: A fairly large, geographically distributed high-technology manufacturing organization had suffered long delays in bringing an important and already-announced product to market. Because the product was so critical and already over a year late, more than the usual number of people attended the monthly status meetings. The functions in the development process were distributed worldwide, and all were represented by individuals either present in a large conference room or participating remotely using a speaker phone.

The following exchange took place at one meeting, well into what promised to be an endless technical debate.

Scene: Marketing headquarters, Connecticut.

VICE PRESIDENT [exasperated; shouts into speaker phone]: Enough! Who can tell me when the damn product will ship?

[Several moments of silence elapse, then a voice through the speaker replies.]

JOE BURNS: This is Joe Burns. I'm the development manager in Dublin. The product will ship on September twenty-sixth . . . this year.

[Nervous laughter.]

[At this point the senior group manager, also in Connecticut, eager to regain control, leaps in.]

SENIOR GROUP MANAGER: OK. Great! September twenty-sixth. Everyone happy?

[Much mumbling in the room and through the speakers, indicating global assent.]

SENIOR GROUP MANAGER [triumphantly]: The product goes to volume manufacturing on September twenty-sixth.

[Uproar. Everyone talks, shouts at once—in the room, through the speakers. The loudest voice wins, from New Jersey remote.]

CARL: Wait a minute. This is Carl from the support group. The date we want is when Alpha test starts! Volume ship is too late for us to begin support.

VICE PRESIDENT: I thought he meant the first major customer installation would be in by September twenty-sixth. This is too late.

SALES MANAGER IN AUSTRALIA: Hold it. I told you we've already promised deliveries to the customer Beta test sites. When's that?

JOE BURNS [clears throat loudly]: This is Joe again. The twenty-sixth date is when we'll complete the final build. There's still quality review before Alpha test. I have no idea when we'll get to volume ship.

That meeting ended with shared information, but no satisfaction.

Fortunately, the senior group manager's offhand revelation of his personal context for interpreting "ship date" had forced the group to recognize that each person had a different interpretation of what the date meant. The interpretation reflected the goals, responsibilities, and promises that went with their roles in that project. The lesson is pretty obvious: Make sure that contextual information is shared continuously during the project, before misunderstandings arise. And, as we'll see, there are ways in which extended project teams can do just that, even in widely distributed projects.

Functional Organizations

During the past ten years, tremendous progress has been made in understanding organizational dynamics and design. The perspective here is limited to the issue at hand: what causes and what can prevent barriers to information sharing in organizations.

The causes are extensions of the same tendencies that constrain information sharing between individuals. We are suitably appalled to discover that noble social, economic, and even military efforts are dashed or at least delayed because of ignoble attitudes. Issues of territorial ownership, of power and control as well as land, are prime barriers to organizations working together. In World War I, maneuvering over control between General Pershing and Marshal Foch kept the United States out of battle for months. That scenario was repeated in the squabbles between Generals Montgomery and Eisenhower in World War II. People tend to hold to local or parochial goals and contexts, rather than to extended group goals. This is why keeping the goals and purposes of a simultaneous distributed work project continuously before the entire group is a key function of leadership.

A key barrier results from organizational unwillingness to give up traditional technologies and methodologies. Responding to innovation from another organization is often taken as an admission that the group itself could have been doing things better, or lacks creativity itself.

Organizations are jealous of what they've learned and of their learning style. The Not Invented Here (NIH) syndrome—through which the organizational immune system keeps outside agents at bay—is basic, elemental, and entirely normal. For example, a user interface engineering group may reject an animated specification because they've always worked from paper specs; it may be difficult to get them to accept even what seems to be a logical and obvious change, and impossible to convince them to accept what another group proposes as a better way. (8)

Much current work in networked organization models involves building understanding and approaches to these barriers. We'll discuss some of those approaches in later chapters.

Cross-Functional Teams

In our project team example, representatives of various functions tried to resolve the meaning of "ship date" in the already late product. They also had to achieve their goal of reducing the time from initial product conception to volume customer ship. Concurrent engineering efforts require open communications—information sharing—across different functional groups in the network. To achieve aggressive goals in a distributed, changing environment, the functional groups involved need to understand each other's contexts: goals, methods, criteria of success, and priorities in the product cycle.

All groups must be aware of barriers that impede the open flow of necessary information. A barrier in the engineering/manufacturing process lurks in the perspective each group has on project methodology and timing. Designers seek perfection; they want to iterate design cycles until they are absolutely sure they have it right. Working in parallel, the manufacturing side wants to get hold of the design as soon as possible so their own people can design the manufacturing process. This functional tug-of-war over product data is not attributable to sinister motives on either side; it's an unavoidable clash of interests that can be addressed only by keeping the overall goal before people in all the functions: working as a team, not as a solo professional unit.

The network can help address such barriers by giving both sides access to the same product data base, enabling them to evolve their work in parallel without each closing off the other's activities. Also, working electronically through design and testing using simulations helps avoid the state change from electronic simulations to physical prototype early in the process. Capturing the design in physical form tends to fix manufacturing on a particular snapshot of design; commitment at this stage by manufacturing makes it difficult for downstream changes in design that are bound to follow testing.

Of course, convincing design engineers to "stay electronic" is another barrier at work here. Physical prototypes have always been the norm. People who have gained expertise through the look, touch, and feel of the real thing, find it difficult to depend on an electronically simulated rendering. A similar reluctance to give up physical experience affected the U.S. Navy's programs to automate carrier landings a few years back. Although the electronically guided landings had a 100 percent success record, pilots just would not give up control; they would not trust electronics to do what they were physically trained and skilled to do.

Multiple Enterprises, Global Initiatives

At higher levels of cultural aggregation—industries or multiple enterprises, tribes, nations, and language groups—even more barriers exist to information sharing.

We've already seen that understanding a language does not mean understanding context. It's difficult for local government agents to discuss border violations with members of cultures that do not understand the concept of edges. Such cultures do exist; they describe spatial distinctions in terms of directions and areas. For some of them, the prow or keel of a canoe is not a concept; they speak instead of the "front of the side."

Cultural differences can be dramatically demonstrated. In the 1960s, two films were made about Navaho silver crafting; one by an American member of an anthropological team visiting a Navaho tribe, and the other by a Navaho silversmith from the tribe. The American team showed the Navaho carefully working the silver until the piece of jewelry was complete. The Navaho's film began with his setting out early in the morning to dig the silver ore, to refine it, and finally, briefly, to fashion the jewelry. To him, "making jewelry" comprised the entire process; all stages of the creative journey were important. In the view of the anthropologists, making jewelry meant just that—working the metal with the tools. (9)

Enterprises are cultures. Some support "open" information-sharing contexts; some believe that information should be filtered, focused to ensure that only the people who are perceived to need it, get it. Like differences mentioned earlier, the issue is not which of these modes of information sharing is better, but how information sharing is handled between enterprises that differ fundamentally in their attitudes toward information sharing. These are relative positions: as companies mature they tend to establish more rigid information-sharing protocols. This enables them to achieve the control they need to manage the complexity of a large institution, but it inhibits flexibility and departure from historical process, that is, innovation. Ironically, at a time when the keys to competitive success include flexibility and adaptability, a countertendency toward rigidity is becoming visible in some quarters.

A similar stiffening can be seen in a phenomenon that used to be so freewheeling that it coined the term *Happening*. Rock concerts have come a long way from their random, crowd-stimulated early days. Now, the information (music) is constrained by high-tech trappings; programs are fixed and predictable. At each stop the same songs are sung in the same order.

It seems that rock-concert audiences have found this mode of getting the message acceptable. Maybe they are becoming more tolerant of structure.

In the aerospace industry, a multienterprise teaming model has been mandated by the government, but, as they say, the map is not the territory. As they begin to try to actually work together and share information, enterprises will need to learn each other's cultures to reach understandings. Some aerospace contractors in a major Department of Defense program have developed work models that hinge on a partnership with suppliers and information systems vendors. In this instance the "partners" contribute their principal skills: building aircraft structures, engines, and avionics, and processing information, as equal stakeholders.

Other contractors have always kept, and will continue to keep, their internal information systems known only to themselves, both for security reasons and to preserve control over what they feel to be essential to their uniqueness.

Whichever model they choose, these companies will soon be sharing information with each other.

SUMMARY

The capability-based environment can, does, and will exist in spite of all these barriers to information sharing. In fact, the strength of the CBE springs from those differences that, left to run their random course, result in destructive barriers.

Our ability to understand how to share information across all kinds of barriers will come through an understanding of some of the forces at work, and through the experience over the next decades of working globally. It's often painful to learn through experience, but that's the only kind of learning that will work in situations that are people-intensive and complex. Theory and research will make important contributions in the areas of cognitive models, context sharing, valuing information, and models of cross-cultural information sharing. The problem is a dynamic one. We must learn by attempting to maintain the unique values of different cultures in business, while gaining the capability for broader communications. We must aggregate, interpret, and share our knowledge.

NOTES

1. Frederick P. Brooks Jr., *The Mythical Man Month* (Reading, MA: Addison-Wesley, 1975), pp. 18–25.

2. In *Managing Cultural Synergy* (Houston: Gulf, 1982), Robert T. Moran and Phillip R. Harris point out how differing cultural perspectives affect the analysis, causes, and solutions of business problems, and offer guidelines and exercises for building people's skills in cross-cultural interactions.

3. Marshall McLuhan, *Understanding Media* (New York: New American Library, 1964), pp. 23–45.

4. Neil Postman, *Conscientious Objections* (New York: Knopf, 1988). Postman includes the trivialization of serious business by the media in his discussion of "Future Schlock," pp. 162–174. This year, many voices have been raised protesting the blurring of the line between the reality of the Persian Gulf war and television's representation of that war as real-time drama.

5. Leonard Bloomfield defines dialects in *Language* (Chicago: University of Chicago Press, 1984), pp. 48–52. See also Charles Savage, *Fifth Generation Management* (Bedford, MA: Digital Press, 1990).

6. See Ben Shneiderman, *Software Psychology* (Cambridge, MA: Winthrop, 1980). Shneiderman discusses the phenomenon that makes it difficult to write in a language somewhat like, but not exactly like, your native natural language. This is called proactive interference, "the confusion between what you know and what you're trying to learn." (p. 199)

7. For an overview of the major cognitive models and styles, see K. Patricia Cross, *Accent on Learning* (San Francisco: Jossey-Bass, 1976).

8. Dr. Harvey Robbins, in his highly readable *Turf Wars* (Glenview, IL: Scott, Foresman, 1990), describes "turfism" as the antithesis of information sharing, pointing out that it makes more sense for organizations to fight with the competition, not each other. Peter F. Drucker, in *The Frontiers of Management* (New York: Harper & Row, 1986), points out how the Japanese systematically turn NIH to advantage by recasting imported techniques, such as JITI and Quality Circles, to

"embody Japanese values and Japanese objectives" (pp. 220–223). See also George S. Odiorne, *The Change Resisters* (Englewood Cliffs, NJ: Prentice-Hall, 1981).
9. Sol Worth and John Adair, "Navaho Filmmakers," *American Anthropologist*, Vol. 72, No. 1 (1970): 9–34.

Chapter 6 | Enterprise Networking

In the capability-based environment, networking is a commitment—through all levels of the enterprise—to the design and use of electronic, voice, and video networks to perform purpose-driven, information intensive, distributed work. Here again we mean the extended enterprise, reaching laterally across all stakeholder constituencies.

Networking describes individuals teaming across distance and time, across cultural, functional, and national boundaries (all work-inhibiting barriers). These workers use high-performance electronic communications to apply their individual and combined knowledge to the building of time-sensitive, complex, information-based products and services.

Networking is a social, not an individual, activity. Team effectiveness, not individual efficiency or productivity, is the appropriate metric. Distinguished from but clearly related to electronic networks, networking shares some attributes with its technological counterpart. Both networks and networking involve connectivity between working nodes: the former links intelligent devices; the latter links people. This intersection in a common language makes it possible for an organization to plan and design effective network communication paths based on the networking relationships needed to get the work done. Networking modeling can define network requirements.

In this chapter we'll look at the attributes of networking in the capability-based environment, along with some of the attitudes and roles that networking teams need to develop. Specifically, we'll discuss:

○ The networking model
○ The elements of networking
○ Networking in action
○ Networking events

to emphasize networking as a social, not technological, activity.

The Networking Model

To do any kind of work, we need a model of the world. This is especially true when groups of people work together: a common framework of beliefs and vision is necessary at some level, or else there's no sense of progress. A team needs to know rules, processes, and goals. If your tennis partner ignores the foul lines, uses a hockey stick, and assumes that the goal is to drive for distance, there is little likelihood that you can work together toward a reasonable outcome.

Electronic networks and digital information mask the realities of time and space from users in the network. Electronic networking requires extraordinary efforts from team members to establish and maintain a shared framework. Distance and location are no longer anchors; people and information are merely "out there."

Similarly, our concepts of time and "time zones" are challenged. In the network, the store is always open. Financial traders use networks to follow the sun from Wall Street to Tokyo to London. Retail information on the day's demand is networked to European and Asian centers so the next manufacturing shift can start with precise information on the following day's mix.

What frame of reference, then, can we offer networkers? What are the visible markers to which people can anchor their perceptions of their work world? One approach is to provide interfaces to the electronic network through familiar images: screen representations of people or functions with whom you communicate electronically; doors or drawers that you "open" to lead us to information; maps and models that help you "navigate" your communications links. These are all valuable, but in a way constrain electronic communication within the boundaries of physical communication, rather than help move electronic communication to its potential.

We propose a different framework, based on the human, social, and cultural principles of commitment and trust. Commitment must begin at the highest level of the enterprise, with management supporting the vision of distributed, information-based work and flexible, networked organizations. Through the enterprise, management must build and maintain a visible commitment to teaming, to the open sharing of information, to the understanding of the different perspectives in the human network, and to the primacy of group goals.

These commitments have a common prerequisite: trust. Workers will share information only if they trust those with whom they communicate and believe the information they access and receive. Trust is the strongest weapon we have against communication barriers; indeed, trust is largely a letting go of communication barriers we have built. (1)

This commitment and trust will not just happen, and it will not persist without support. We'll talk about implementation later. Now we'll describe the elements of networking from a perspective that will aid networking design and implementation.

The Elements of Networking

The Networking Institute, a Massachusetts-based consulting organization that has pioneered the application of networking theory in industry, models the elements of networking as nodes, links, purposes, leadership, and benefits. The relationships and interactions among these elements motivate and support the interpersonal communication instrumental to successful distributed teaming. (2)

Nodes

The locations where participation in networking occurs are called nodes. These are logical, rather than physical, places because they include functions, like finance, that are not tied to one place and allow people to access the network from a variety of locations: office, home, car, or airport clubroom. Networking nodes, then, are the logical counterparts to physical network nodes, but are not tied to specific places or devices. Nodes identify the stakeholders in capability-based environments; they represent all the perspectives, information sources, and work resources that contribute to enterprise value.

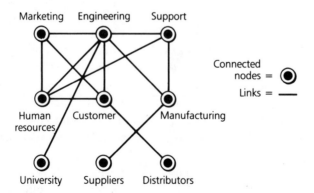

Figure 6-1 Elements of Network Model: A Network for Product Design

Links

Nodes are connected by logical communication links. As network technology links devices, networking links are the relationships that unite the group into an information-sharing community. Logical communication links vary with the purpose of the communications. In the network analog, links vary according to the kind, volume, and frequency of information to be shared between nodes.

Purpose

Clarity and visibility of purpose is essential to building and exercising networking capabilities. In the CBE, the ideal is to provide networking potential across the enterprise with total peer-to-peer physical and logical linking. In reality, investment choices must be made on the basis of priorities: purpose provides the rationale for determining which nodes should be connected by what kind of link. As purpose changes or is clarified, the networking topology shifts to respond.

The success of networking activity, measured in the degree to which team goals are achieved, depends on clarity of purpose as well. Unless distributed networkers carry with them a strong sense of the overall purpose, or goal, they are likely to drift off center. Their contributions, decisions, and perceived information needs will not be focused on what's best for the team goal, and they will be more likely to impede than to impel progress.

Leadership

In networking, leadership—not administration or control—is the key aspect of management. Leadership is provided by a person or persons who keep the networking purpose clear at all times, and should help break down the barriers that inhibit the required links. Again, there is an analog in the technical world of networks with the new emphasis on the comprehensive roles of network management. We'll discuss these roles in Chapter 9.

Benefits

Purpose must be reinforced, even justified, by a clear expression of benefits to the enterprise, to the team, and to the individuals. Networking is difficult. It challenges our customary and comfortable ways of working as individuals or in face-to-face teams. The commitment to succeed in this new and challenging environment will be developed and sustained not through idealism or altruism, but through a constant appreciation of the benefits networking will generate across the networking community.

Networking in Action: Distributed Teaming

Earlier, we indicated distinctions and relationships between physical networks and the social activities needed to extract work value from that infrastructure. Similarly, we need to distinguish what we mean by distributed teaming from the conventional image of high-performance teams. Such distinctions highlight the extraordinary demands placed on groups working in the networking enterprise environment.

Most of us have had personal experience with teams, two or more people working or playing together to achieve a common objective. If we look at some common examples of high-performance teams—flight crews, professional sports teams, or hospital emergency room staffs—we can isolate some of the conditions that enable a group of individuals to come together and perform effectively.

Effective teams share characteristics that define their "teamness"—the qualities that make the team activities add up to more than the sum of its parts, or members. These qualities, listed below, focus largely on standards of skill and the mutual meeting of expectations.

O Members are trained and certified against established standards.
O Their roles and expectations are clearly specified.
O The concepts of trust and interdependence are well understood and influence the performance of each individual on the team.
O Work processes and procedures are rigid and well defined.
O Tools or equipment are common or standard, and procedures are reduced to checklists and other standardized references.
O Individuals are replaceable from a pool of equally qualified resources.
O The work environment is fairly stable and does not require frequent changes and adjustments.
O Rewards and recognition criteria are clear and most often affirm the efforts of the entire team.

All of these team attributes contribute to achievements that often are greater than the total output of each individual acting independently. But to ensure high performance for teams, it is essential to control the majority of the variables that influence their output potential. Traditionally, this control function has been managed by moving the team members to a common location. There they receive special training to reinforce their individual skills and build the trust and confidence they need to work together. Simulators, scrimmage matches, disaster exercises, and other derived techniques artificially stress workers' environment and provide the opportunity for individuals to merge their identity into the team. Checklists must accompany even the most routine and repetitive tasks. There are instant rewards for team achievements—spot promotions, incentive pay, trophies, and championships. Results count, and it's no wonder that organizations commit huge amounts of time and resources to creating and refining team-based work processes.

Distributed teams range in scope from small stakeholder units within a group or division, through extended enterprise or multicorporate teams, to full-scale corporate alliances. In all cases the teaming is characterized by team members' bringing different qualities to bear on shared goals, while retaining other personal, professional, and organizational goals, processes, and motives. All teams face similar cultural challenges.

Although distributed teaming has some of the high-performance team attributes discussed above—the acceptance of trust and dependency being one—it differs in other critical ways. Teaming, in this context, requires highly refined interpersonal skills and techniques independent of the job skills an individual brings to the team. Think of the chaos that would result if the members of a 747 flight crew, each a fully qualified pilot, acted independently in every flight situation. The distributed teams we depend on in the CBE often represent cross-functional business segments who would normally see and respond to issues in very different ways.

Job skill without communication skill, specifically electronic communication skill, is "light trapped under a barrel" in the simultaneous distributed work environment. (3)

Despite all our experience of and familiarity with the concept of teams, in the CBE many of the traditional techniques for building effective teams do not work, because it is often impossible to physically collocate the team members. We depend on the network to provide the common link for dispersed team members to work together and share their knowledge and expertise.

Distributed teams are dynamic, often constituted on an ad-hoc basis— "scratch teams." Frequently, an individual serves on several teams at the same time. To meet this complexity in the CBE we refocus management and leadership roles, and for this reason team management and development of a teaming culture becomes a full-time responsibility for line and staff managers. Team makeup is crucial to the success of any teaming activity. Film and theater directors have long known that the actors make the drama, much as team members will make the project: success is usually determined in the casting process. But building distributed teams is still an inexact science. Clearly, the goal product or services and the basic work processes of the organization have a lot to do with "casting." But equally important are commitment to electronic information and communication, trust, openness, and the ability to tolerate the stresses of time and distance when doing shared work.

In our model we make a clear distinction between networks and networking. This is to highlight the relationship between the physical network infrastructure and the special management and worker activities required to extract work-related value from the network. A similar situation exists when we consider teams and teaming. In an environment where the majority of work depends on accessing and sharing distributed information and knowledge, making a similar distinction helps to isolate the opportunities and barriers that effect creating and empowering teams.

Teaming is the optimum means of creating value within the realities we have discussed throughout this book: time compression, distributed resources, increasing dependency on knowledge-based input, the premium on flexibility and adaptability in organizations, and the fact that most of the information needed in today's work environments is in electronic form.

Teaming participants should exhibit the following characteristics:

- ○ Respond well to unstable environments, constant change, incomplete objectives, requirements, or specifications.
- ○ Build on group knowledge to address new situations.
- ○ Readily and proactively share knowledge and information.
- ○ Develop trust through communication and exchange of knowledge.
- ○ Are flexible and adaptive in stressful, time-compressed situations.
- ○ Accept the dynamic nature of the team, its scope, members, and goals; accept and adapt to rapid change.

Teaming is the behavior required for a team to overcome the barriers that affect their performance. In the work environment these barriers include:

- ○ Time compression that is constant and relentless.
- ○ Team resources that are physically distributed.
- ○ Work processes that are increasingly complex and more dependent on knowledge-based inputs.
- ○ Lack of organizational flexibility and adaptability.

Engineers and marketeers look at a product from completely different perspectives. The engineer is attracted to conformance to specifications, performance, and fit and finish. The marketeer sees the product in terms of messages, competitive position, and industry leadership. When cross-functional specialists become members of a team, their effectiveness is determined by their ability to contribute their special skills and perspectives to support the objectives of the team. And this is where teaming and networking come together and define a new culture to provide effective techniques and solutions.

A good example of the value of teaming is evident in the phenomenon of "teaming specialists" that has become a trademark of fast-track work.

One of the advantages of simultaneous distributed work is that specialists, wherever their physical or organizational location, can participate precisely when they are needed. There are many advantages to reaching out to specialists rather than gathering them in. By remaining at their home sites, specialists can continue to be in touch with home-base innovation, building their capabilities with the rest of their colleagues. Given the emerging capabilities of network learning, specialists do remain in contact with distributed sources of innovation as well: research institutions, consultants, and other innovating groups across the global enterprise. Another advantage of the reach-out model is that a specialist can be used in projects only when he or she is needed. A compiler expert or a chip designer can participate as part of the development team when those skills are needed. There's no need to incur the overhead and tie up an expensive resource with a close bonding of the individual to the project.

Additionally, specialists in a specific discipline can be brought together virtually, rather than physically, to address knotty problems that arise in the development cycle. Their "bonds" are based on communication capability and knowledge, not proximity. But these specialists, whether working independently in parallel or cooperating to simultaneously solve a common problem, must have open communication. Information and knowledge, wherever they reside, must be quickly accessible. The tighter the time frames, the more pressing the need for input and feedback capabilities that approach immediate, real-time communication.

We'd be remiss unless we said a few words here, in addition to the discussion in Chapter 9, about managing and leading distributed teams. Again, there is a distinction. Management is a responsibility, a role accepted by a person who commits to supporting the environment in which work happens, and in many cases, helps define work goals and processes. Managerial commitment is essential to the success of teaming initiative.

Given the blurred boundaries between organizational authority, changing group membership, distributed modes of work, complex technology infrastructure, and general lack of knowledge of what really works, to manage is to adventure in this new world.

The primary purpose of management is to define and articulate the visions that represent the best interests of the organization. A clear vision is the first requirement for clarity, and clarity overcomes many barriers that inhibit communication. Management is also responsible for developing strategic plans and for providing the resources needed to fuel the work processes. Management must identify and empower qualified leaders who will direct the various efforts called out by the strategy, and finally, management must evaluate results, reward success, and buffer the organization against outside interference.

Leadership, on the other hand, is not a position, not a fixed role but an attribute that can be demonstrated by one or more workers at any level in a teaming situation. A leader is responsible for maintaining the clarity and visibility of project goals across the team and for building and supporting the networking links that will sustain the environment.

Leadership in the CBE provides the bridge across management and the work processes, team resources, and the product or services that represent value. The leader gets things done. Obviously, a leader must have technical skills to be credible, but here we want to focus on the special leadership attributes that are essential in the CBE.

The leader is the agent for managing complexity. Complexity is a fact of life, and things rarely get less complex, regardless of our efforts to the contrary. The normal reaction to complexity is specialization, but specialization requires vertical development and the "stovepipe" mentality common in most organizations. An effective leader recognizes this and ensures that the team is properly constituted with a group of specialists equal to the complexity of the task and equipped with the tools and information they need to operate.

Leadership, then,

○ Provides the catalyst to bond the group into a productive team. The leader
>   ensures that management's vision and strategy are clearly understood
>   ensures that the task is well defined
>   creates an action plan

      sets goals and expectations

      recognizes outstanding performance

      deals quickly and fairly with individual and group problems

○ Becomes the feedback channel from the workers to management so that the vision and strategy are always in phase with the current capabilities of the organization.

○ Is responsible for initiating the special teaming and networking techniques necessary to ensure positive results in the information-based distributed work place.

○ Is required to recognize innovation. When a well-constituted and motivated cross-functional team addresses a problem, the leader should expect creativity. The leader must be sensitive to these creative flashes and make sure that the team is free to "push the envelope," as test pilots say. When a breakthrough is made, the leader ensures that management is aware, that rewards and recognition are given, and that this new knowledge is introduced to the rest of the organization.

Finally, the obvious—but most difficult—leadership attribute in the capability-based environment: the leader must make decisions. We have discussed at length the fast pace that must be maintained in today's work environment. We also know Murphy's law, which states that anything that can go wrong will go wrong. A leader who can and will make decisions is critical to maintaining the fast pace of the environment. This means that the leader must have a relationship with management, formal or implied, that gives him or her the authority to make decisions within specified boundaries.

This issue can easily become an insurmountable barrier for an organization in transition to the CBE. Either management will not delegate decision-making responsibilities, or they will put administrative protocols in place that inhibit real-time decisions. In fact, in many organizations decision making has become a victim of growth and bureaucracy at all levels. The effectiveness of leaders can and will be measured by the quality and timeliness of their decisions.

Our point here is that leadership is not a position on the organizational chart. It is an attitude, a perspective on a teaming effort, and requires special skills acquired through training, experience, and commitment. In the CBE culture, proven leaders will be highly valued. They will directly influence the survival of the organization.

Networking Events: A New Perspective on Meetings

A key goal of networking in the capability-based environment is to accomplish simultaneous distributed work. The success of this work model depends on continuous sharing of information and continuous shared understanding of information—on communication, meetings, and conferences. Data and information can fly among processes, people, and databases at incredible speeds. Communication among people takes more time; it's not as simple as just shipping the packet from point A to point B. People must painstakingly go through feedback, error checking, disambiguation, misunderstanding, irritation, secrecy, omission—a host of ancillary activities that are necessary if both parties are to "get" the same message. We need to address designs for people sharing information with as much care as we devote to designing how computing devices share data.

A meeting is an event in which people share (or withhold!) information. Conceptually, then, meetings are the hallmark of the networking environment. Most teamworking time is spent either in centralized (collocated) or distributed (electronically supported) meetings. Many of us, when we're not meeting with other people, meet with our own information: on the desk, in the books, or at the computer terminal. Here, through our own knowledge, we create or add value to information in the form of documents, spreadsheets, designs, and simulations that ultimately will be shared with others—at meetings. (4)

It's important to state all this up front, because a favorite excuse for alleged low productivity is "too much time spent in meetings." Information work demands meetings; we learn, coordinate, and integrate our work with the work of others in meetings. The outcome of a meeting should always be a more realized information process, service, or product. So, rather than reduce the number of meetings, we should make sure they happen every time they are needed—continually in some cases—and that they accomplish the intended purpose.

As we know, meetings, being interactions among individuals, tend to evolve other than as planned. Often they involve the wrong people, and exclude the people who should be there. Participants lose attention and drift. Meetings are often inconclusive. Often the outcome is ignored or forgotten.

Meetings can be classified in terms of space and time. In the space dimension, meetings can be *face to face* (with collocated participants), or *distributed* (with geographically separated participants). In the time dimension, *synchronous* meetings involve simultaneous exchange of information. *Asynchronous* meetings enable participants to offer and receive information at their convenience.

Face-to-Face and Distributed Meetings

Face-to-face meetings, including luncheons, chance meetings in hallways, informal work discussions, presentations, and reviews are the energizing activities of any group. And the protocols of face-to-face communications are unique cultural expressions of groups. Managers know the way they communicate, formally and informally; contributors in groups quickly learn their managers' and each other's styles and build a set of expectations about how to send and receive face-to-face communication.

Intergroup meetings also have protocols. These are based on the nature of the meeting, and more important, on who's hosting it. A technical management committee expects one kind of presentation; a financial forecast review another. Agendas, histories, and personalities all cue participants in the behavior patterns of the meetings. Even "styles of evidence" and "listener context" guide the meetings. For example, Committee A may be impressed by return on investment, past and future, not on vagaries such as product leadership or architectural completeness. The senior manager of strategic research may not like abstractions; better to give that person examples. Instead of alluding to "team performance enhancement," say that "the XTI Integration team reached their third prototype base level with all functionality on June 13, five weeks ahead of schedule."

These protocols continue to be in force at the nodes of distributed meetings; when protocols conflict in any way, or when participants in the meeting have different contexts or expectations, communication suffers. Given the intent of distributed meetings—to bring the contributions of a diverse set of stakeholders together—contexts and perspectives will vary. Since it's not always possible to know who is in the meetings—participants are largely out of sight, free to come and go unnoticed except by others at their node—it's not possible to predict difficulties. The issue is not to avoid such circumstances, but to plan for and manage them. It's not enough to run a distributed meeting as if it were any other meeting. All distributed meetings, regardless of the networking application used to support them, require specialized commitments and skills from the meeting leader and participants.

Synchronous and Asynchronous Meetings

In synchronous meetings, whether participants are together at a local site or communicating electronically across distance, everyone is together at the same time, taking turns offering and feeding back information. These meetings are ideal for rapid dissemination and exchange of information, especially when quick decisions must be reached.

Asynchronous meetings allow participants to interact at their own convenience, rather than having to commit to a specific meeting time. Electronic or computer-mediated communication applications such as electronic mail and computer conferencing enable such meetings. In computer conferencing, participants are free to speak their mind, vote, and accept action items as easily as if they had committed to a "same-time, same-space" meeting. Thus, schedule conflicts, time-zone differences, and personal commitments need not affect the sharing of information. Such meetings can occur over distances through electronic information vehicles such as videotext and computer conferencing applications, or in meeting rooms where charts and diagrams are left on the wall to form a physical shared information space.

Electronic Meetings

As we've mentioned, electronic meetings enable participants to fully engage in a meeting, whether asynchronous or synchronous, while remaining at sites convenient to their work. Coworkers, customers, suppliers, and other stakeholders can remain where they have access to their information; they share their knowledge through the network, rather than move themselves to another site. Distance is not a factor in distributed electronic meetings.

Electronic meetings are supported by peer-to-peer connections; for example, telephone and video networks that move information to and from people, as opposed to moving people to or with information. Benefits of electronic meetings include the following:

○ A meeting or conference among two or more people at two or more sites can be set up as quickly as we can dial a phone or log on to the computer system. For example, users of computer-aided design (CAD) models in, say, Scotland can in a matter of minutes discuss and often fix bugs with the engineering group in Canada. No filing, reporting, or waiting until the next cycle is required.

○ Travel time and expense can be reduced in many cases. However, there is strong evidence that overall, travel expenditures are not reduced, just redirected more productively.

○ Expert knowledge can be brought to bear on issues and problems no matter where the experts are, or in whose organization; their participation can be episodic, knowledge based, and administratively informal.

○ People can confer without leaving the office, or current work locale. This is a much less formal and more productive alternative to a central conference location.

○ Information can be shared with a great many people in one event.

○ Time of decision cycles can be reduced.

○ Changes can be effected simultaneously across the organization and across the information base.

○ Feedback to information shared is exchanged in real time. This is important when we consider the time-value of information and the dependence of our work processes on having the right information, in the right form, at the right time.

○ The technology base of distributed meetings makes it possible to record information and retain it in accessible form.

○ High-level personnel who need to be everywhere at once can work from their physical location, participating in an electronic information exchange anywhere the network reaches.

○ New opportunities can be seized, not lost, by getting to the right decision makers wherever they are, whenever they are needed.

One common use of the electronic meeting is as a pre-meeting, to build shared context expectations among the anticipated participants of a large face-to-face conference. The pre-meeting provides a cost-effective, convenient forum for clearing the air, enabling the main meeting to progress with more clarity and efficiency. This is especially important in stakeholder meetings, where people from different, perhaps even competing, organizations will be participating. In many industries, competing contractors must hold lengthy meetings to cooperatively build information-based plans and designs. They must be sensitive to one another's meeting styles and expectations, terminology, and protocols. Not having the advantage of seeing the looks on their co-participants faces when they are heading down a dangerous path can be a drawback. But a well-moderated computer conference can provide a neutral ground to sort out concerns, agendas, and expectations before people travel to the site for the face-to-face meeting.

This is not to suggest that electronics distributed meetings should replace collocated, face-to-face meetings. Face-to-face meetings may be the most essential activity of any group. The way these meetings are conducted, their purpose, and their expectations are all deeply rooted in a group's culture. And we must keep in mind that a distributed meeting is actually a linking of collocated meetings: the dynamics of the meeting as a whole depends on how well each node manages its own meeting process and successfully integrates into the overall meeting. It is important to consider face-to-face meetings as well as distributed meetings, and determine how each can best contribute to the new work model.

SUMMARY

Networking applications can substitute for much of the communication that is lost when people are separated in time and space. However, by representing only pieces of the spectrum, the technology tends to miss things. Any kind of distributed meeting is hampered by the fact that people can't see each other, don't know each other, and in some cases don't even know who is at the meetings. In face-to-face meetings, much social control comes through eye contact, and voice tone and volume. In electronic meetings these features work only within the groups participating face to face (or eye to eye) at the host site or remote sites. Even audio and video conferencing lose many of the dynamics of face-to-face contact. But with attention paid to potential pitfalls, a well-thought-out approach to electronic meetings can leverage an organization's overall capability base.

NOTES

1. Charles Savage sees trust as perhaps *the* critical prerequisite for successful teaming. For an excellent study of the technologies, processes, and implications of collaborative work see Michael Schrage, *Shared Minds* (New York: Random House, 1990).
2. The Networking Institute, Inc., 505 Waltham Street, West Newton, MA.
3. Problems arise when teaming members desire to exert influence on each other in cross-organizational, non-hierarchical environments. For a recent discussion of the many faces of personal influence in organizations, see Allan R. Cohen and David L. Bradford, *Influence Without Authority* (New York: Wiley, 1990). Chris Argyris, in *Organization and Innovation* (Homewood, IL: R.D. Irwin, 1965), examines the beliefs, fears, and behaviors that are barriers to building trust and accepting innovation in organizations. Dr. H. David Shuster sees teaming as the key

to quality in *Teaming for Quality Improvement* (Englewood Cliffs, NJ: Prentice-Hall, 1990). In "The Practical Guide to Joint Ventures and Corporate Alliances," Robert Porter clearly articulates principles that are key to successful alliance management, whether at the corporate alliance or multifunction team level. Quoted in *IEEE Engineering Management Review* (September 1990). See also Shneiderman, *Software Psychology,* Chapter 3.

4. For a comprehensive and readable study of meetings, see Helen B. Schwartzman, *The Meeting* (New York: Plenum, 1989).

Chapter 7 | Enterprise Networking Applications

We have envisioned the enterprise as a network of constituencies—stakeholders—that must come together to meet today's time-sensitive, quality-focused, global business challenges. This union is accomplished through designed electronic networks and networking techniques, by way of computer-mediated communication through networking applications. We've already mentioned some of these applications, such as the telephone, electronic mail, and computer conferencing. Here we are speaking of enterprise-level applications: the "effects" of the applications must be available to all stakeholders in the extended enterprise. This can mean a single, backbone application or information-sharing service that is shared by all constituencies; for example, a proprietary electronic mail system. In an alternative model, applications or services from a variety of information system vendors can mutually exchange and understand information passed between communicators if "open systems" protocols are observed. The primary example of this model is the ubiquitous telephone, through which voice information can be exchanged whether one or many telephone systems are involved.

In this chapter we'll look more closely at how enterprise networking applications further the information-sharing work of the enterprise.

Overview of Networking Applications

Networking applications can be categorized according to:

○ The representational form of information they support: voice (sound), text and graphics, image and video.
○ Whether they enable synchronous or asynchronous communication: support real-time interactions or effect communication at the conve-

nience of the participants, saving the trouble of getting everyone on line at the same time.

This classification has been a traditional lens through which "groupware" (the generic name for computer-based group communications and information access applications) has been viewed. Robert Johansen uses the matrix in Figure 7-1 to position groupware applications in relation to appropriate temporal/spatial contexts. (1)

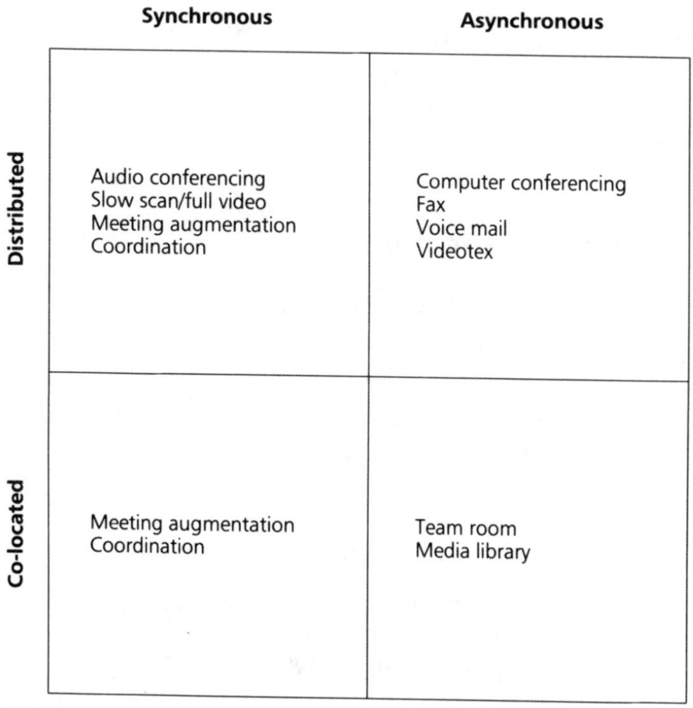

	Synchronous	**Asynchronous**
Distributed	Audio conferencing Slow scan/full video Meeting augmentation Coordination	Computer conferencing Fax Voice mail Videotex
Co-located	Meeting augmentation Coordination	Team room Media library

Figure 7-1 Groupware

Beyond this general scheme, applications may be particularly useful in one or another communication situation. For example, using electronic mail to announce an important ad-hoc meeting to a wide distribution list gets the word out efficiently to a lot of people. It is somewhat more formal than a phone call, but less formal than a memo or an announcement in a computer conference.

Here we will look at these key networking applications:

○ Voice applications
    Audio teleconferencing (synchronous)
    Voice mail (asynchronous)
○ Text and graphics applications
    Electronic mail
    Computer conferencing
    Videotex
    Shared text and graphics editors
    Bit-mapped multiwindow displays
    Fax
○ Image and video applications
    Still and slow-scan video
    Full-motion video
    Hypermedia

Voice Applications

The basic networking technology in our high-tech world is the telephone. Telephone equipment and services have reached an extraordinary level of versatility and accessibility. There are phones in most places in the world; voice access through the network is ubiquitous. Audio applications can connect people synchronously and asynchronously wherever they may be: in distant offices, train stations, cars, or airplanes.

Audio Teleconferencing

Audio teleconferencing, the synchronous linking of three or more people through the telephone system for peer-to-peer voice communication, is somewhat more complex that the usual one-to-one telephone call. Ideally, a teleconferencing service establishes and manages the links, making sure nodes don't drop off during the meeting. State-of-the-art audio teleconferencing is an effective and relatively inexpensive way to link small or large numbers of sites, with small or large numbers of people at each site, in real time. (2)

The spectrum of teleconference support for distributed meetings ranges from informal, ad-hoc, three-way conference calls through private or public telephones, to large, planned audio teleconferencing events managed by a teleconferencing service.

With high-quality equipment and facilitation skills, teleconferencing among multiple groups of people can be as useful as the phone is for two individuals. The telephone provides immediate feedback, the semantics of intonation, capability for holding attention, as well as flexibility and availability, because worldwide, the network is in place.

Conventional wisdom holds that 40 percent to 50 percent *reductions* in travel have been reported after audio teleconferencing becomes available. However, it is likely that the primary benefit will be in the acceleration of the work process, rather than savings in travel cost. Audio teleconferencing is extremely useful for time-critical, highly interactive discussions on specific subjects that do not require visuals. For example:

○ Reviewing status of action items.
○ Reporting a problem with a delivery date that needs immediate attention.
○ Getting agreement on the readiness of a distributed support group to deliver services.

Information expressly packaged for audio delivery can be distributed to large distributed groups. For example, the pharmaceutical industry often augments doctors' lunches with audio teleconferences in which a scientist or engineer who has developed a new drug presents the pharmacology to the assembled doctors. They can thereby remain current on the latest in pharmaceutical research and availability. This way, hundreds of doctors (potential customers) can be reached simultaneously at very low cost.

Voice Mail

The asynchronous counterpart to telephone conferencing is voice mail. Analogous to electronic mail, this application uses "store and forward" and "tone-coded routing" technology. Participants send, receive, and manage voice messages at their own convenience. Voice-mail users can send messages to distribution lists, access date- and time-stamped incoming messages, and leave messages as to their own whereabouts and how they can be reached. The systems are wholly automated; subscribers use the telephone keypad to call up system functions as well as address calls.

We are encountering voice mail in many of our daily interactions. When we call to cancel a magazine subscription, refinance a mortgage, or discuss a design issue with the chief engineer, we may find our call being routed by directed keypad entries. If no person is available to accept our information, we can leave a message in the proper "voice mailbox," analogous to an electronic mailbox or even a regular mailbox. The value of voice mail is efficiency. If the caller can't find the right person at the given time, he or she can leave a message at the right mailbox. On the receiver side, the message is retrieved when the person returns. Voice mail automates routine clerical tasks and ensures that no called-in information is lost.

Text and Graphics Applications

As with audio applications, data communications that support the exchange of text and graphic information are available wherever a subscriber can gain entry to the computer network. Your office is where you can log on to the computer system. There you can exchange messages, participate in meetings, and read the latest organizational news. You are connected informationally with your peers, not tied down to your physical office.

Electronic Mail

Electronic mail (e-mail) enables any subscriber in the system to communicate in writing, synchronously or asynchronously, with any other subscriber who shares access to the network. Messages are generally informal and can be sent easily to wide distribution lists. Messages can contain text, graphics, images, and other data, depending on the sophistication of the system. (3)

Computer Conferencing

A computer conference is a written asynchronous discussion or meeting involving any number of participants in a shared network. The term *computer conferencing* is actually too restrictive, for the medium is used for a wider variety of purposes:

○ Informal discussion places for organizations, interest groups, social organizations.
○ Open and scheduled issue resolution forums.
○ Virtual office hours for students to meet with teachers in distance learning settings.
○ Information exchange before and after synchronous distributed meetings.

○ Anonymous self-help groups in the workplace or in society as a whole.

Conferencing involves accessing the information space, selecting the desired meeting, reading what other participants have been saying about the topic, and entering into the deliberations with one's own written contributions. Admission to a specific conference can be open or controlled, as determined by the conference moderator (a participant who has taken on the responsibility for leading and managing, including opening and closing the conference). Moderation, or chairing a conference, is a new role in organizational electronic communications. Computer conferencing is important and interesting because it is a technology that depends on continuous, knowledgeable human interaction.

Computer conferencing has played a significant role in simultaneous distributed work projects, providing a continuous electronic location to find resolution to key issues. The meeting is always in session. (4)

In a computer conference you can ask a question to the group at large. You may have no idea who will supply the answer. But with an organizational agreement on naming of conferences, and guidelines for finding the right place to contribute or look for information, the conference can predictably support round-the-clock information exchange.

Videotex

Videotex has been called the electronic newspaper. Essentially, it is an enterprise application that enables access to information as screen pages of text and graphics from anywhere in the computer network. Subscribers can see pages of regularly updated information about activities of interest: announcements, news from home, or financial reports. Videotex is also valuable as an electronic publishing mechanism: manuals, policies, and catalogs can be published in videotex format.

Shared Text and Graphics Editors

Within our definition, shared text, graphics and image editors are communication devices; they enable distributed users to simultaneously see and manipulate shared data and information. Team members separated by a campus or an ocean can simultaneously (almost) revise a simulated model image, a blueprint, or a paragraph of a specification. With shared editing capability, a designer at one site can electronically highlight a point of information, while someone at another enters modifications.

Success with shared editors is not dependent solely on technology: there must be agreement in place among participants on who has the authority to write to the screen at a particular time. This is analogous to "who holds the chalk" in a traditional classroom or conference setting. In distributed computer-aided-design applications, for example, this kind of activity becomes quite complex, requiring shared protocols for calculations and for manipulation of models. Ideally, groups of users in shared editing situations should have all the capabilities of working collaboratively with information that they have working alone at their desktops.

Bit-mapped Multiwindow Displays

Bit-mapped multiwindow displays, while not strictly communications artifacts, are essential for optimizing the use of networking applications. The precision and flexibility of bit mapping and windows enable a level of information work otherwise constrained in single-screen, character-cell presentations. For example, multiwindow displays:

○ Provide a spatial layout of information, as well as graphics. Windows are useful syntactic indicators when working in distributed mode ("Now let's compare that text with the drawing in the upper-left window").
○ Enable users to juxtapose displayed information from a variety of applications, peers, or parts of a single document for comparison and association.
○ Allow users to multiprocess information; to simultaneously work on several ideas, jumping from one displayed or accessible window to another, when an association or relevance presents itself.

Fax

Fax enables the accurate transmission of an image through the telephone from one location to another, or several, locations. Because so much information is still in paper—not digital—form, and because the telephone network is everywhere, fax has become an extremely popular application. Fax is often used to transmit late-breaking paper information to remote sites during teleconferences. With portable faxes so easily available, it is possible to use them in any meeting room, office, or even automobile, where a teleconference is taking place, as long as the site has two outside telephone lines.

Image and Video Applications

Still and Slow-Scan Video

Slow-scan video (SSV) refers to the capability to transmit images from one site to another through the use of video still cameras at speeds slower than full video. A key advantage to SSV is its ability to transmit over common voice lines, avoiding the high costs of video network transmission. Thus, SSV is an inexpensive way to widen the scope of teleconferencing to include video, as well as text, voice, and graphic information.

SSV has been used extensively in applications such as computer-aided manufacturing. Conferees can share still representations of people and information: images of concrete objects, not just paper. The capability is useful when, during meetings, new visual information needs to be shared—information that is not yet represented in the data system, slides, or paper that can be faxed. Of course, pages from documents can be shared as images as well, for discussion or revision.

Full-Motion Video

But the big news of the 1990s is full-motion video. This is the capability to use standard video, as we know it from television and film, in support of business activity. The press is full of success stories of corporations who are using their own satellite-based business video networks to communicate across their distributed organizations. Major corporations have in place private video networks with multiple transmitting nodes and hundreds of receiving nodes. To enhance simultaneous distributed work processes across the stakeholder community, customers and suppliers of these corporations are being included in the networks.

With video you can transmit a well-structured message to a large number of people simultaneously. You know that your audience gets the message, and that they get it all at once; and with additional teleconferencing, you can get instant feedback, again in a formal setting.

Appropriate use of video can result in improved bottom-line performance. In such situations there can be significant time and cost savings, minimized interruption of work and geographic commitments, and timely sharing of extremely important information.

Video conferencing has been used extensively in communicating key organizational messages:

○ A customer service headquarters can reach 8,000 field personnel simultaneously to "personally" deliver new corporate sales directions and initiatives.

○ A CEO, in his New England media center, delivers a congratulatory message to 400 Australian area salespeople. They get to talk with him directly by audio hookup.

○ Major product announcements with images of the product and marketing strategies get to an entire worldwide sales, support, and customer organization; no one has to wait to read about it in the papers.

○ University courses are broadcast to all engineering sites in a manufacturing organization. Employees can see the courses during lunch and call in with questions. Or they can see the videotape when it's more convenient. And everyone on the computer network can discuss issues in the televised presentation with instructors who hold electronic "office hours" by participating in ongoing computer conferences.

The main caveat with full-motion video conferencing and still and slow-scan video is that it is not a casual medium; its use must be well-designed and executed, and preparation time can limit its effectiveness for fast-breaking events.

Hypermedia

We've mentioned the roles of hypertext and hypermedia in the capability-based organization. (5) Hypermedia can link ideas and information representations in an information base laterally or vertically. That is, you can "jump" laterally from an agenda to a related report to a relevant airline schedule by following links; or you can "zoom" on a single document to greater or lesser detail, whether it be from topic to statement to backup data in text.

Videotex can provide this capability to some extent, but navigation is across static pages of information, rather than along dynamic pointers to information that can range in granularity from a symbol or character to an entire document in an information base.

With hypermedia members of a team can navigate through volumes of written specifications, following only those threads relevant to their search, jumping to illustrative simulation models or videotape demonstrations where needed. Hypertext and hypermedia can enrich the capabilities of other networking applications, such as electronic mail and computer conferencing, by linking information in meaningful ways within and across the applications.

For example, several computer conferences may have information on the downside effects of a marketing strategy. Hypertext links can logically associate those information items in a context of "all comments on going for market share with product X," rather than leaving each information item in the context of the particular conference topic within which it appears.

To extend this further, hypermedia links can connect relevant information from computer conferences with graphics contained in electronic mail messages and with video clips of key executives speaking to the issues. Again, the context is a sharp focus on the *situation,* not the local framework in which each piece of information originally appeared.

The most comprehensive use of enterprise networking applications is found in distributed meeting augmentation systems. This describes a suite of applications that provide multimedia high-bandwidth communications,

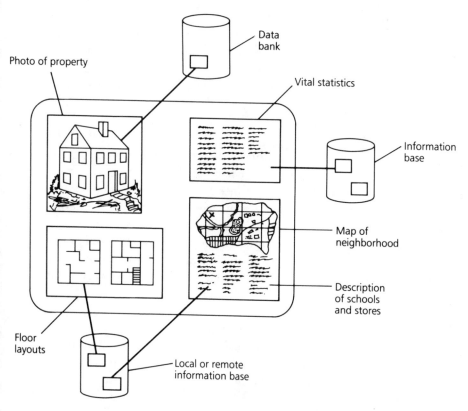

Figure 7-2 Hypermedia Linking of Text, Graphic, and Video Information

support for meeting dynamics, and recording of meeting deliberations in formal distributed meetings.

An augmented meeting involves a trained facilitator using a computer workstation at one or more of the conferencing nodes, accessing, capturing, and displaying information being generated or discussed in the meeting. The workstation display is projected on a screen for everyone in the conference room to see. That same display is transmitted in real time to all participating nodes, where, depending on the size of the group, the display can appear at a workstation or a wall projection. The windowing capability of workstations allows for juxtaposition of information, such as versions of specifications, or supporting arguments for various decision alternatives. In addition, multiple display windows enable the group to keep before it the agenda, clock, list of action items/commitments, map of who's participating in the meeting, and any other important background information. And the facilitator can keep all the information current with no disruption to the meeting.

At remote nodes the shared screen information is supported with teleconferencing links. When necessary, remote participants can ask the facilitator to "pass the chalk" to them so they can make a written contribution to the shared electronic display from their own workstations. The information can be discussed by all present, captured as files, interrelated by hypertext linking, filed in commonly accessible databases, and distributed to other participating nodes.

Electronic blackboards, having the capability of digitizing, filing, distributing to other nodes, and printing out text and graphics handwritten on the board, are also used extensively in augmented meetings.

The primary value of augmented meetings lies in "information economy": more information generated in the meetings is retained in accessible form (storage of information is not of much value; access to it is). Also, the meetings have persistence. The proceedings don't disappear and become forgotten when the meeting ends; all information and interaction can be continued in electronic form for follow-up. There are a number of advantages:

○ Minutes can be generated at the terminal in real time, displayed on the screen, revised and accepted, mailed by e-mail to distribution lists, and/or stored in computer conferences or other shared information spaces. No state change of information from paper to electronic form need be endured.

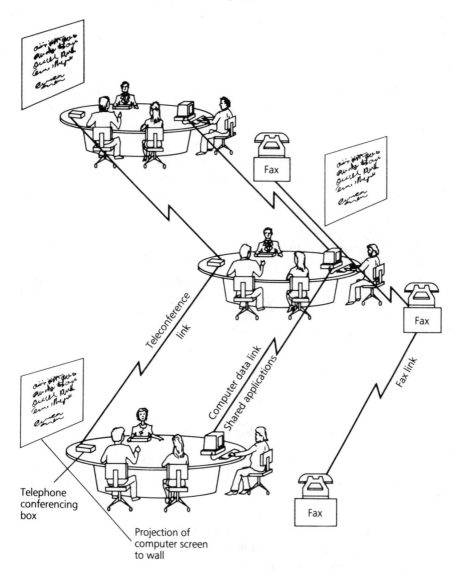

Figure 7-3 Augmented Meeting

○ Deliberations, decisions, and commitments are "published" in the room as they happen. Using instant feedback, misunderstandings and ambiguities can be cleared up immediately. By using so-called coordination software programs, or e-mail follow-up, commitments can easily be tracked.

○ All participants at all sites have access to all on-line data and information. (6)

A major contribution of augmented meetings is the ability to coordinate activities and to record and track commitments. "Coordination" software is available now that supports structured approaches to group work, including time and commitment management, information access and routing control, and decision support. Such programs all come with built-in philosophies of what is right for a group's coordination processes. Organizations must use good judgment in incorporating such support into their work process: the perspective inherent in the software must be appropriate to the organization's culture.

Along with the advantages, however, there are some short-term drawbacks to using augmentation applications. Groups must agree to formalize meetings—to design the meeting process in such a way that meeting information can be captured, attributed, and tracked. Introducing formality must be done with great care, as people are extremely sensitive to being forced into new meeting protocols. Human systems consulting is recommended to ease the transition into new meeting forms, no matter how appropriate they may seem to management. Also, the technology and facilitation can be intrusive. Meeting participants must be put at ease in this possibly threatening environment.

Networking Design

As with any other aspect of simultaneous distributed work, networking design must be based on the needs of the work community, including:

○ Connectivity needs of distributed work teams.
○ Types of information to be moved.
○ Appropriateness of technologies to social realities.
○ The availability and interoperability of various audio, data, image, and voice applications.

Such care in design is necessary because effective networking does not happen by accident; it is not as easy as picking up the phone. Yet, with the appropriate technical, methodological, and social infrastructure, sufficient predictability can be brought to the process. Midway through some particularly excruciating time-crunch, we don't hear those show-stopper words:

"We need to review these color specs with Singapore ASAP; anyone got an idea how we can do this?"

A well-designed communications infrastructure can reduce information barriers between people. With agreed-upon applications and protocols for their appropriate use, networking is easier and more natural. Rapid feedback, both positive and negative, helps resolve ambiguity and diffuse disagreements. By spending less time dealing unproductively with the routine aspects of planning, setting up, and managing distributed communications, people have more time to devote to individual work and to the quality of information sharing.

Only a group engaged in a specific project, knowing the forms of information that need to be shared and the priorities for work, can determine what networking applications are most productive for its teams. While managers can determine that there will be such a networking design and that it will have certain goal and metrics, it is extremely important that the teaming individuals participate in the distributed meeting design.

The model offered here suggests a basic networking design to support simultaneous distributed work in the capability-based environment. The applications are available today and will continue to evolve rapidly. Therefore, organizations must design their networking infrastructure with an eye toward tomorrow's needs and technological capabilities, as well as today's requirements. With even a small part of a networking design in place, an organization can begin to expect, rather than hope, to handle communication needs as they arise. A networking enterprise should evaluate its communication needs in terms of the kind of information it expects to communicate, the nature of the situation (formal/informal, urgent, sensitive), and whether synchronous or asynchronous communication is appropriate. The assumption is that the team will be distributed.

Once the required information sharing "map" is developed, the nodes where people work—their workstations, terminals or phones—will be linked to the nodes with which they must communicate. The nature of the links (phone line, data line, video channel) will be determined by the purpose, therefore the nature, of the information to be shared.

A Networking Design for Team Building

Certain networking applications are suited to particular kinds of work, or stages in typical work processes. For example, Robert Johansen has applied such applications to the essential process of team building.

Johansen offers the matrix shown in Figure 7-4 that maps the appropriate networking applications to traditional stages in the development of high-performance teams. (7)

Such networking designs have been applied successfully on worldwide projects ranging from development of computer hardware to the creation and publication of equipment user manuals.

The general design of such products calls for initial face-to-face "kick-off" meetings, where participants can get to know each other on a human-contact level. Usually these initial meetings last a day or two; but on occasion they are extended into more lengthy context-building periods with individuals actually working at each other's sites: workers live in each other's organizations and cultures to build an understanding of the perspectives and processes of the groups with whom they would be teaming. Whatever the length of this kickoff period, no distributed project in our memory has succeeded without such "context-setting" meetings.

The information-sharing activities of the project can then be carried

	Synchronous	**Asynchronous**
Distributed	Change notification and feedback Goal clarification Role verification Commitment restatements	Build group knowledge base
Co-located	Team start-up Trust building Commitment making Teaming renewal	Site specific policies, training

Figure 7-4 Team Building Matrix

out primarily through continuous availability of networking applications that suit project needs in terms of kind of information to be exchanged, the formality required in the exchange, the urgency of the communication, and the preferences of those participating. For example, a computer conference may be kept open for the duration of the project to hold the discussions and negotiations concerning design changes. This not only provides a convenient facility for debate, but constitutes a permanent record of design changes over the course of a project.

Another common use of computer conferencing and bulletin boards is to continuously support the social context for their teaming efforts: conferences evolve that may have nothing to do with the subject matter of the project: restaurants in Ireland, skiing in New England, best West Coast Beaches—all contribute to the teaming effort by creating a level of shared interest—the beginnings of a culture—that helps people understand each other better, and therefore understand each other's project-related knowledge and information better.

On the other hand, status meetings, project reviews, and resource planning meetings need rapid recognition of issues and commitment to action; they can best be handled through regularly scheduled teleconferences or augmented meetings.

As the projects progress, the face-to-face context needs to be reinforced. This has led to the creation of the role of "circuit rider." This is a knowledgeable, trusted project member who literally carries the news, controversies, and ideas from teaming node to teaming node. Instead of many people traveling to other sites to "get the feeling" of what's going on, one or two people "live on a plane," linking the people at the sites, acting as messengers, ombudspeople, chaplains, and lifelines to those who may work far from their home site throughout the project.

Only by experimenting within pilot projects will a group learn which applications best support its processes. But whatever the menu of application, successful distributed projects will have one feature in common: the communications will have been designed from the start.

SUMMARY

Networking applications provide the window into the communication system of the extended enterprise. Most of the technology is new, the social aspects of the simultaneous distributed work situation are even newer, and designed implementations are rare.

But successes so far have had one thing in common: the networking was designed. Communication is too complex to leave to chance. Through processes such as augmentation, the risk of introducing new kinds of communication can be reduced, while the appropriateness and performance of the application is evaluated. With a predictable distributed communication infrastructure in place, and an enterprise commitment to networking applications support, teams can do their work with minimal energy invested in the routine of communication. Interpersonal communications can be sustained across the organization as naturally as a personal phone call today, and the networking enterprise will prosper.

NOTES

1. Robert Johansen, "Groupware and Collaborative Systems: A Big Picture View," a report prepared for Globecom '89. For an excellent study of what groupware is, what it does, and how it can bring value to your group, see Johansen's, *Groupware: Computer Support for Business Teams* (New York: The Free Press, 1988).

2. See Robert Johansen, *Teleconferencing and Beyond* (New York: McGraw-Hill, 1984); Lorne A. Parker and Christine H. Olgren, eds., *Teleconferencing and Interactive Media* (University of Wisconsin Extension Center for Interactive Studies, 1980); and Robert Cowan, *Teleconferencing* (Reston, VA: Reston, 1984).

3. The Electronic Mail Association defines electronic mail as: " . . . non-interactive communication of text, data, image or video messages between a sender and designated recipients by systems utilizing telecommunications links." Quoted in Caswell, *E-Mail*, p. 2.

4. Graham Galer of the Shell Planning Group describes the role of computer conferencing within the Royal Dutch/Shell group of companies. See *Computer Conferencing in a Multinational Company,* a report delivered at the American Association for the Advancement of Science 1990 Annual Meeting. The report is available from SIPC (PL/24), Shell Centre, London SE1 7NA.

5. See Douglas C. Engelbart, "Authorship Provisions in AUGMENT," pp. 107–126. For a thorough examination of the past, present, and future of hypermedia, along with an annotated bibliography, see Jacob Nielson, *Hypertext and Hypermedia* (San Diego: Academic Press, 1990). To experience an ultimate vision for hypermedia, read Theodore H. Nelson, *Literary Machines: The Report on, and of, Project Xanadu Concerning Word Processing, Electronic Publishing, Hypertext, Thinkertoys, Tomorrow's Intellectual Revolution, and Certain Other Topics Including Knowledge, Education and Freedom* (Ann Arbor: XOC, 1981).

6. N. Dean Meyer, and Mary Boone, *The Information Edge* (New York: McGraw-Hill, 1987), Chapter 11, "Augmented Meeting Support." For a discussion of augmented meetings at the Greyhound Financial Corporation, see "Business

Meetings by Keyboard," Claudia H. Deutsch, *The New York Times,* Sunday, October 21, 1990, p. D-25.

7. Robert Johansen, "Groupware and Collaborative Systems." The Team Performance Model™ is the work of Allan B. Drexler, David Sibbet, and Russell H. Forrester. It is quoted in *Team Building,* W. Brendan Reddy and Kaleel Jamison, eds. (Alexandria, VA: NTL Institute for Applied Behavioral Science, 1988). For more information on the model, contact Graphic Guides, 832 Folsom, San Francisco, CA.

Chapter 8 | Enterprise Networks: Anatomy and Physiology

Earlier, we saw how the successful construction of the Panama Canal ultimately depended on the creation of the proper infrastructure to move the dirt: the railroad. In the capability-based environment, where the chief material is digital information, the infrastructure that moves the information is the enterprise network. It is important to think of the enterprise network not just as technology, but as a strategy driven by the need to provide information access to the workers who need it.

Modern networks are complex technologies that require trained and motivated specialists who are fully committed to the design, procurement, and operation of the system. But successful networking requires that all key players share a common understanding of essential network assets, because those stakeholders share the responsibility for ensuring that these critical resources will serve the design objectives of the organization.

Viewing the enterprise network as a strategic concept, we can describe it as a vehicle for capability in terms of a few high-level specifications:

○ The network must incorporate an architecture designed to support peer-to-peer, open information access between all work groups in the enterprise.
○ High-performance local area network (LAN) technology will be used to provide network access to workers and to provide access to other LANs through the enterprise backbone network.
○ The wide area network (WAN) backbone will provide channels to interconnect local area network segments and to provide access to the outside world.
○ The various network segments, the LANs, WANs, and various con-

trol elements that they utilize will comply to approved standards to support efficient use and exchange of information.

○ The enterprise network will be constantly monitored and controlled by a network management system that compiles and displays the network's vital signs and allows management to deliver the services needed to sustain the value-generating activities of the organization.

In his explorations of complex organizations, Harvard Business School professor Robert Bartlett uses a model developed for the study of human organisms. Bartlett uses the biological taxonomy of anatomy, physiology, and psychology to isolate key attributes of organizations. (1) Like humans—and organizations—modern networks are complex and constantly-changing organisms, so Bartlett's technique is useful for developing a perspective of how the network relates and contributes to the capability-based environment.

Applying the model to networks, we can relate anatomy to the various products and configurations that comprise the enterprise system: LANs, WANs, and network management systems. The physiology of the network relates to activities, processes, and functions that allow the network elements to work together as a system. We use connectivity, interoperability, manageability, and performance as indicators of network physiology.

In enterprise networks, psychology—the science of mental processes—becomes a deliberate design and management commitment, which ensures that the network-based capabilities are responsive to the organization's needs.

In this chapter we'll look at the first two elements of the model, network anatomy and network physiology. Chapter 9 will discuss network psychology, the science of real-time involvement in network capability processes.

Anatomy of the Enterprise Network

Our organism is the enterprise network, comprising all network resources, or segments:

○ Voice systems, including private exchanges, local wiring loops, trunks, and tie lines that interconnect locations.

○ Data systems of LANs and WANs, public and private packet networks, wire, coaxial cable, microwave and satellite radio, as well as fiber optic data distribution facilities.

○ Fax and video imaging systems.
○ Management and control resources required to sustain network operations.

Because of the physical similarities among all networks, we can concentrate on one—the data network—and extend its attributes across the other segments.

Local Area Networks (LANs)

LANs are a collection of wires, coaxial and fiber optic cables, electronic repeaters, active and passive gateways, portals, equipment cabinets, operating systems, and monitoring devices selected and integrated to move data among users who share either physical proximity or common interest. LANs provide the basic building blocks needed to begin the communication process: connecting the knowledge worker to a capability-based environment.

LANs are reminiscent of the Shmoos that cartoonist Al Capp introduced many years ago in the comic strip "Li'l Abner." Shmoos were cheerful, obliging creatures that could change into whatever met people's needs:

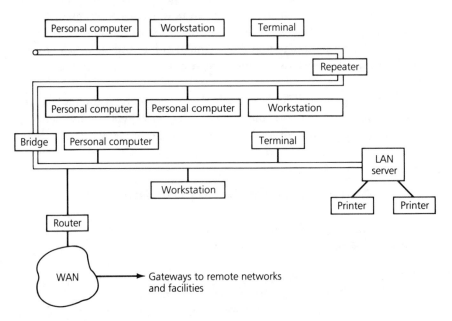

Figure 8-1 The LAN

gourmet meals for the hungry, designer clothes for the trendy, and dollars for the needy. LANs are capable of doing almost anything innovative network managers and users design them to do. In many ways, the availability of LAN technology is what makes the advanced and information-dependent work process we use for simultaneous distributed work possible and practical. The high-performance LAN has evolved as the most effective way to process digital information for use within the boundaries of a localized work environment, and to provide practical and cost-effective connectivity to the extended enterprise.

Properly designed and employed, LAN technology contributes directly to all the "effects" required to sustain capability. It can facilitate information access, it can provide communication channels to link workers into distributed teams, it can be flexible and support growth, and it can be easily changed as circumstances require. The performance potential of a well-engineered LAN can sustain the tempo of the most sophisticated work process, expanding and contracting as the boundaries of the enterprise change. LAN technology is extremely reliable and easy to configure, so it can provide the confidence and flexibility needed to keep pace with a rapidly changing environment. LANs are used to interconnect with networks serving the rest of the enterprise community and with the outside world, using devices called gateways and bridges. They can provide management with effective control and a wide variety of options for more creative, secure, and efficient use of their information resources.

LANs come in all sizes and flavors, from tiny nets serving a few personal computers within an office space to networks linking thousands of users and machines. LANs support routine administration applications, like word processing, spreadsheets, and order entry; they also enable graphic and simulation applications that control the most sophisticated automated processes.

The majority of LANs in use today fall into two major configurations: LANs that connect users of large and mid-sized computers into a "computer network," and a newer configuration known as the personal computer LAN, or PC LAN, which has evolved to provide the growing personal computer user community with a lower-cost networking alternative. PC LANs add networking power to personal computers, significantly adding to their utility and functionality.

LANs use a wide range of technologies and can be configured to support most work situations, physical plants, or application requirements. Consequently, they vary significantly with respect to their transmission speeds, the number of devices they can support, the distances they span, and the capabilities and services they offer.

Wide Area Networks (WANs)

Simultaneous distributed work, by definition, implies geographic separation. An obvious requirement for the networking enterprise is that geographic barriers be overcome, allowing knowledge workers to interact as distributed teams. As the LAN serves as the basic building block to provide information workers with the communication and access they need at their workplace, the wide area network (WAN) provides global access and communication.

Wide area networks are not a new concept. Telephone networks, private or public, have always made a distinction between local distribution segments and long-distance toll segments. Both these segments have evolved separately and developed specialized technologies to improve their quality and reliability, as well as their financial return on investments. For example, multiplexing, the technology that is used to derive multiple voice channels from a single wire pair, was developed to increase the traffic capacity of the long-distance toll segment.

For most organizations, telephone services are the largest consumer of network resources. However, as the use of digitized information continues

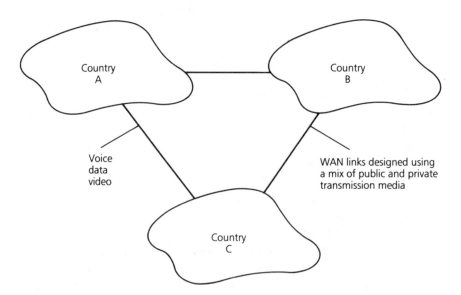

Figure 8-2 The WAN

to increase, the ratio of voice and data information transported over networks will change. In some cases even the voice signal is digitized at the telephone so that there are no analog signals on the network. Further, in the enterprise WAN segment, voice and data requirements are frequently integrated to share and make the most efficient use of transmission resources: creating a backbone network segment. However, voice communication will always be a major consumer of WAN resources, and the special technical requirements for distributing voice service throughout the enterprise play a major part in the design of the capable organization.

The enterprise WAN must be designed to serve flexible, adaptive organizations. And it must not only support but encourage work processes and programs that depend on an open access to information by widely distributed teams of knowledge workers.

The WAN must accommodate the daily administrative and configuration activities of the network necessary to keep information flowing through the enterprise. The network manager must be able to add to or replace any segment or component of the WAN system without affecting the overall performance. This facilitates the introduction of new elements into the system while still providing continuity with the other segments.

In a capability-based environment, WAN architecture must also cope with several other variables, conditions, and dependencies. For example, networks grow constantly and in totally unexpected ways. Quite common today are examples of network growth driven by corporate mergers, marketing partnerships, expansion into new territories, joint ventures, and any number of relationships that require a network to expand rapidly and not compromise services.

Physiology of the Enterprise Network

The successful networking enterprise acquires its skill and capability from the blend of network technology and network applications and from the relationship this combination has to the organization's networking needs and work processes. The relationships that bind distributed work to network tools are reflected in these attributes:

- ○ Connectivity.
- ○ Interoperability.
- ○ Manageability.
- ○ Performance.

By focusing on these attributes, which reflect the physiology of the network, we can build a common ground between network users and network providers. On the one hand, these attributes describe the technical characteristics and operation of the physical network, including topology, design, installation, operations, and maintenance. On the other, they define the characteristics and requirements for effective networking.

The common attributes provide common reference points to facilitate the communication and understanding needed to build partnerships between the technical staffs who provide the services, the managers who define the requirements and provide the resources, the workers who use the systems to create the products and services that generate value, and the vendors who must increasingly establish cooperative relationships with their clients and help them address the impact that their technologies have on the organization.

For example, connectivity defines the physical network for the telecommunications manager, the pattern of information flow for the information systems staff, the links between the organization and the customers for the business manager, and relationships with coworkers and information resources for the workers.

This conceptual common ground structures relationships between tools and work and enables communication between work mechanics in each area. Such a language is extremely important if the highly complex and quickly evolving network infrastructure is to respond in nearly real time to the evolving capability requirements of organizations.

Connectivity

Connectivity describes the physical and logical linking of information users—workers—through whatever transmission media is appropriate for the device and application used for specific a task. Connectivity includes the processes and techniques to ensure information integrity, and provides the foundation for the development of specialized distributed information applications to serve the enterprise.

Connectivity is the essence of flexibility, when we include capacity, or bandwidth, as a principal design element. When an enterprise is fully "connected," management can seize and develop opportunities confidently without affecting operations.

As a networking and knowledge work support attribute, connectivity enables open communication: the flow of ideas between workers, directions from managers, needs and requirements from customers and suppliers. It is the conduit for social interactions that supports the physical workflow through the enterprise.

Connectivity can and must be deliberately designed so that information can be presented in the forms required by the workers and the processes they support. (For example, workers who process insurance claims need client information on their screens as they check current status and enter necessary details to service clients on the spot.) When an organization is fully connected, all workers have channels to access so they can move information among individuals, machines, or centers of activities by using the right combination of physical transmission media, routing techniques, and system integration options.

Unfortunately, to meet the expanding requirements, the expedient solution is often simply to add wire. Need another telephone line? Pull in another pair from the private branch exchange (PBX) mainframe. Need to access another data base? Run another cable to the computer room. This common solution rapidly becomes a major problem rather than a practical fix.

On a recent visit to a large aerospace manufacturing design center, the network manager provided a vivid example of life in the "add-a-wire" environment. The enterprise communications center is built over a typical computer-center raised floor. The manager lifted a panel to reveal eighteen inches of cable conduit so full of wires and cables that the floor panels would not seat properly. The plant had been installed randomly over several years, and few, if any, accurate records were available. Since pulling new wires was less costly than isolating and repairing or removing old cable, the actual condition of the plant was a mystery. The final irony was that so much of the plant was in constant use, the option of removing the entire rat's nest and starting over with a new cable network was impossible.

LAN connectivity includes the physical and electrical characteristics of the network. For guidance in these areas we look to industry standards. Fortunately, there has been some solid progress in developing and approving industry standards, but this is an area where small compromises tend to grow into big and expensive problems. The bottom line is that network connectivity must respond to constant growth and change to meet ever-increasing performance requirements, as well as striving for the most reliable integration into the enterprise. These are complex tasks, but commitment and compliance to standards is the best way to minimize risk and avoid greater difficulties and expenses.

Several approved standards are used to define the various physical, logical, and performance characteristics of networks. These are based primarily on the Open System Interconnection (OSI) model sponsored by the International Standards Organization (ISO). The OSI model is the only internationally accepted framework of standards for system interconnection. To ensure network interoperability, new procurement, and future expansion the network must conform to approved standards. This practice will also help differentiate vendors who have based their products on proprietary technologies from those whose products meet the standards. Integration problems will result as these "non-standard" segments need to become part of the capability-based environment.

The OSI framework is a seven-layer model. Each layer performs a different function and defines the accepted protocols by which open systems can communicate with each other. The conventions also set the rules for how the standards are to be implemented.

Each OSI layer provides services to the layers above it and uses the services of the layers below. These layers, active in every network node, establish and maintain relationships with the corresponding layers of the node to which they are connected.

The layers are independent of each other in the sense that a change in one layer does not affect operations of protocols in neighboring layers. For example, if a change is made to the physical transmission medium (layer

7	**Application**	• Application-oriented functions • Management functions • Provides a distributed information service
6	**Presentation**	• Data formats, codes, and representations • Syntax selection and conversion • Compression and encryption
5	**Session**	• Dialog control and synchronization • Initialization, support of recovery, and termination
4	**Transport**	• End-to-end control of data transport • Reliability and quality • Optimization of network resources
3	**Network**	• Forwarding packets toward final destination • Routing and switching • Establish, maintain, and terminate connections
2	**Data link**	• Reliable transfer of blocks of data between adjacent systems • Error detection and recovery • Synchronization and flow control
1	**Physical**	• Control of data circuits • Cable and physical circuitry • Electrical signaling

Figure 8-3 The OSI Model

1), such as a change from a cable link to a microwave radio link, this will be transparent and will not affect the operation of the data link (layer 2). Changing the physical connection does not have an impact on the operation of the transmission protocols.

Open system standards now dominate the development of hardware technology, software applications, and connectivity and integration models. If applied carefully, they provide senior managers and network designers with the guidance and confidence that they need to expand network boundaries to meet the changing needs of their users.

In the WAN segment connectivity is most often provided through the use of permanent facilities: lines and trunks leased from the common carriers, private or leased microwave links, and fiber optic systems linking nodes of heavy network activity. The connectivity decisions are based on determining the most cost-effective transmission media that will provide the performance required for the anticipated traffic flow. Distance, transmission frequency and volume, security requirements, reliability, regulatory factors, geography, and electrical characteristics of the data being transferred also influence decisions.

Interoperability

Interoperability enables well-connected environments to communicate. In the network, interoperability prescribes the electrical and logical integration needed for network devices to work together. This in turn allows information to flow reliably through the enterprise across different vendors' systems and applications. By specifying interoperability criteria for selecting vendors and suppliers, management can determine who offers the functionality that best meets the requirements of the work. Finally, interoperability releases workers from rigid technical and communication boundaries so that we do not have to "force fit" solutions or work around the best options.

The reality is that information systems and their network support are frequently procured against specific requirements: an accounting system, a manufacturing computer support system, and an administration network. But in the networking environment, where interdepartmental resource sharing and information exchange is required, these diverse systems must be made to work together.

New developments and techniques now make it practical to interoperate among various information media—for example, combining database information with the telephone system to provide enhanced customer services and to support telemarketing activities.

In today's work environments there is a dazzling variety of information processing and handling equipment in daily use, such as central computer mainframes, minicomputers, word processors, personal computers, workstations, high-resolution graphics plotters, copiers, high-speed printers, and intelligent data-storage devices. A network will return value in proportion to the ease and flexibility it provides workers to access these various devices. Users should be able to make a simple request for the information or service they need and feel confident that the network is working for them.

For this level of interoperability, selecting standards-based solutions is again the best strategy to protect investments and ensure that the network has the flexibility and adaptability to respond to the dynamics of networking. Solutions that comply with open standards expand the network manager's options and help the organization realize the full potential of its network investments.

There are other ways of achieving interoperability in the WAN segment. Common solutions use devices called gateways and routers. These devices are software modules or sets of modules that transform the operating conventions of one network into the conventions of another. For example, a WAN that was designed using the propriety protocol of one network vendor would use an X.25 gateway to gain access to a public packet switch data network, which uses the standard X.25 protocol. The gateway effectively links two dissimilar network environments together. Gateways are also used to link competing vendor network segments.

The design goal for interoperability is that any device connected into the enterprise network will have access to all distributed resources on the network and connect to the enterprise WAN with a working peer-to-peer networking relationship. This introduces another dimension, the "manageability attribute." This provides the means of controlling the open network, and ensures that "openness" becomes a virtue and that access to information is managed in the best interest of the organization.

Manageability

Manageability is a combination of systems, processes, and techniques enabling the network to be controlled and monitored, easily changed or modified, and made secure, without degrading operations or interrupting service to the organization. Manageability enables planning for new communications and making effective cost-management decisions.

Manageability generates confidence—confidence that the assembled network technology is working as designed and is under control. It is the attribute that ensures that network managers have the data, tools, and support personnel to monitor performance, identify potential trouble spots, isolate faults quickly, and direct remedial action. Network operations managers need to be able to detect, isolate, and fix problems rapidly, monitor performance metrics, and have effective and reliable control over all system components.

Manageability and control are the keys to a successful networking enterprise. In general, the manageability attribute includes the products and services mix that enables the network to support the work of the organization. Because the network is an intrinsic part of all work processes in the capability-based environment, network availability becomes more than a monthly statistic: it becomes an imperative.

Some management considerations are unique to WAN operations. One is the special interaction required with vendors who supply wide area telecommunications lines, the segment of the WAN where the majority of faults and troubles occur. One company that specializes in providing network operations services for their clients estimated that more than 90 percent of the problems they isolate are line faults. When the WAN extends through international borders, managing these vendor and supplier relationships calls for statesmanlike skills. Fortunately, we now have special tools and services available that can expedite the detection, isolation, and diagnosis of these problems and help the network manager maintain a high-quality, reliable service.

Network managers can use the backbone network segment to begin integrating various network technologies such as voice, data, image. Using high-speed communications services that have become extremely reliable and cost effective, they can integrate multivendor systems and applications used by the enterprise.

Network growth planning is an ongoing process through the life of the system. It is necessary to select a network architecture that is not artificially limited to an arbitrary size or a set number of user nodes. It is not unusual for companies to suddenly find themselves managing very large networks. There are many examples of private networks that service thousands of nodes (fully functional computing devices with networking capabilities internalized or included as peripheral equipment). One corporate network currently has more than 50,000 nodes providing service to more than 100,000 workers worldwide. Each month, they add dozens of new nodes.

Network size issues absorb a large part of the network manager's daily operations activities—for example, decisions to lease high-capacity transmission links or to purchase fiber optic or microwave radio segments between large user centers to bypass the common carriers and eliminate the recurring costs of leased lines, are influenced by size and capacity requirements.

Every network resource should include life-cycle service and support, locally and wherever the network reaches out to connect the various segments of the enterprise. Today, for many organizations regardless of size, this means worldwide support, and service and support means much more than routine repair. The operative term is *life-cycle;* it comprises the entire scope of activity—from design, through the installation and testing phases, into the daily operations and modifications required to keep the system synchronized with current developments. It includes the training of users and support personnel, the introduction of upgrades, and network growth support. It provides the manager and his staff with sophisticated tools and specialized technical assistance. Life-cycle service and support helps solve system integration problems. It also helps the manager and users develop new applications to extract more investment return and adapt more completely to distributed and concurrent work processes.

Because network management is so essential for the networking enterprise, we will look at this activity in more detail in the following chapter.

⌐ Performance

Performance criteria and metrics are the basis for evaluating the impact of the network on the organization's work.

Network performance is measurable, and that is what makes this attribute so important. In the final analysis everything, including our enterprise network and our SDW processes, must add value. And value is most appreciated when it can be counted, measured, compared, or defined in graphic and real terms. Managers need this attribute to have a base point: to compare one thing with another, to justify a new proposal, to evaluate an opportunity, to get more resources, to identify and reward success, and to correct performances that are not up to par. In networks, performance is defined in terms of response time, transmission errors per unit of time, mean time between failures, time to repair, bandwidth, frequency response, numbers of derived channels, and any number of similar characteristics that can be counted, measured, and recorded.

For network managers, performance data provide an excellent basis for comparing proposals from alternative vendors. The only requirement is that they ensure equivalent comparisons and that the specifics are important to the network environment.

Financial performance is one distinct area of performance that is common to every network element and is frequently the principal factor in network purchase decisions. In a networking enterprise, the overriding financial consideration is the cost of owning and operationing information systems and networks over time. Initial procurement costs are, in fact, significantly lower than the combined cost of daily operations and the cost of incremental changes driven by growth and modifications to these systems throughout their life-cycles.

As networking becomes more understood and practiced throughout the organization, it will become much easier to balance cost with metrics that reflect the relative value of the services the network provides. We will recognize these new metrics because they will be accompanied by the pain associated with the failure of an essential and critical network service.

The overall performance of a network is a function of the transmission medium, the communications controller technology used, the number of users connected and their traffic requirements, and the characteristics of the devices used to configure, extend, and interconnect LAN and WAN segments. Performance is also influenced by increasing numbers of users added to the network. It must be able to constantly grow and adapt to accommodate new users and applications, and constantly deliver required performance. This is a constant fact of life in the networked enterprise. In large LANs, for example, it is common for the majority of users to be active at any given time. The designers must make sure that these networks are robust enough to accommodate these peak service demands.

Knowledge workers expect quick response to their request for data, and they quickly develop very low tolerances for network delays or errors. In a LAN environment, it is not uncommon for workers to simultaneously access large tables of numbers for the generation of a graph, create and distribute short electronic mail messages, or use a CAD/CAM application on a workstation to do engineering modeling and simulations. Each of these applications consumes resources from the LAN performance bank.

LAN performance is normally a measure of its bandwidth capacity, measured in megabits (Mb/s). For example, a 10 Mb/s LAN has the theoretical capability to handle a combined traffic load of 10 Mb/s. There are technical reasons why this theoretical capacity cannot be reached, but in practice the statistical distribution of user traffic is quite low. Vendors constantly stress-test their products and publish results that indicate that well-engineered LANs are rarely stressed beyond 20 percent of their potential.

Although these statistics are comforting for today's environments, there are clear indications that user demand and complex work processes will require order-of-magnitude improvements in the very near future. Vendors are using 100 Mb/s fiber optic technology for this purpose and although this may be difficult to imagine now, there will be applications that will stress this performance level even as these new-generation LANs are becoming available for operation.

Performance is a critical variable. Testing and evaluation of performance characteristics is a constant priority for network managers. Node and network hardware, transmission media, and all the ancillary support systems and services are selected so that any local node or component failure can be quickly isolated, diagnosed, and repaired, and the network returned to full service without disrupting any other elements of the enterprise network system. For this, network managers use special control and monitoring devices and applications, a trained and responsive network operations staff, and a product selection strategy based on approved international and/or industry standards. This allows the network to grow and interoperate with other elements without the need for excessive and complex integration or conversion effort and expense.

It is difficult, if not impossible, to predict the rate and nature of growth and change in a dynamic work environment. Therefore, it is best to acknowledge and accept that it will always happen, it will never be constant, and it will always be greater than planned, budgeted, or thought possible. Networks must be easy to configure, and the configurations must be easy to modify and expand. The system must be able to add nodes wherever and whenever users need them, and components must be easy and cost-effective to move when necessary. Network systems must scale easily from very small to very large, and occasionally back to very small, without any serious impact on the user community.

SUMMARY

In this chapter we have discussed the enterprise network in terms of its anatomy and physiology. These are complex concepts, and organizations need to depend on specialists to ensure that their investments and requirements for information transport and access are met. But the capability-based environment requires that all the key players have a common basis for communication. We think that visualizing the network in terms of basic building blocks (LANs, WANs, and network operations/management; and the functional attributes connectivity, interoperability, manageability, and performance) provides a practical and common foundation for translating individual, team, and group requirements into technical specifications.

Networking also requires that the network manager play a more comprehensive role in the enterprise. This is reflected in the broader scope of activities and responsibilities as network management becomes system management—a new psychology that we will explore in the next chapter because it has such a critical impact on organizations.

We know of no network—installed, tested, and implemented in the user community—that looks exactly like its original design specifications. Most differences are due to the natural and constant change endemic to networks. There are many opportunities to avoid problems and cost by simply accepting that change is a constant condition and ensuring that vendor and equipment decisions address flexibility and adaptability, that compliance to standards is specified where possible, and that clear objectives and expectations are mapped to the requirements of the capability-based environment and the work processes it supports.

NOTES

1. In Bartlett and Ghoshal's "biological analogy," the physical structure is with anatomy, system information flow with physiology, and cultural values with psychology. See *Managing Across Borders* (Boston: Harvard Business School Press, 1989), pp. 201–207.

Chapter 9 | Enterprise Network Management: Psychology

The third aspect of the Bartlett biological metaphor is psychology, which we equate to the science of managing the network processes to meet networking needs. Network management is emerging as the critical, real-time activity that keeps the capability-based environment in business. Management does whatever it takes to ensure that workers have access to the information they need, when and where they need it through the network. *Whatever it takes* is the key phrase. Realizing how dependent organizations and work processes are on information access, senior management is just beginning to appreciate the magnitude and importance of network resources.

The capability-based environment is dependent on networks, and business and organizational strategies depend on network access and availability. Therefore, network management must assume a leadership position. In this environment, nontechnical managers work side by side with the network experts, and each must be able to understand the other's perspectives as they make informed decisions on network issues such as resource allocation and mission priorities.

This chapter does not focus on the tools and techniques for managing networks, nor does it serve as an operations handbook for network managers. But it does provide a holistic perspective of what it means to manage an enterprise network, both for network managers who see their organization moving toward networking capability and for other key members of the organization. Organizational survival depends on the access and use of information, and this in turn depends on the availability and performance of the network.

Network Nirvana

It may be useful at this time to build a mental map of what Network Nirvana—the ideal enterprise network—might look like. We suggest something that resembles a connect-the-dot puzzle. Each dot represents a center where work happens: the shops, the production lines, the offices, the plants, the branches, the individual contributors, and all network resources required to support the activity of the work group and workers. The spaces between the dots represent the geographical separation between offices, floors, buildings, cities, or countries. Connections between the dots represent network links, the lines representing the appropriate transmission medium: leased lines, T1 services (high-speed transmission services offered by public carriers), microwave, and fiber optic cables.

The network incorporates an architecture and operating system designed to support peer-to-peer, open information access to each work group in the enterprise. Within the dots are high-performance LANs, which provide workers with access to enterprise information resources and to specialized networking applications. Each dot is linked to the network backbone segment, which has been optimized for cost and performance effectiveness. Selected dots are configured to serve as wide area nodes and include gateways to the entire organization and to the outside world. The various network segments and the communications media they use are fully

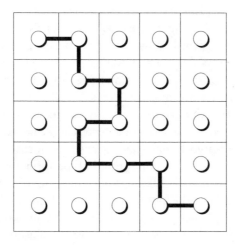

Figure 9-1 Network Nirvana

standardized and integrated to allow efficient use and exchange of information from whatever sources, in whatever form, to whatever destination at any time. The enterprise network is constantly monitored and controlled by a network management system that compiles and displays the network's vital signs and allows the network manager to deliver the service levels needed to sustain the value-generating activities of the organization.

Everything connects and interoperates because everything conforms to approved standards. Everyone can have open access to information. Management has the flexibility to add connections or change relationships (reconfigure the dots) to match the dynamics of the business. In other words, this utopian model network is a flexible template that represents the flow of information from work center to work center, team to team, individual to individual, constantly adapting to the changing dynamics of the simultaneous distributed work processes.

Keep this model in mind as we take a more conventional look at the major network segments. Our network ideal incorporates the flexibility and open access that must be the design goal for the enterprise network as it approaches the capabilities required in the CBE. Also keep in mind that many organizations already have network infrastructures that look and perform very much like this model.

Managing the Enterprise Network

Normally, network management deals with a complex technical environment. The typical enterprise network comprises all types and sizes of network segments furnished by multiple vendors, and a wide variety of process applications as diverse as CAD/CAM, financial spreadsheets, and electronic mail. Information is used simultaneously by work centers located around the world that are interconnected by all varieties of private and public transmission facilities. Since all this has to work for the enterprise to be successful, network management is central in the networked enterprise.

Traditionally, network management has been focused on network design and operation activities: monitoring link performance, optimizing the cost performance of links, isolating line faults, doing some applications management, specifying the physical and logical architecture of the network, ensuring compliance to standards, and restoring service to the users in the event of failure. Network managers ensure that information security is maintained, even as the network facilitates access to the information. They provide help, training, and guidance to users, and they identify and qualify internal and external support resources. They must perform all their duties while the network is dramatically and constantly changing in size and function, as new simultaneous work processes, wholly dependent on the availability and performance of the network, are implemented.

Today, with the CBE concept, the greatest change in the network manager's activities comes with a new leadership role. That role includes providing the organization with the knowledge, confidence, and counsel needed to effectively use information and network access to move the organization into the capability-based environment. The network manager must be proactive in bringing intimate knowledge of the network into the mainstream of enterprise planning and capability developers.

As the network becomes an integral and essential part of the enterprise, as workers move into information-based networking, network management shifts to a form of systems management where the physical network is transparent to the users and the processes it serves. This paradigm requires a much broader perspective and fits nicely within our human model as the psychology of the enterprise network.

The Need for Comprehensive Network Management Architecture

Several factors combine to create the need for a comprehensive network management architecture.

○ Multivendor network segments become integrated into the enterprise network; technical and operational differences among these segments add increasing complexity.
○ Suppliers propose new technologies and more cost-effective solutions.
○ User demand and the introduction of new work processes stress existing facilities.
○ New business strategies require major network expansion and change.

Network managers have to contend with these and any number of equally disparate and sometimes opposing realities. They must have the ability to view and control the network as an integrated system, as well as the specific tools required simply to operate and maintain network piece parts. These capabilities will evolve from a carefully crafted and comprehensive network management architecture.

Networks are usually designed to mirror the organization they serve. Since most organizations traditionally tend to be modeled as hierarchical, with information flowing from the top down following established management reporting structures, networks and their management systems are often designed to follow the same predictable, highly centralized, and well-structured model.

However, distributed organizations—based on lateral, peer-to-peer, relationships designed to be flexible and fluid and to share information in real-time across all boundaries—need equally responsive network support systems. Designing networks for these alternative organizational models would not be a problem if they could be designed from scratch. But most organizations are somewhere in between, generally moving from the hierarchical to the distributed. For these organizations, network management issues have become very complicated.

In the distributed enterprise environment the question of centralized or distributed operations management has a new significance. Today it is possible to operate worldwide networks from a central location. There are clear advantages that make this alternative very attractive. Qualified technicians and the special tools that detect and isolate problems are expensive and in short supply. Coordinating service restorations with telecommunications and equipment suppliers is easier when there is consistency and focus throughout the process. Also, collecting trend data and monitoring performance is more reliable when the operation is centralized.

In reality, even in the most sophisticated network control and operations centers, there are many tasks and procedures that require the attention of a local, on-site manager who understands the local situation and conditions. A manager who is familiar with the skills and resources of local vendors and service providers can move quickly to explain specifications and requirements. A person familiar with the user base can spot trends and report on user satisfactions or changing needs. Pilot programs and the start-up phases of new applications are common examples. Therefore, the optimum situation is to have the flexibility to select centralized and/or local network management options, and to demand this capability as a selection criterion for network management architectures and operating systems.

Most organizations have grown their enterprise network resources quite haphazardly as separate networks were installed to solve specific problems. As these disparate segments become integrated, by technology or purpose, preserving a holistic perspective of the network becomes very difficult, but increasingly critical.

Operations and Management Attributes

Fortunately, we have a set of definitions that covers both the technical and the management responsibilities of the network manager. These definitions can be used to determine current network management status, and can provide a basis for future planning and priority setting.

The activities are based on the recommendation made by the OSI committee as they attempt to provide the industry with basic and internationally accepted guidance. There are no approved standards as yet in network management, but many preliminary agreements have been reached by various subcommittees. Vendors have begun to define and propose solutions for managing the enterprise network system. They feel that the networks will adapt to these standards as they are approved.

The template we use defines six activities: the five selected by OSI and a sixth that we have included because of its increasing importance and because of the special relationship applications have with distributed networking. We feel this is a comprehensive template that can cover all significant network management activities. The activities include:

○ Network fault analysis and resolution management.
○ Configuration management.
○ Performance management.
○ Security management.
○ Accounting management.
○ Applications management.

Network Fault Analysis and Resolution

This category encompasses most of what is defined as traditional network operations: the tools, procedures, and services used to identify problems and verify the results that ensure network service is restored.

Fault analysis and resolution also covers the interaction among users, internal operations staffs, and outside service suppliers and vendors, who play a role in maintaining the integrity of the system. In the distributed environment the critical variable is restoration time, because work depends on network availability. Each network will have its own peculiar dependencies, but finding those that have the greatest impact on time-to-restore will provide the manager with clear pointers as to where investments and priorities should be placed.

For senior managers, successful fault and trouble management converts to confidence. A network control center that has the capability to display system status, isolate faults, demonstrate current operations activity, show potential trouble spots, predict the impact of management plans through network simulations, and graphically relate cost to physical resources can introduce a sense of reality to the people who make major decisions. It can give management the sense that a resource on which they are critically dependent is under control. This sense of security is much like the feeling that passengers have when they enter an airplane, glance into the cockpit, and see the captain and flight crew checking and monitoring the flight systems and controls.

Configuration Management

The activities in this management segment are focused on setting, compiling, and recording selected information about all components and features in the network. For the enterprise network this is the seminal task. Everything else depends on, or is affected by, this activity. Modern networks now do many of the configuration tasks automatically, but even in the most sophisticated systems many configuration procedures and data recording must be performed manually. Without accurate and complete configuration data, every network management task takes significantly longer, has greater risk of failure, and implants a future trouble situation.

Maintaining accurate configuration data starts with the design phase and continues through the life cycle of the network, a difficult and expensive investment. However, in spite of the difficulty and cost, configuration data are the best insurance available for the network manager and users. Configuration data, being essential to the rapid restoration of failed systems and for constant and satisfactory service level, provide an excellent rate of return on investment.

Configuration management starts at the physical layer, the cable plant. Careful systematic planning is the key. Basic rules include:

○ Accurately labeling and documenting active and spare wires and cables.
○ Carefully planning and documenting wire and cable routes within the facility.

○ Avoiding installation practices that will prevent or hamper easy access or cause unnecessary wear or exposure.

○ Properly selecting equipment closets and connection frames or patch panels to provide secure access and room for expansion.

○ Planning redundancy where practical for service expansion to ensure the highest possible reliability if main cable runs should be damaged.

○ Inspecting any new or modified cable plant to verify the quality of the work and to ensure the accuracy of the configuration documentation.

The design of network topology, which is the combination of the physical plant configuration and the locations of major network components such as nodes, bridges, switches, and other active devices, also has a major effect on network performance and reliability. Configuration management issues around topology include determining the exact operational requirements that the network or network segment will be required to support. Issues such as system interfaces, projected traffic volumes, and interconnections between different media or systems within or outside the enterprise should be resolved as part of the configuration planning process.

As a network grows, topologies become increasingly complex. At some point in the growth curve, it will become necessary to automate the topology configuration process. Several tools are available for this, and most vendors have professional services available to ensure compliance to standard architectural and design criteria or to determine the most robust configuration for custom applications.

Large enterprise networks are often divided into discrete segments to maintain required performance standards and to simplify configuration management. In digital networks, many vendors have automated the routing process within their own operating systems so that the system chooses the best, most cost-effective path for the information packet to use at the particular moment. A message entered into a node on one network segment automatically selects the most efficient and/or cost-effective route to the addressee, regardless of the addressee's location in the network. The selected routing options may include various types of network links using several different transmission media.

Additionally, some vendors offer adaptive routing to guarantee network availability. Adaptive routing selects alternative routes for delivering traffic when primary routes experience failure or congestion.

Routers are used as forwarding agents and know how and where to forward packets toward their destination. The router maintains the address listings and must be updated every time changes are made to the network topology. Topology maps showing the location of all routing devices with their interconnecting links are a valuable management tool and can serve as a point of reference for planning change.

At some point in a network's growth, it becomes necessary to introduce a configuration process that provides continuity between separate areas or segments. This requires that each node have a discrete name and address. This is an administrative problem and merits careful review of operational and security specifications as well as business plans that will indicate future network requirements.

Network configuration touches all the bases and is at the heart of network management. Technical specifications and requirements for all equipment and software must be carefully considered; organizational policies, current activities, and future plans must be understood and complied with, and relentless administration practices must be maintained to assure a dependable and responsive enterprise network.

Performance Management

Performance management includes the equipment and programs needed to monitor the vital signs of the network. A network with poor or erratic performance cannot serve the purpose for which it was installed. Individuals, the key factor in distributed work, will be discouraged from using the network to support their work. Degraded network performance will dampen users' enthusiasm and their ability to find innovative and improved work processes. The effect of poor network performance on user work habits can be more debilitating than not having the network in the first place.

Performance characteristics are built into the network during the design phase. Performance management variables include:

○ Selection of line speeds.
○ Power and number of nodes.
○ Transmission medium selected.
○ Addressing and routing architectures defined.
○ Applications used.
○ User training.
○ Network monitoring.
○ Management experience.

Performance issues usually surface when users complain that their expectations or needs are not being met. The network manager has no option other than to find and fix the problem, never a simple or inexpensive task.

The keys to maintaining required performance include:

○ Understanding the network environment and the work processes that use the network facilities.

○ Selecting and configuring the resources to meet the needs of the users.

○ Continually monitoring network operations using tools that react to performance parameters.

○ Budgeting for growth and improvement.

○ Constantly fine-tuning each segment of the system.

Several sensitive design areas have great impact on the performance of a network. As circuits become congested, performance suffers. Circuit performance is a function of bandwidth, and bandwidth is expensive to rent or buy. Bandwidth judgments should be made after considering growth patterns, user demands, and future application plans. Topologies must be designed to accommodate those work applications, now or in the future, that will require the most network bandwidth. Only careful planning can help ensure nonconstricting traffic routes.

Network managers can use distributed information networking techniques and resources to help control and manage bandwidth requirements—for example, installing a LAN to support a work center. This can provide high-capacity bandwidth through the use of highly efficient communication media such as coaxial cables with simple terminal connections.

The LAN can then be interconnected to the WAN segments for further distribution using specialized and cost-effective bandwidth tariffs. The ability to mix and match transmission media and network service segments gives the network designer several options to manage the bandwidth requirements of the total enterprise system. The options selected will be determined by performance requirements and cost.

Performance Management Metrics

During the course of daily network operations, the network manager examines a wide variety of technical and performance data. To be useful, this data must be compiled and organized into meaningful management information.

Reliability and Availability

There is a clear distinction between reliability and availability that the network manager must constantly consider. Reliability is a measure of the network's ability to function without failure. Availability is a measure of the network's ability to serve the purpose for which it was installed—from the user perspective. A network that is not available to users because of frequent scheduled maintenance may have impressive reliability statistics, but may not provide adequate support to users in their work processes.

Maintainability and Recoverability

Maintainability—the ease with which a network can be kept functional, and recoverability—the users' ability to continue work when a network anomaly interrupts their work sessions, are also key metrics. Both are the responsibility of the network manager and must be carefully specified and planned into the design and modification of network segments.

Monitoring and Trend Analysis

A network manager must both anticipate and react to problems. Fortunately, several excellent tools and services are available to assist the network manager in the constant monitoring and trend analysis that is required. Monitoring tools, often integrated into network management systems, signal line degradation and alert the operations staff to potential traffic bottlenecks. Other tools provide for disciplined and informed response to alarms and alerts that indicate failed circuits or excessive errors. They constantly test and monitor circuit activity and identify options to redistribute circuit loads and improve performance.

Today, many large network users are turning to service suppliers who have invested in specialized monitoring capabilities that can detect anomalies in circuit performance quickly and are equipped to accurately isolate and diagnose the fault anywhere in the network. High-performance circuits often degrade over time. These conditions must be detected and reported to the circuit providers because of the compounding effect this has on the overall performance of the network. These value-added services can often expedite responses from suppliers more efficiently than reports initiated by the user.

Senior managers play a key role in network performance. They must understand that incremental improvements in performance are very expensive. Therefore, they must carefully consider the impact of their plans and decisions on the network's ability to deliver performance. They must understand how modifying various segments of the network can involve long procurement lead times and can generate ripples through the entire system. Recognizing this, many organizations have created senior-level staff positions to ensure that network requirements are integrated into the earliest planning stages.

Security Management

This is a priority issue for the networking enterprise. Recent, well-publicized events demonstrate the vulnerable nature of networks. As sharing resources and information becomes a characteristic of work processes, everyone must become aware and responsive to the risks associated with using networks and the network-supported work processes. The network manager and all responsible process managers must decide how to maintain the balance between easy, unrestricted access and the restrictions that can be used to control and protect critical information.

Perfect security would consist of an infinite number of defenses and configurations against all possible attacks. This is impossible. There is no perfectly secure network. But good security is possible. It starts with commitment and planning at the top management levels, and ends with every user on the network. It includes special technologies where required, and total commitment to simple and obvious administrative practices. It also includes constant vigilance.

A practical way to focus on security is as a multilayered system such as the OSI model discussed in Chapter 8. The lowest layer is physical security. A locked door on the cable vault or the equipment closet and the use of shielded or fiber optic transmission cables and wires that reduce radiation are examples of physical security measures that control unauthorized access to information.

Physical security also includes measures to guard against damage to buildings, computers, data files, and voice circuit switching facilities.

These measures are basically common sense and are used in proportion to the sensitivity of the information and the source of the risk. At the transmission level, for instance, the option to use a low-cost microwave radio link or a relatively secure but expensive fiber optic link could finally depend on the sensitivity of the information. Diskless workstations, network resident operating systems, or restricted peripheral device access are options to consider in managing security at the user location.

In LAN configurations, nondedicated servers post a risk because every time the server is turned off and on, the opportunity exists to defeat the network's software security safeguards. Controlling who can upload programs and copy data protects against the risk of injecting software viruses into the system. A skilled programmer, if unmonitored, can insert commands and procedures into a software program that will be extremely hard to detect and could disrupt operations for weeks. Network equipment that is not physically protected cannot be made secure. Many users have assigned these tasks to the network manager when they have an architecture that allows remote management access.

Security of Applications Software

Following the OSI model, we move on to higher levels of security. There are many products and services available from suppliers who have recognized the need to incorporate security safeguards into their operating systems. A practical model for selecting options is based on the military model: access based on the need to know. Workers should be provided with the minimal tools and network privileges they need to do the job. Controlling these privileges limits deliberate or negligent mischief.

Security procedures for protecting software applications are basically accounting practices and audit procedures. These procedures begin by creating files, known as controlled program libraries, in which all programs are kept. Only selected individuals are nominated to make changes to these libraries, and these individuals are required to document all changes and modifications to the programs.

Controlling User Access

The next step in data security is to focus on the user. Access controls set limits on an individual's access to network resources. The most common access control is the password, information that only a specific user knows. Passwords are frequently supplemented with user IDs, authorization tables, and access rights list.

Because passwords are passive measures, additional options include automatically generated audit trails and alarms embedded in the software used to control the application program and the data.

External Threats

Guarding against data interception by outside parties is called communications security. The threat of outside interception through wiretapping or emission sensing is most often associated with national security or corporate espionage. The technology used for this purpose is sophisticated and very difficult to detect and protect against.

Communications security is normally segmented into line security, transmission security, cryptography, emission security, and technical security.

Line security protects lines used locally to carry data and voice transmissions against wiretapping or other types of physical interception.

Transmission security protects the information itself as it passes through various network segments. For example, cryptography is a method of encoding information so that it becomes unintelligible to anyone except the intended recipient. Cryptography can be applied at the link, session, and user levels, with each application providing added protection.

Emission security protects against the interception of information by monitoring electrical fluctuations, radiation, and other modulations of the transmission signal.

Technical security includes techniques to protect against non-network intrusion devices. These devices include microphones, carrier current-bugging equipment, visual or optical surveillance equipment, and telephone bugs.

Of all the network management functions, security has received the most attention in recent months. There is fresh evidence of what a few dedicated hackers can do with their personal computers and modems. In addition, it is clear that senior managers need to feel comfortable about the state of network security before they lead the organization into information- and network-based work processes.

Accounting Management

As the cost of networks increases and becomes a major expense category for the organization, network managers need to understand and plan for the financial impact of these investments. In distributed networks, this becomes a complex exercise, because the enterprise network manager must probe for the cost elements that may be buried in departments and groups who have independently invested in network systems used in their work processes.

A major dilemma for the network manager is getting the network to do more work, serve more users, support more applications, and, at the same time, perform these miracles at reduced cost.

The cost side of the cost/benefit equation is calculated using daily and periodic operating expenses. These include bandwidth purchase and leasing, capital expenses for equipment and plant facilities, network software, installation and service contracts, consultant fees, operations center personnel and associated support services, and administrative overhead.

Even more difficult to quantify is the added value of networks to the organizational value chain. Metrics for productivity, efficiency, accuracy, or timeliness are very hard to find and subjective at best.

All cost must be projected over the expected life cycle of the item. Studies show that there are significant differences in life-cycle network costs between flexible peer-to-peer architectures and inflexible architectures and topologies. The latter configurations generate greater requirements for high-cost operations personnel and maintenance support.

There is research available to help us accurately establish the cost of networks. A study by the Index Group, a Boston-based consulting firm, identifies the five significant cost components specific to networks. (1) These include the costs associated with equipment, software, personnel, communications carriers, and facilities (wiring and space, for example). Further, they identify three distinct stages in the life cycle of the network where the relationships change between the cost elements:

○ The acquisition phase, where the majority of capital cost associated with the original procurement of equipment and resources is allocated.

○ The operations phase, where maintenance, annual licenses, software fees, routine monitoring and operations, network problem correction, user liaison and administration, and monthly tariff charges generate cost on a recurring basis.

○ The incremental change phase, which is characterized by cost generated by user adds, moves, and deletes, and by the cost of making required operating system software version changes.

As a result of the study, the Index Group developed a practical model to help the network managers segment the cost of their network as a function of their cost management activity. In addition, the study makes several basic observations: (2)

○ The real cost of networks starts once they have been paid for.

○ Personnel costs are substantial and are responsible for approximately 60 percent of the total cost of the network over the lifecycle.

○ Communications costs are high, but not as significant over time as cost associated with people.

○ The topology of the network, whether distributed or centralized, has a significant influence on cost over time.

The model itself is quite simple and has been tested in a wide range of network configurations. It works, and we recommend that all network managers use it to review their current installations and as a reference to evaluate network proposals submitted by different vendors.

Several useful commercially available software applications can help the network manager track various financial attributes within each network segment. These programs capture cost elements and usage information that can be used to recover cost from the systems users.

Organizations must decide how they will manage their network investments. In a typical situation, the organization might budget for the design and procurement of the wide area backbone network segment and charge these expenses to general capital expense categories. To recover these costs from profit centers, a usage tax can be calculated, or fees can be assigned for all connections to the backbone network. Voice, data, and image subnetworks are connected to the backbone using common standards. A fee structure can be developed to support these services, reflecting higher cost installation and recurring charges for high-speed leased circuits.

Management must develop policies that reflect reality: all network connections do not cost the same, usage requirement will differ from group to group, and some groups will receive greater benefits than others from connecting to the backbone.

There are many other methods and fee-structure models for recovering network cost, but in the networking enterprise care must be taken not to make network access prohibitive. If users are forced to find alternative methods to obtain and exchange the information they need, they will. Today many users access the network through workstations and personal computers. They share network resources, frequently across traditional organizational boundaries. This method of access complicates cost recovery. Ultimately, the enterprise network becomes a utility, and network managers must charge for services and commodities as in any other utility business. The network manager and the organization need a coherent accounting policy to accommodate the complexity of the network system environment.

Applications Management

Recommendations for managing applications are not formally part of the official OSI network management structure. However, in a distributed environment the ability of the network manager to extend control and monitoring services into the applications layer provides major benefits.

System-wide applications required to create the distributed, peer-to-peer networking environment are resident over the entire network. Programmers who write specific work-related applications need only use standard network interface instructions to ensure that their applications will have network-wide functionality.

For example, consider an application written to support an order-entry process that involves the participation of several remote departments of the organization. This process requires a series of sequential transactions as the electronic order forms and information are processed through the various departments. As each transaction is completed, the communications layer application automatically inserts the logical link-routing instructions needed to move the order to the next department. All the communication processes are transparent to the users, and system-level logical link processing is responsible for the establishment and control of the link, and for its breakdown when the order-entry transactions are completed. This example demonstrates how a typical user application, and the system-level communications protocols that are part of the enterprise network architecture, perform together to support a work process. It emphasizes that the network manager must have the resources to monitor and control the interaction of local and system-level applications, using the network to monitor and isolate faults should these distributed applications develop problems.

SUMMARY

The explosive growth of network-supported devices, the increase in network users, the variety of creative applications pulling the network into new work processes, and relentless pressure from management to control cost is the new reality for the network manager. The network is changing, and every indication suggests that the process is accelerating. Network users, no longer intimidated by technology, have begun to demonstrate how network-based services can improve the quality and productivity of their work. Senior management also has new incentives for greater involvement with the network. The high cost and critical dependence of information resources in organizations give senior managers no alternative but to participate in the network design process, operations, and procurement strategies. They are beginning to understand that network investments are critical to the goals and objectives of the organization.

Network management is receiving a great deal of attention. In many organizations, network managers have become key members of the senior management team. They participate directly in strategic planning, adding value because of their understanding of what can be accomplished within available network resources, and receiving insights as to what will be required from the network to support future requirements.

The principal network vendors have addressed the issues around network management. There are several new products that integrate required tools and processes into a single management system. This is a major improvement for operations staffs, who previously had to familiarize themselves with several different devices and procedures required for their multivendor network environments. Frequently, this included inconstancies from the same vendor.

These new network management systems provide the operator with instant notification of alarms and faults. Once detected, problems are indicated on topographical maps and diagrams, and entered into configuration files that display the proper names and specifications of affected network elements, which then show physical locations and the proper contacts for service restoration actions. Some even interface with voice and radio systems to page stand-by service personnel and use electronically synthesized voice messages to inform them of the problem.

Although these new products can and do improve network operations, organizations that are moving to enterprise configurations and planning to use network-supported work processes must look into the next generation of network management. The evolving network management systems will integrate all network resources using open-system specifications and will provide the robust framework to ensure that the network can support the dynamic conditons demanded by simultaneous distributed work processes. Demand for basic and enhanced services is growing faster than the network can support, and this trend will only accelerate.

Today, network managers are concerned about the quality and reliability of the network services they deliver. They reference the shortage of qualified personnel, the increasing complexity of systems and configurations, and the increasing financial and productivity impact of network failures. Network managers need better and more effective tools, more automation in network systems, and more effective ways to work with third parties and service vendors to sustain their current service levels and to support the requirements of the emerging capability-based environment.

Furthermore, senior managers do not always see the value networks provide to their most critical business processes. Often the network is perceived as an expense, a bottomless pit for resources. They ask: How, when, and where will the organization benefit from network investments? What form will the return take, who will benefit, what will be required to sustain the benefit over time, and how much will be enough?

Network managers must demand that their enterprise network management system provide clearly defined interface specifications to which any vendor can interconnect. They must specify that all network domains—voice, data, and image—are included, that the system is expandable to ensure that it will not restrict their network growth and configuration options, and that there is a support organization and development commitment sufficient to protect past and future investments. This is not a simple prescription, but given the technology available today, it is reasonable; given the networking challenges of today, it is essential.

In the final part of this book we use the network attributes to frame key points that management can use to identify and evaluate their current network resources and to plan their acquisiton strategy toward the capability-based environment. Clearly, this network overview will not qualify nontechnical readers to assume the responsibilities of a network manager. However, it will serve to place all the key players on a common ground to begin the dialogue needed to build productive relationships.

NOTES

1. See Michael E. Treacy, *The Costs of Network Ownership* (Index Group, Inc.).
2. *Ibid.*

Chapter 10

An Architecture and Process for the Capability-Based Environment

Looking back over the realities of the environment, the nature of distributed information work, and the increasing time pressures on organizations, it's clear that organizations must be able not only to apply the networked information available to them to their current work, but to ensure adaptiveness or flexibility into the future. In this chapter we'll look at one perspective on creating a unified vision for networking; network technology; capability for simultaneous distributed work; and capability to meet future work challenges.

The model we use is based on the work of Doug Engelbart, who asserts that capability can be attained only if organizations first have capability to build and maintain flexibility—to proactively address that next level of complexity as it comes over the work horizon. (1)

Such recursiveness—building the flexibility to build flexibility—delights Engelbart, an electrical engineer and knowledge systems architect. Earlier we noted Engelbart's observation on the viability of flexible organizations; how becoming the cat, not the dinosaur, should be high on the list of organizational capability goals. Over the years Engelbart has, with a small, usually distributed team, evolved and articulated an architecture and process that provide the means for developing that capability infrastructure. The architecture embodies a systemic view of information work methods and information technology; the process is a variant of a basic circuit feedback loop in which you improve your work capabilities by improving your capability to improve. We'll sort this out later on.

Achieving flexibility is largely a matter of overcoming traditional barriers: inertia and the serial problem/solution perspective. Inertia is resistance to change. Energy is needed to put a fixed body into motion, and some organizations don't have that energy. Even if they do, the "stop-to-start" activity takes time, and therefore costs money. Athletes know this; they always keep moving, not in precise anticipation of what the next response must be, but in the knowledge that they will be more likely to react appropriately if they are moving, rather than still. Watch the way a goalie defends the nets, always in motion, avoiding being caught "flat-footed."

Reactive problem solving constrains an organization's responses. The work system only knows to "do," not "adapt." A bus driver knows that the fare is $1 per ride; for convenience and safety, the coin box is designed to accept the $1 fare in exact coins only. It cannot adapt to the exact fare in paper money presented by a tourist, who expects an amount-of-money payment system, not amount- and kind-of-money. The customer is not satisfied.

An organization can overcome the straitjacket of inflexibility through a continuous learning and improvement process Engelbart calls augmentation. Within this framework, distributed, knowledge-intensive organizations can continuously increase their abilities to perform complex information work in rapidly changing environments.

Engelbart's work provides an existence proof of the capability-based environment; as such, it is drawing wide attention from industry, particularly the high-technology manufacturing and information systems sectors. For these reasons we devote this chapter to this prototype framework. We'll look first at the augmentation architecture, built on dynamic, interacting human and tool subsystems; then at the process, a design for organizational learning through the piloting of team networking methods and applications.

The Architecture

Engelbart's capability architecture goes beyond the scope of traditional information architectures by incorporating both technological and human system components. As we might expect, the technological side has received more attention over the years than the human (or the social, cultural, psychological, and skill) side.

As an engineer and a technological innovator, Engelbart knows the technology potential well. His contributions to computer-based information work have included the introduction of workstation windowing capabilities, the mouse, groupware, and hypermedia. Over many years, Engelbart developed all these tools within the context of augmentation;

each was part of the overall system of technology that would support simultaneous distributed work. However, most have found a life beyond their original conceptual home and are in common use today. Some have arrived, like the mouse and windowing; others continue to evolve as their value and potential are better understood—for example, hypermedia and groupware. (2)

Engelbart and his associates at the Stanford Research Institute began building a prototype of the technology system more than twenty years ago. That system, known today as Augment and owned by the McDonnell Douglas Corporation, continues to be viewed by many as the archetype for systems that support teaming communities committed to simultaneous distributed work. It is in this light that we focus on Augment here, not as a product but as a prototype of what a networking technology can do in support of complex, distributed information work.

Augment is a hypertext-based system that includes in its effects most groupware capabilities (e.g., electronic mail, shared information spaces [computer conferencing], shared screen editing, extremely powerful hypertext editing) as well as access to professional applications (spreadsheets, CAD modeling, desktop publishing). The user interface features windows and multiple text input and navigation devices such as keyboard, mouse, and "chord." The chord is a five-key device that looks like a piece of piano keyboard; it has all the functions of a standard terminal keyboard, but can be operated with one hand, leaving the other free to run a mouse: truly a "whole-brain" setup.

Realizing that the universal characteristic of technology is to evolve faster than other knowledge domains, Engelbart, among others, is currently emphasizing the human-system side. Being people-based, largely culturally dependent, and highly unstructured, the human-system side has seen less directed evolution. Here the focus is on people sharing information to add value, learning new work methods, and sustaining a nurturing social environment in the workplace. While the understanding and evolution of human systems is recognized as having profound importance for organizational capability, only the bravest, most stressed organizations are willing to take on the challenge. More human systems investment is needed to bring the systems into balance.

The Human System

Organizations have culture, language, methodologies, and policies. Key capabilities identified for augmentation include:

○ The ability to contact large, geographically distributed projects.
○ The ability to bring technological tools to bear on the routine work that traditionally takes up 80 percent of a knowledge worker's time, freeing the worker to concentrate on the specialized tasks that represent 80 percent of that worker's value.
○ The ability and commitment to create, access, manipulate, and share information.
○ Flexibility in designing work and creating appropriate organizational structures.
○ Ways of creating shared contexts to enable common understanding across various constituencies.
○ Methods for building trust and commitment to networking.

In short, augmenting the human system leads to individual and organizational learning, and ultimately to individual and group knowledge.

The Tool System

Tools, in complex, distributed, time-critical environments, must push the boundaries of information and knowledge communication, processing, and representation. An augmentation tool system would provide, for example:

○ High-bandwidth data; text, graphic, voice, and image communication among individuals, groups, and machines.
○ Information access based on key words, phrases, or even character patterns as well as by association through hypertext links.
○ Administrative support through electronic signature and security capabilities.
○ Distributed project management support.

Augment prototypes provide many of these augmentation tool features.

Process: Augmentation

No organization, be it a small group or a society, can develop to full potential unless both human and tool systems evolve synergistically. For example, in terms of moving information, electronic mail and computer conferencing implementations have succeeded wildly in already distributed environments, but tend to fail when first introduced into environments where face-to-face or even telephone communication drives the work process. The human system—the goals, motivations, and conceptual framework of the people who are the key stakeholders in the work system—must be considered with the technology. We can no longer afford to look at the problem serially, at the "impact" of technology on the workplace. At that point, it's already too late. Human systems need to be addressed simultaneously with tool systems. (3)

With the assumptions that balanced development, or coevolution, is a requirement for organizational capability, and that most innovation occurs in the technology-system sector, organizations must simultaneously work toward:

○ Understanding human-system needs; and prototyping, evaluating, and possibly adopting technological support to meet those needs.
○ Continuously tracking technological innovation and testing its ability to increase human-system capabilities.

The process that directs the interaction between the human and technology systems is based on continuous, systemic piloting of innovative technologies and methods within the organization's operational groups.

Pilot participants are drawn from all stakeholder organizations involved in a particular project. The teams Engelbart focuses on are high-performing and culturally and functionally varied. He draws membership from multiple functions, divisions, and enterprises. Pilot teams are not removed from their everyday work and put in ivory towers or glass rooms

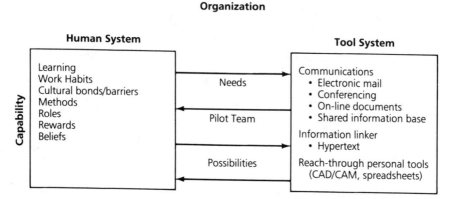

Figure 10-1 Interactions Between Human and Tool Systems

to research new methods and tools. On the contrary, they retain their operational responsibilities, at agreed levels of commitment, as well as participate in the piloting. They simultaneously learn and apply the learning to pilot work and to their organizational work.

Direction or orchestration of the coevolution comes from highly trained teams of augmentation coaches—fluent in the organization's mission, values, work designs, tasks, and technology—who focus on developing specific capabilities with pilot teams of seven to twelve workers.

Augmentation means changing work, and such change is both threatening and disruptive in the short term. When a group chooses to invest time in discovering new ways of working, it cannot devote as much time to the current work: productivity takes a hit. In the long run the new capabilities will more than compensate for short-term dropoff; but to survive and see long-term benefits, the group must assure (and be assured by) upper management that the direction and mission of the enterprise supports the organization's venture into augmentation.

The base of knowledge that members bring into and build in the pilots is leveraged in two ways. Simultaneous with their participation in pilots, team members carry their new knowledge of process and technology back to their organizations, effectively diffusing the learning in real time. In addition, the pilot coaches who manage the pilots form teams among themselves to exchange knowledge both about the capabilities they've developed and their experiences as drivers of the augmentation process.

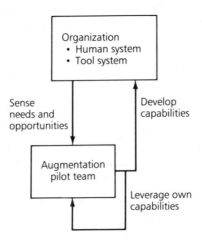

Figure 10-2 Augmentation Process: Leveraging Capability

These continuous, ubiquitous pilots, then, serve the capability-based environment by helping organizations:

○ Decide where to invest to develop human and technological capabilities.
○ Gain practical experience with new processes.
○ Build the organization's capability to build further capability.
○ Diffuse new ideas through the organization.

This approach has the advantage of minimizing the resistance of organizational immune systems to new capability. By having members of the work groups actually bring in the new knowledge, the "Not Invented Here" syndrome is neutralized: the new learning is "invented here."

Another traditional barrier to innovation that augmentation helps avoid is the impact of new methods and technology on the organization. Here, the impact of innovation is part of the focus for study in the piloting teams: the human-system side of the equation. Technology and human-system relationships are understood before the innovation is carried to the work group, so there are no surprises. Integration into the work process, under-

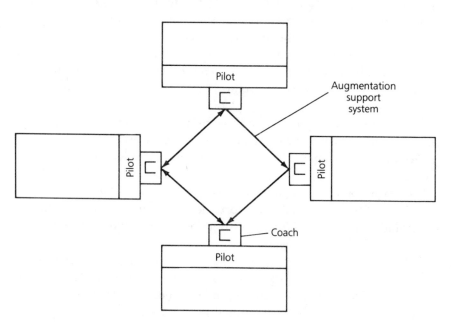

Figure 10-3 Recursive Augmentation

standing of benefits, and training are all first-order concerns, not after-thoughts.

Since piloting is the tactic for simultaneously evolving the human and tool systems, we'll look more closely at the process through the following example. A manufacturer of electronic components sees a future in which continued success will require anticipation of and reaction to market changes, coupled with fast-track development and manufacture of high-quality products. The company leads the creation of a multiorganizational team that includes membership from:

○ Its own marketing, design, manufacturing, and support units.
○ Prospective customers.
○ Suppliers.
○ Information systems vendors.

A cross-organizational management team, knowing that real-time information sharing will be critical to success in this new environment, creates pilot teams to build capability for doing the work. Theirs is not a research activity, but application prototyping, with applications defined to encompass knowledge of both human-system and technology-system variables. The teams pool their experience and share their knowledge. They build prototype information support systems, based on electronic mail and hypertext, that bring the capability of linking key people and key pieces of information in meaningful ways. The team develops addressing, information navigation, and security protocols that provide a base level of the desired capability.

Then the pilot group exercises the prototypes, using the group information management and communication system themselves. They focus on issues of shared context that will be meaningful across the environment agreeing on distribution lists and on categories and labels for public folders. They reach consensus on ways to link information within the collective information base. They map out corresponding functions in the different stakeholder groups, establishing distribution formats and routing conventions for electronic documents.

While this work goes on, team members bring the developing knowledge back to their base organizations, applying potentially appropriate methods and technology, structuring and retaining knowledge of their own group. They see how useful the stored knowledge is and how people feel about using it. What changes does the new technology cause to the human side? Are there new roles? More trust in each other's knowledge? Willingness to follow group information, navigation paths, and flow?

Then, as changes are made in the human side, what new technology support might be needed? Perhaps the work is graphic, or image based. Hypertext won't do; hypermedia is needed, bringing linking capabilities to graphics, video, and even recorded voice or music.

Team members share the learning with coaches running other pilots, and bring feedback to the original stakeholder team. Over time the team will have incrementally delivered new capabilities to the sponsoring stakeholder organization and to their own proprietary base organizations. Furthermore, based on this knowledge, they will have augmented their own capability to work as a stakeholder pilot team, and significant value will accrue across the stakeholder environment:

○ Cross-functional groups will better understand each other's work contexts.
○ Potential customers can contribute to product design, ensuring that it will more closely meet their needs.
○ Suppliers will be ensured of real-time knowledge in product changes.
○ Information systems vendors will gain insight into the kinds of products they should supply to support simultaneous distributed work.

For our electronic manufacturer, all these benefits will endure beyond the scope of the immediate project. When the next challenge comes along, requiring participation in a project of twice the complexity in half the time, knowledge of technology and methods of managing and sharing information will already be in place—or more likely, will still be moving forward.

Capturing Knowledge and Innovation

In the augmentation model, the interactions of the human and tool systems, as well as the record of the pilot organization's evolution through augmented states, are captured by the information system through the artifacts of a *Journal* and a *Handbook*.

The Electronic Journal

The Journal is a shared information space, a sort of hyperlibrary, that contains the whole of the group's information corpus: actual electronic texts, images, and tables. The Journal is indexed and is accessible by everyone in the group. Determining who needs to access the journal is, of course, a human-system activity; perhaps a team task, if not a specific new role. Storage and access policies are shaped to meet the needs of the group. In some situations, storing all communications and project information may be the appropriate convention. This would include electronic mail, specifications, memos, deliberations in computer conferencing files, agendas, and trip reports. Other groups may be selective about storage and access; their situation, for privacy or security reasons, may require agreeing on certain protocols to screen what goes into the "public" record. In either case, the Journal becomes a permanent record of the information basis of the project or situation.

The Journal should include information from organizational documents, from other organizations, and from outside intelligence, such as scanned-in newspapers, books, and trade literature. This may require yet another role: that of the Knowledge Manager. This person, or persons, would be responsible for an electronic library, including acquisitions, access, publication, and review of available materials. The Knowledge Manager

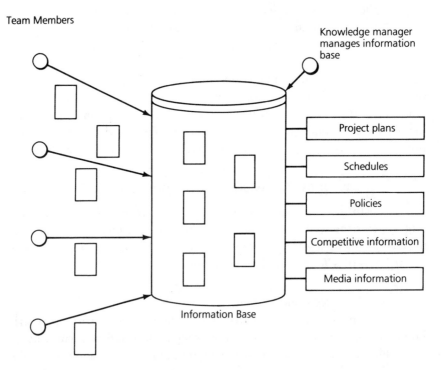

Figure 10-4 The Electronic Journal

must know what to acquire, and therefore must know the organization—its purpose, history, goals, direction, and culture. The Knowledge Manager uses this knowledge to build the group's own knowledge base.

The Handbook

As the Journal is the electronic library, the Handbook is the electronic artifact that structures the information held there into the group's intelligence. (4) It's best to think of the Handbook as a logical capability—a framework—rather than a physical entity (an actual book).

Using hypertext links, the Handbook enables users to view the organization's information from a variety of stakeholder perspectives such as: organizational, work group, individual specialist, and individual-specialist-as-part-of-a-work group. The richness of the Handbook concept lies in its potential for providing a continuous window into organizational knowledge. The Handbook provides the rapid access to knowledge that distinguishes the flexible proactive organization from the reactive organization.

The Handbook always represents the current state of the organization, providing contexts for the vast amounts of information available to it, enabling shared meaning, shared directions, and shared associations within the organization.

The Handbook enables individuals in a work group or larger organization to remember and learn, with some degree of predictability, from the group's experience. In the present (and future) business environments, marked by extreme complexity and rapid change, it is essential that organizations do not waste time in relearning, rediscovering, and redeciding brought about by faulty memory access. Having the capability to record and retrieve both information and processes enables the organization to respond to environmental changes and opportunities quickly and with a higher probability of success, since the basis for the response would be experience and learning.

Moreover, mistakes and omissions are as much a part of the Handbook as historical information. Knowing what path not to take is as important as knowing what worked.

The Handbook is also a reference guide for all the information new group members need about their environment. What's the group's record? How do workers get a raise? A vacation approval? What are the policies, the taboos, communication paths, pragmatics, and goals?

For example, a group may have a policy that its members keep daily or weekly activity and progress reports in a shared document space. Any stakeholder in the organization can see a snapshot of that dynamic progress

report from a specific perspective: management might want top-level progress against commitment information; a person in resource development
might want to view the report from the perspective of time spent in employee education; new members of the group could access historical information about the group, current policy and protocols, and pragmatic
information about how to get what they need.

Since the Handbook is integral with the organization's work system,
it is always up to date, providing real-time access to:

○ Relevant environmental information.
○ Organizational structures, roles, processes, culture.
○ All system-user information.
○ Individual preferences, skills, and interests.
○ Project and product plans, deliverables, and histories.
○ Indicators of environmental change.
○ The keys to appropriate organizational response to change through
   adaptation of structure, processes, or tools.

Since the Handbook must be responsive not only to the informational realities but to the cultural, organizational, and personal realities of groups, it
does not evolve automatically. Its access paths must be built and maintained by a key information worker in the organization: the Handbook
Integrator.

The Handbook Integrator is a new role, an evolution from centralized,
technology-focused Management Information Systems (MIS) activities to
the sociotechnically proficient knowledge work performed in the local organization or work group. It is a role that exists today in its infancy, in
the concept of Computer Conferencing Moderator and Videotext Information Provider. Other manifestations will follow as the role becomes a
key organizational staff position in the coming years.

No Handbook will ever be full, or even fully defined. Recorded learning, or knowledge, consists not just of discrete things, but of entities that
are valued in and because of the various contexts in which they appear.
Even the absence of an entity in a crucial context has value, if only as an
indicator that work needs to be done or that old methods are unproductive.
For example, after enough weeks, empty "Action Item" fields in the minutes of project status meetings suggest that attendees are, or should be,
getting direction from other sources.

The Handbook, then, consists of entities and contexts, of ideas and

Team Members

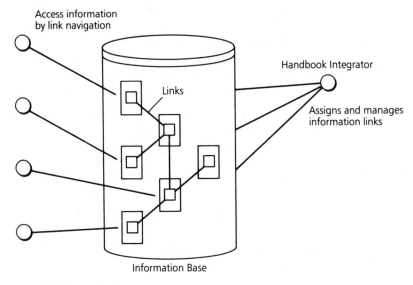

Figure 10-5 The Handbook

actions that worked or didn't work, of facts and probabilities and guesses and mistakes of the past that might have value in current and future contexts.

Leveraging Capabilities Across the Organization

Learning and innovation are spread through organizations, out of the pilot groups, not by chance but by a designed process:

○ Augmentation team members share their learning from interactions with individual knowledge workers in their pilot groups. They capture the pilot's successive augmented states in the pilot Handbook.
○ Key change agents from an organization's pilots share Handbooks and create an augmented organizational Handbook that is a source of intelligence for all members of the organization.
○ Change agents from a variety of organizations form cross-functional augmentation teams. They build and share Handbooks, continuing to build and make available increased capabilities to an ever wider segment of the enterprise.
○ The recursion continues to an agreed corporate, multicorporate, industrial boundary.

The Handbook is a logical electronic artifact, and the actual scope and method of sharing new knowledge is limited only by the imaginations of the groups involved. The knowledge can be accessed by category, context, content, chronology, or source group in any number of ways, electronically. Knowledge is available instantaneously anywhere in the network, to any stakeholder in a group or any stakeholder group in a larger organization.

For example, the personnel group's manager, having just reviewed an innovation made by the group's own augmentation team, can send a message like this to the appropriate distribution list:

"Follow these hypertext links in the Handbook and you'll get:

○ A description of the new planning process.
○ Review comments.
○ Link addresses to the electronic conference we have opened for feedback on the process.
○ Link addresses of the actual executable software."

Here the Handbook serves as the group's electronic knowledge space, as well as the shared information space. And it delivers what the group needs to react instantaneously to an opportunity.

Augmentation in Practice

Recently, augmentation pilots were conducted in the National Aerospace Plane (NASP) planning project, which involved five major aerospace companies.

The project was "managed" by one company, serving as "first among equals" within the new Department of Defense project model of a team of prime contractors collaboratively doing the work. In one segment of the project, five teams researched heat-tolerant composites for engines and airframes. Each participating organization worked at its home site; each had membership in all the teams headed by the other corporations.

The Augment system provided "core knowledge work" capabilities for the multienterprise teams: mailing, shared-screen conferencing, shared document and information space (the Journal and Handbook), structured document processing and publishing, access to specific professional applications such as 3-D modeling programs, electronic signature and encryption, and project management—all on an integrated hypertext base.

Augmentation focused on the "contract data requirements" for the project—activities reports specified in the contract. Even under relatively simple management conditions, such reporting is time consuming. Acquiring, coordinating, and transmitting accurate data periodically can occupy entire staffs. Given the basic Department of Defense requirements, plus the inter- and intra- enterprise requirements, reporting on this project appeared prohibitively complex.

For example, monthly—sometimes weekly—reports needed to be received by the Joint Program Office at the managing Department of Defense site. These reports were aggregated by project area (e.g., composites, logistics, airframes) and submitted by the contractor responsible for that area. That same information needed to be delivered to the management of each participant in each area, but aggregated with the information for other areas in which the participant had primary or membership responsibility. New report schedules, destinations, contents, and aggregations emerged sporadically: the problem for one set of reports could not simply be solved and moved from the critical path. (5)

Since "can't be done" was not an acceptable response for this complexity, augmentation teams began working with NASP management and users to develop the capabilities that would enable the groups to continually evolve to meet reporting requirements.

Rapidly prototyping with Augment and developing the group Handbook, facilitators and users carried out the work processes and the technology support that would enable the desired effects. A messaging capability based on the roles, information capture and flow, security, and periodicity of the report emerged that used hypertext links to reduce duplication of information. This capability automated collection and distribution lists for information capture and routing, and signatory capabilities for validation.

The final task of augmentation teams, true to the recursive nature of the model, is to instill augmentation capabilities, not just the results of augmentation throughout the organization. With decentralized self-evolution capabilities, the organization will get to catlike agility, instead of dinosaurlike torpor.

SUMMARY

This excursion into augmentation has been aimed at presenting one vision of how organizations can evolve their capability to do distributed knowledge work. We recognize that many well-thought-out, detailed models exist for aspects of the augmentation architecture. Organizational learning, knowledge-worker teaming, and piloting processes have been investigated in some depth. On the technology side, networks and groupware recently have been subject to enormous attention by the information systems and research communities. Far from trying to obviate that work, we offer Engelbart's model as an overarching framework for these methods and technological artifacts. Augmentation stands as an example of how it can all be put together to achieve a strategic organizational goal: the building of work capability that can address the challenges of the present and the future.

NOTES

1. Engelbart continues his lifelong commitment to building organizational capability at the "Bootstrap Project," affiliated with Stanford University. Project researchers, consultants, information systems users, and vendors representing dozens of organizations have met regularly for over a year to collaborate on developing continuous improvement processes in distributed, knowledge-based organizations.
2. Engelbart, "Authorship Provisions in AUGMENT," in Greif, *Computer Supported Cooperative Work,* pp. 107–126.
3. The interactions between culture and technology are repeatedly evidenced in the transportation sector. In recent years, officials in Rome have been struggling to control the automobile emissions pollution that is destroying many of the city's monuments. Rome's problem is largely due to the fact that most commuters make the trip between home and work four times a day: they go to work, return home for the afternoon siesta, go back to work, then return home in the evening. Many are government workers, and the government has looked at two possible ways to reduce traffic volume (as far as we know, abolishing siesta is not an option):

○ Better mass transportation.
○ Moving offices outside the city closer to workers' homes.

Either option is technically possible, but Romans have a strong cultural belief that work is a place in the city that you drive to; therefore, neither solution is gaining much popular support.
For a scholarly yet pragmatic examination of the cultural (organizational) barriers to coordinating public transportation in the San Francisco Bay area, see Donald Chisholm, *Coordination Without Hierarchy* (Berkeley, CA: University of California Press, 1988).
4. The Networking Institute has developed and begun applying a sophisticated model of group intelligence that fits with Engelbart's handbook process. See Jessica Lipnack and Jeffrey Stamps' unpublished work, *How Groups Think* (West Newton, MA: The Networking Institute, 1988.)

5. The vertical dimension of management should be mentioned here as well. To facilitate communication and clarity in distributed teams, and to bring the best knowledge quickly to bear on issues and decisions, "participative management" is recommended. In this model the hierarchy is flattened by having managers "up and down the line" participate in the communications exchanges—face to face or electronic—at higher and lower levels than they would normally. That is, instead of primarily meeting with their own staff or manager or peers, managers participate in the work meetings at higher and lower levels of the organization. See Ackoff, *Creating the Corporate Future*, pp. 65–70. Also, Calvin Pava calls this the "reticular organization." See *Managing New Office Technology* (New York: The Free Press), pp. 123–128.

Part III | Simultaneous Distributed Work

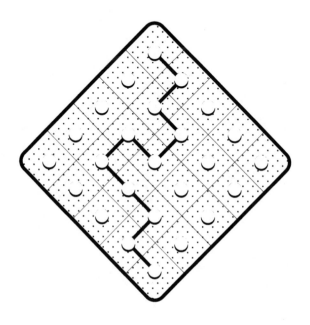

Chapter 11 | Simultaneous Distributed Work: Goals and Processes

The optimal value of the capability-based environment is its ability, over time, to initiate and sustain successful simultaneous distributed work initiatives. The environment supports work in the appropriate stakeholder community through state-of-the-market technologies, processes, and work methods in any business climate and in any business—be it manufacturing, service, education, government, or any other value-generating activity.

Simultaneous distributed work (SDW) is symbiotic with the capability-based environment. It actualizes the potential of the environment, simultaneously feeding back knowledge into the extended enterprise and aggregating into knowledge at the work group, the distributed team, and the enterprise level—wherever the network provides access to information, people, and knowledge.

In this chapter we'll look at the emergence of simultaneous distributed work, a phenomenon that responds to today's business priorities for competitiveness and profitability. This is not to say that today's—and tomorrow's—key business concerns are suddenly different from the traditional "better, faster, cheaper business concerns." What is different is the rate of change in acceptable performance within those categories. It's not unusual these days to hear companies, even entire industries, set goals for 100 percent quality, reduction in time-to-market from years to months, and reduction in costs of up to 60 percent.

First, we'll discuss how today's challenges in the dimension of quality, time-to-market, and cost instigated the early simultaneous distributed work efforts. In the latter part of this chapter we'll describe some key aspects of the SDW model.

Enterprise Goals Driving Simultaneous Distributed Work

Time-to-market, cost, and quality are abstractions we use to measure the value of products and services both from the producer's and the consumer's points of view. These attributes are not separate entities; they interrelate. One can argue that from the customer's point of view, reducing the time-to-market contributes to quality in the time dimension (the customer gets the right product when it's needed). From the producer's perspective, shorter development cycles reduce time-to-market and cost as resources are consumed over a shorter time period. Quite often the shorter cycles contribute to product quality from both perspectives as well.

Time

There are obvious benefits in getting to market more quickly than the competition. Actually, while time reduction usually comes to mind, the real goal here is to "control" time-to-market. You want your product or service to be available, in volume, when its availability will best accomplish your business goals: profitability, recognition as innovator, market share, coordination with the leading edge of the demand curve. In most cases, sooner is better than later. Customers usually want products as soon as possible, to satisfy their needs as consumers or to provide their own competitive edge as they use your product or service in their own value-adding process. Today's market windows are narrow, and the sooner you

Figure 11-1 Relationships Among Business Goals

reach the market the more profitable your product will be, as competition tends to lower prices.

On the other hand, being late to market can cost millions of dollars per day in lost revenues. Given the rapid changes in market needs, being too late could mean you have no product at all, no matter how high you finish on other quality and cost scales.

Cost

Reducing cost has become a requirement for remaining competitive. Resources—time, people, tools, and dollars—are expensive. Earlier time-to-market can significantly reduce costs, as resources are consumed over a briefer time span. As large organizations scale down over the next decade, this freeing up of scarce resources will help keep organizations productive; more value can be generated with fewer resources. Shorter cycles also mean more frequent project starts, making it possible to take advantage of cost-saving innovations in tools, materials, and products. (1)

Productivity resolves directly to profitability. By controlling costs, an organization has more leeway in controlling prices. It can follow the best business strategy without being constrained to a high, narrow price band. Go for market share with lower price, or go for profit; both are possible because of cost reduction. (2)

However, random efficiencies have little effect on the lasting productivity in large, complex value chains or networks. To dramatically contain costs, we need to develop processes that help us work smarter. We recall a key attribute of the capability-based environment: the commitment to retaining over time, the knowledge, the history, upon which such qualification is based in accessible form. This means knowing what worked, what didn't; knowing the unexpected hazards of subcontracting a key module in a communication system; knowing what distributed team can be depended upon to go the extra mile to work patiently and creatively with new, perhaps unwilling, team members during crunch time—regardless of the location, function, or organizational culture of the new team.

Simultaneous distributed work, as it compresses the time consumed in development, makes the organizational learning that accompanies that development available sooner to other projects. This is especially true if the piloting principles described earlier are used systemically in the environment. The accelerated learning from project A can be shared in real time with projects B and C. This brings learning to bear in other areas more quickly than possible with the traditional "post-mortem"/"what-did-we-learn" approach to codification of organizational knowledge, and has direct and positive results on bringing innovation to work processes and to products.

An obvious way to reduce cost is to reduce waste by eliminating rejection and reworking of unacceptable goods and services and excluding excess or irrelevant materials from inventory. From another angle, these are quality issues. Cost savings can be achieved by assuring quality at every step of the way, continuously qualifying parts, people, products, and processes to fit the expectations placed on them. This congruence of work and product to specification and expectation increases the ratio of product output to work input at all levels.

Of course, the customer is not concerned with your cost of producing the output, except as it affects the price. And that means the price over time, including maintenance, changes, even disposal. (One can of paint may be a dollar cheaper than another, but it may need priming now, touching up in a year, and it may cost you double the price to get rid of the hazardous empty can.) Again, it's a matter of expectation for cost to the customer over the life of the product.

We turn next to quality.

Quality

Increasing global competition has put pressures on enterprises to deliver products and services that get high marks from customers in all dimensions—cost, timeliness, and functionality. Because of its pervasive influence across all these areas, quality has become the driving product and service goal in the 1990s.

At this point, it's important that we define the way we use the term *quality* here. Quality is the degree to which a product or service meets or exceeds customer expectations. Granted, this obviates "absolute" characteristics of quality: our relativistic definition implies that satisfying junk food surpasses the quality of a brilliant but gamey pheasant-under-glass-for-two that no one wants to eat. The point of business is customer satisfaction, not self-expression. The absolutes of quality—function, aesthetics, innovation, robustness—are all couched within expectations. (4)

Every output along the value chain must be considered a product worthy of the quality concerns usually restricted to the final product. This means that every output must be designed to assure that it meets the expectation of its consumers: the next stage in the value chain. Meeting consumer expectations should become a predictable pattern; only in certain circumstances is unpredictability valuable. For example:

○ To attract attention to an activity or product. There's the Budweiser beer commercial on television in which someone asks for a light and is handed a candle, or floodlight, or something equally inappropriate, instead of a Bud Lite. This incongruity draws the viewers' attention to the fact that just asking for a "light" won't necessarily get you the beer you want or the beer the sponsor wants to sell.

○ To confuse the competition. If a bank traditionally comes out with new services a given number of weeks after periodic Federal Reserve announcements, the competition will get the clue and announce competitive services a week before. So the smart bank varies its offerings so as to not give away competitive advantage.

We can approach quality as subsuming several attributes of products, including time-to-market and cost, from the twin perspectives of the customer and the producer. (See Figure 11-2.)

For the producer, quality derives from setting and achieving organizational expectations within the attributes. We've discussed the advantages of early time-to-market and reduced cost. Equally important is the functional quality of the products or services, how they do what they do better—how better mileage, better sound, or faster claims settlements distinguish one company from its competitors. Here's where innovation becomes an important competitive edge.

On the other hand, following a planned strategic direction, or product architecture, helps protect investment in knowledge and tools. We don't advocate stifling innovation; but an organization that designs electronic business forms one year, roller bearings the next, then elects to bank its

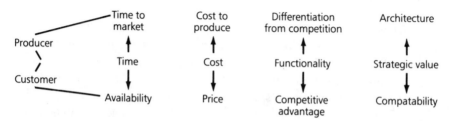

Figure 11-2 Quality Expectations

working capital the third year builds no capability. It does not leverage its unique resources, knowledge, tools, and processes.

On the customer side, the same attributes have different manifestations. Availability is what concerns the customer. Usually, the customer will fit a new product or service into a context of critical dependencies: you want the new camera before your vacation, the roof before the floor, the process control machines before the composites start arriving. Here, timing expectations form a web of contingencies; all must be met for the customer to be satisfied.

The customer's quality perspective continues through price, competitive advantage, and compatibility, all of which contribute to the perception of value received.

Achieving aggressive quality goals is a function of sustaining simultaneous processes and eliminating mistakes and the associated rework at all stages of a project within all aspects of an organization. This could include:

○ Cost estimating materials accurately, and allowing enough tolerance so that a product design can reflect financial constraints from the start.

○ Personnel recruiting doing its job so the right personnel requests are signed, the right leads established, and finally, people with the right capabilities for a project are on board at start time, when they're needed.

○ Decision-focused meetings happening as planned, with essential information always available electronically to those who need to know, so that through electronic conferencing the meeting can be held no matter where the people are located.

○ Disseminating decisions instantaneously across networks; and making those decisions, and the deliberations that led up to them, accessible electronically in the future. This saves time on the next project when analogous situations come up.

When an organization delivers according to expectations of quality and timeliness, trust develops. Often in simultaneous distributed work, geographically separated, largely unseen members of cross-functional teams must collaborate around common data, each deriving function-specific information from that data. A spreadsheet with product endurance data developed by the Australian simulation unit may have production implications for manufacturing personnel in Ireland; marketing personnel in Los Angeles may interpret the data as fodder for benchmark comparisons. If each has trust in the accuracy of early data generated by the Australian materials team, they can get to their own tasks early, and with confidence. Again, quality expectations contribute to reducing time-to-market by supporting simultaneous distributed work.

Characteristics of Simultaneous Distributed Work

Next, we'll highlight key activities, philosophies, and organizational priorities that characterize simultaneous distributed work efforts. Many of these are familiar, being essential to the capability-based environment itself; others are specific concerns of working in simultaneous mode. In order, we will discuss:

○ Concurrent task performance.
○ Concurrency management.
○ Electronic information.
○ Universal distributed data access.
○ Communications among stakeholders.
○ Knowledge sharing.
○ Total product quality.
○ Architecture and design.
○ Simulation.
○ Personal and social environments.

Concurrent Task Performance

In the perfect world, the same project done serially and simultaneously could be modeled as shown in Figure 11-3. An initiative in which all activities start at Day 1 and proceed simultaneously should finish in the time it takes to complete the longest nonreducible project task: this is the philosophical goal of simultaneous distributed work.

The advantages of the simultaneous model are clear: the simultaneous project is completed in half the time it takes to complete the serial project. However, we must remember that this is an idealized state. As long as we break down tasks to reduce their duration and move the subtasks into parallel performance, we seem to be able to increase the number of projects done within a fixed time period with limited people and resources. As we'll

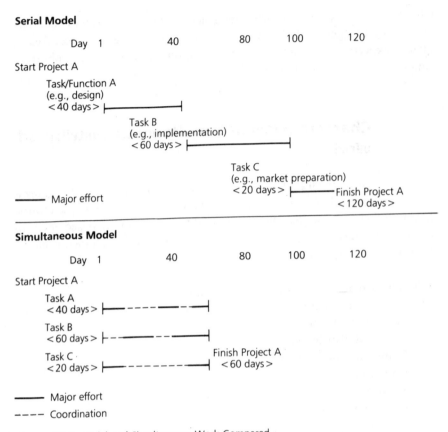

Figure 11-3 Serial and Simultaneous Work Compared

soon see, this often isn't possible, but for the moment we'll stay theoretical and look at the implications of the model.

Figure 11-3 illustrates that in simultaneous distributed work, all tasks or stakeholder activities do begin and end together: at Day 1 and at the finish. While all task efforts are continuous in the simultaneous model, level of effort varies between direct project work and maintaining continuous liaison with other project teams. This can free people to work on parallel projects. This lateral participation can accelerate the spread of learning innovation into new projects, getting them off the ground faster. Project teams learn quickly, as knowledge is brought to bear from all quarters over a short period of time. Following the augmentation model, several projects can contribute learning simultaneously, effecting a quantum jump in the knowledge base of a new effort. Innovation and learning from each project can be transferred to parallel or succeeding efforts defined by people whose heavy contributions to one project have slacked off.

Serial work takes longer, and while task participation is episodic, resources are still tied up for much of the duration because of interdependencies and rework: designers really can't take off after their initial design is complete, because there may be problems that require redesign during the project.

In practice, a project will take longer than the time it takes to perform the longest irreducible task. First of all, no matter how closely people work together, it takes time for the output of one task to be processed as the input of another task. Time is consumed in communication between people working on interdependent tasks, even (perhaps especially) in parallel processes.

Finally, in complex projects, there is no certainty about the length of tasks, only probability that the tasks will be completed by a specific time. Using various planning techniques, it's possible to determine the probability of the best case, the most likely case, and the worst case scenario for the time to complete each task. The more tasks involved, the more probable it is that one or more task will be late. Any one late task, any one late contribution to the shared value being built in the project, will impact all other tasks. All tasks are dependent, and all are on the critical path. All will be late if one is late.

Statistics show that in any complex set of tasks, one or more of the tasks will probably be late. The probability of one or more being early is far lower. This predictable suboptimization is known as *merge event bias*—the triumph of reality over intuition in simultaneous work.

On the other hand, simultaneous distributed work models offer opportunities for innovation in work processes that can reduce the traditional length of time tasks take to complete. For example, an illustrator can see the text of an annual report as it is designed, written, and laid out. He or she can therefore develop illustrations in real time with the writing and layout processes, getting direction and feedback. Similarly, the constraints of illustration can provide valuable feedback to writers and designers that will make the annual report a more effective communication object. So, while it's statistically improbable that simultaneous distributed work can reach the limit of perfection, extraordinary time savings can be achieved, with equally impressive improvements in quality.

Concurrency Management

We've mentioned new priorities for management and leadership in conjunction with the capability-based environment. Simultaneous distributed work carries even more management challenges. It thrives on increasing complexity, that is, more relationships between disparate entities in ever-shorter time spans. Complexity is not an unwanted by-product of simultaneous distributed work. Because it is both stimulus and capability, complexity lies at the heart of the process. The agenda of simultaneous distributed work is to get all requisite complexity on the table and keep it there continuously for the duration of the effort.

Complexity does need to be managed. This requires skill to keep disparate teams, perspectives, and aspects of the design together in spite of the forces of suboptimization and parochial interest.

We can see some of the management challenges as we zoom in on the theoretical model of simultaneous distributed work just discussed.

First of all, the manager needs to make sure the capabilities, both technical and social, are in place. A, B, and C each may comprise team members who are widely separated geographically. A, B, and C may be, probably will be, separated from each other. The manager needs to orchestrate the project. Like the distributor in a gasoline engine, the manager needs to get attention and energy to the cylinders that are firing; to keep the engine running smoothly, economically, though driven by energy generated by opposing forces. The manager must know the various stakeholders and consistently and clearly represent group goals in ways that make sense to their unique perspectives.

Management needs to sustain concurrency, ensuring that real-time contribution and information communication is supported by the technological network.

Electronic Information

The cornerstone of simultaneous distributed work is a commitment to electronic information—moving images, animation, text, sound, and graphics. We've seen how changing from one physical (paper, solid model) form to another, or from digital to analog and back introduces significant cost to the overall effort. State changes consume time, introduce errors, and quite often create a bottleneck that enables barrier bureaucracies to arise in the backwaters. Given the capabilities of electronic networks and network applications, acceptance of electronic information within the organization is an attitudinal rather than a technical problem. With the rapid evolution of scanning technology, it is possible to render all hard copy text and images into digital format. The critical element is in gaining the organization's commitment to trust and work with electronically accessible information, even if it goes counter to tradition.

Paper is inadequate as a communication medium because it is unmanageable and inaccessible in the large volumes generated for complex projects. Supercession and revision cause additional problems, especially in lengthy documents. Aircraft manufacturers have the problem of keeping current hundreds of thousands of pages of maintenance documentation for each aircraft at every site the aircraft may land. The only way to get the most up-to-date information—specifications with all changes, aircraft history, and supplier information to all possible sites—is by access to a maintained electronic information base via an electronic network.

Consider, for example, a production manager who decides to subcontract essential parts of a product to external suppliers. Design engineers use an electronic model to generate specifications, also electronic, for tolerances, weight, functionality, and materials. These specifications must then be submitted on traditional paper forms to the purchasing department, which then reformats, legalizes, negotiates and extends the request for bid. The potential suppliers reverse the process, converting the paper request into electronic format for their own modeling and proposal generation. They revert to paper for their response, at which point the process starts all over again, largely conducted by semiautonomous purchasing departments on either side of the fence. Anyone who has gone through this has felt the frustration of watching errors, delays, and added costs introduced to the seemingly detached development process or the program itself.

Initiatives are well under way to accelerate the development of all-electronic business and support processes. For example, Electronic Data Interchange standards are being developed to enable suppliers, distributers, and customers to conduct transactions across networks: communicate through price lists, purchase orders, invoices, and other documents that remain in shareable electronic form, saving time and money as well as maintaining accuracy.

A much more comprehensive strategy toward the all-electronic environment has been undertaken first by the Department of Defense and now the Department of Commerce: the Computer-aided Acquisition and Logistics Support (CALS) effort. The intent of CALS is to stimulate the development of near-paperless environments for the acquisition and support of major weapons systems (e.g., aircraft, missiles, ships, tanks) over the life cycles of those systems. This networked computer environment will be based on standards that ensure interoperability of information and increase the quality of work processes as well as systems. Industry, taking its cue from the Department of Defense, is adopting CALS for similar reasons.

Processes are put in place to transform data into appropriate representations: shared specifications and design documents, simulated design models, production processes, and even realized products themselves. Recent computer innovations have enabled workers to:

○ Build a data representation of a product.
○ Carve ceramic molds with data-driven robots.
○ Spray metal into molds using data-driven nozzles.

This has wholly removed the time-consuming and error-prone step of hand carving wax models as forms for the ceramic models, reducing the process time from the usual six months to "a few days." (6)

Universal Distributed Data Access

It is as important for the information in simultaneous-distributed work processes to evolve in digital state, as it is vital that the information be available to all project or program stakeholders with the need to know. The implication here is that there be one set of data centralized or distributed according to the needs of the project. In complex, time-sensitive projects, stakeholders will interpret data from their own perspectives, but they must all be linked to common, valid product and process data.

The data base is the logical center of gravity for the project. There must be clear rules for extracting, modifying, and deleting data at all levels. These must be clear processes, not so Byzantine as to dissuade knowledgeable stakeholders from recommending them, or burdening changes with such bureaucratic overhead as to make it impossible for them to be timely.

Proposed changes must be announced simultaneously to the entire stakeholder community; stakeholders must be able to evaluate changes, suggest amendments, negotiate compromises, or even voice out-of-hand rejection, all in real time. Thus, shared access to the data must be overlain with complete cross-functional communication capabilities. Communication access must be fully equal to data access.

Full Communication Among Stakeholders

One manager of an aggressively scheduled distributed development project summed up his group's work challenge this way:

> "We need to work as if we all were in the same room, and we all understood each other's problems."

By having access to a single set of shared electronic information, widely distributed contributors gain the perception that they are working "in the same room," albeit a virtual rather than a physical room. For years, defense industry ad-hoc problem-solving teams ("tiger teams") have been accustomed to convening under one roof to work out problems in one or two weeks. But with the evolution of networks and networking, members of these teams are more often staying home, participating through networks and networking. With networking applications such as shared document editors, computer conferencing, and hypertext information linking, the complex information studied and created by the teams can be stored, associated, and accessed more easily.

With full communication, distributed constituents of a stakeholder team field such as support and corporate finance, sales and marketing, and design and manufacturing can share perspectives at the moment issues arise; feedback can be instantaneous. If a problem arises in the way a component "behaves," the sharing medium can be simulation or full-motion video. Images of broken wires, ugly surfaces, and awkward or ambiguous sections of documents can be simultaneously examined across distances using the same networking communication technologies and networking techniques of the capability-based environment.

If conversation is enough for the required information exchange, teleconferences can be set up quickly to get the stakeholders into the picture. Other options include having computer-mediated deliberations with shared graphics as well as text, or using such applications as electronic mail, computer conferencing, and hypertext linking of information to preserve the discussions.

Such communication capability reduces "information float"—that unproductive "check's in the mail" time between sending and receiving, accessing and retrieving information. Paper doesn't work; the traditional paper information distribution model only accommodates the people who are known to be at a certain place when the distribution occurs. But electronic information can be accessed from anywhere by any person with the need to know.

The technology to effect "anytime, anywhere, anything, anyone" communication is here—or close—although it is somewhat misunderstood, and in some cases expensive. Many companies have their own video networks: they use digital, encoded signals for real-time communication worldwide. Some have daily conferences, linking up project members in multiple, distant sites. As one satisfied user described it: "We exchange virtually full-motion video between New England, Europe, and the Caribbean—two to three thousand miles in any surface direction plus the 20,000 miles or so up and down to the satellite—so, about 44,000 miles in a quarter to half a second. That's as close to real-time as we need to get."

Knowledge Sharing

Building knowledge-based products in short periods of time requires real-time knowledge interactions among stakeholders. When data or information needs to be discussed—for example, when a design change is desirable from a particular stakeholder's point of view—all stakeholders need to contribute to the deliberations from the standpoints of their own knowledge. Unless stakeholders have some idea what the differing points of view are, such deliberations can stall quickly, dooming the possibilities for significant time compression. Robust, available electronic communication helps minimize cross-functional misunderstandings arising from lack of shared point of view and lack of feedback.

To decrease the probability of delay, design team members should be aware of the implications of their decisions on other perspectives, just as the Worldwide Plaza designers discussed in Chapter 1 should have been aware of the maintenance perspective on the rooftop floodlights.

For example, in designing a new money market fund, business planners should understand enough about marketing to supply data that marketing can use in the quality and relevance of demographic analyses and historical comparisons. The financial people don't have to know how to market, but they should understand the marketing context up front to avoid costly mistakes. This holds true of all the stakeholder interrelationships—don't merely "represent your client," as they say on TV's "LA Law," but try to anticipate what's useful to the team. (7)

Total Product Quality

Everyone in an organization should have a product: a report, a spreadsheet, a well-managed group, a set of financial transactions, as well as solid artifacts like door handles, pills, or computer components. (8)

The point is important; while we all might not be directly involved in providing designs, information, materials, packaging, or whatever for the ultimate product that our companies deliver to customers, each of us does have a work product. That product can be ideas, information, influence, decisions, formulas, contributions of knowledge, or coordinating activities. The point of work is output—production. "Production" means more than just what emerges at the end of the value chain and goes on sale: it means what comes out every step of the way leading to that final product. Everyone in an organization must approach their product with commitment to quality.

A person without a product is not a contributor, but a barrier, and should be removed from the organizational value chain. One pioneer in the information systems industry, not given to enduring obstacles, proposed to his management an organizational home for all those people whom he felt were around only to frustrate real contributors with their inaction. He called the new organization NOD—the No Output Division. NOD would be an organizational island where nothing would be accomplished, but at least the obstructing population would be out of the value-adding process and therefore out of the way.

To increase the quality of an organization's products and services while reducing time-to-market and cost, improvements need to be made to every organizational product at every step of the way: quality, time-to-market, and cost are cumulative, not final-stage attributes. We have learned, the hard way, that quality control achieved by examination and rejection of inferior finished products does not assure quality. You may catch all the vacuum cleaners that don't work through 100 percent testing; and you can double-check all those figures in the annual audit your organization has been hired to prepare, but chances are that if visible mistakes have been made in the products, more have been made that don't show. Eventually, these "latent defects" will show, disappointing customers expecting accuracy, reliability, and performance. Only built-in quality will yield quality in the final product.

One perspective growing in influence today is "QFD," Quality Function Deployment or Quality Factor Development. (9) This is a formal process for reducing aspects of a proposed product, service, or process into a fine-grained matrix that ascribes quantifiable quality attributes and goals to all identified aspects of a product. QFD criteria are developed by all stakeholders, driven primarily by what consumers expect of the product: what levels of performance, ruggedness, style, price, or any other attribute they will find acceptable. QFD methodology is widely accepted as a means of bringing all perspectives to the table to focus on all quality aspects of the output. QFD is now taught extensively in manufacturing industries; as knowledge of its processes spreads, it will surely be applied to an even wider variety of work.

Definitions may differ, methodologies may differ, focus may differ, but from every direction the watchword is quality—and the quest is on.

Architecture and Design

Because of cost, complexity, and time pressures, vendors and customers are turning to architecture as the most systemic way of articulating expectations for the way future products and services will behave. We have computing architectures, documentation architectures, user-interface architectures, and weapons architectures. Randomness and unpleasant suprises can be minimized in the evolution of any complex system through adherence to architecture. In the fast-track world of simultaneous distributed work, architecture provides a point of reference for decisions involving design choice, innovation, and often investment.

An architecture is a system of constraints and definitions that forms a framework for providing products and services. Architectures usually evolve to de-facto standards, as in the case of the modern automobile, with its side doors, four wheels, pedal, steering wheel, and dashboard controls. Sometimes architectures emerge as theoretical proposals, with implementations to follow: "ideal workplaces" and "planned cities" fall into this category. Architectural constraints are intended to ensure that the design will work predictably in the anticipated environments. (10)

From an organizational standpoint, architecture expresses in words, pictures, simulations, prototypes, and products the organization's strategic directions. It is an artifact that clearly represents the mission, as well as the product and service roadmaps to that vision, to the entire enterprise stakeholder community. This means fewer forays into nonstrategic business segments, niches where there's money to be made at the expense of more robust revenues from other strategic projects. Architectures make startup decisions easier, and they keep the value-added chain tuned to go after high-payoff, long-term value rather than near-term efforts that may drain resources from more significant initiatives.

From the standpoint of the product consumer, architecture is just as important. Critical investments in information technology, for example, are made today only after organizations are satisfied that new investments will meet work needs across their distributed enterprise, at the present and into the future, while protecting systems they've already acquired.

Architecture, as we speak of it here, must be distinguished from design. Too often architecture—say, in building construction—strays from its purpose, becoming an aesthetic adventure instead of an insurance policy that form will follow function. Some would argue that in architecture there is no place for self-expressive creativity, the domain of design. Architecture is function driving form, and should respect its own architectural limits. (11)

The inability to distinguish between architecture and design can have serious consequences. In our own domain of information technology, we have seen the architecture of the traditional paper-shuffling office be adopted as the constraint system of the electronic workplace. We have desktop computing, with icons of trash cans, concern for page numbers, documents, files, and other syntactic forms of the paper world applied wholly inappropriately to the infinitely more flexible electronic world. We accept the time-proven paper office architecture as the architecture for electronic knowledge work, constraining our possibilities to work in new and better ways with information. The paper office paradigm is an interesting design for some kinds of distributed information work; it is not an architecture for the electronic workplace. Extended enterprises doing simultaneous distributed work need to share a commitment to articulate, understand, and respect architectures.

Other examples of this lack of distinction abound; designs tend to be accepted as architectures. We've all been schooled within an educational architecture that was really a design—for shaping the school year to meet the needs of an agrarian society. The kids were needed in the summer to help pick the crops. Given the general lament about the effectiveness of education, school year innovation, such as classes throughout the calendar year, should be welcomed, not attacked as unwarranted radical change.

Because design—continuous design—is so central to simultaneous distributed work, the next chapter is devoted entirely to describing its role and characteristics. Here we just declare that design is more than the first stage in a simultaneous work effort. It is more than a representation of a planned organization, product, process, or service. In simultaneous distributed work, design is the final entity, moving from first approximation to eventual physical realization. Designing is building through continuous contribution, feedback, and revision by all stakeholders in the process. (12)

Simulation

We have mentioned the availability of simulation tools that enable distributed teams to move smoothly from the initial design, through testing the design and creating modifications of the design through successive cycles until a product is realized. In simultaneous distributed work, "everything" can and should be simulated: the organizational communications channels, resource flow, product behavior, work flow and work processes, documents, and technical systems. Simulation enables us to study behavior under different conditions. Electronic simulation models can be shared like any other information medium; a diverse group can simultaneously see how a part will look, a process will perform, or a function will behave. Simulation processes range from simple "what-if" spreadsheet manipulation to global commodity distribution games to multimillion-dollar flight simulators.

In each case the same electronic design data that define the product and drive its delivery can predict its probable performance. Changes can be made quickly and cheaply anywhere in the electronic design process. This lowers the risk of discovering key defects in expensive, inflexible physical prototypes: hand-built vehicles out in test markets or a published report out for review. No model needs to crash; nor is there need to collate and rekey thousands of pages of manuscript. Simulation can be viewed as a public phase of design, conducted with the designed object existing in the best approximation of its ultimate environment, yet still represented electronically.

Major oil producers, for example, play global distribution games, simulating business models at various price levels for their commodity. What does exploration, drilling, distribution, diversification, and revenue look like if oil is $18 per barrel? If it's $80 per barrel? How much new supply? How many additional supertankers? Here, strategic planning is driven by simulation involving the simultaneous participation of a wide range of stakeholders. (13)

On a more local level, major home builders now use PC-based CAD software to reduce the time needed to design, redesign, deliver, frame, and finish homes. Customers and company representatives work on the design together. Design modifications are sent to all stakeholders—suppliers, town officials, and landscapers. Electronic design reduces this process to hours, rather than the weeks it used to take with hand-drawn, sequential, paper-based blueprints. Changes and the implications of changes can be demonstrated instantaneously (a bay window here would let in more light, but what will it do to the heating load? the landscaping? the roof?). Very quickly all relevant perspectives can be brought to bear on design issues, and resolution can be achieved before any walls are constructed or paper blueprints are distributed.

Electronic simulation reduces time, cost, and risk, while providing information needed for continuous product improvement. In simultaneous distributed work, simulation is not a stage in the development process, as was physical prototyping; now simulation becomes a continuous aspect of shared, continuous design.

Personal and Social Environments

Like all change, the change to simultaneous distributed work models has met with a lot of resistance. This resistance is understandable; there are new costs, impacts, and threats to simultaneous distributed work that are quite obvious to the people who have to do it. For example, acceptance of simulation has not come easily. Primarily, resistance has come from work communities where written specifications and designs were the traditional forms of product definition and description.

Not everyone can change. There are many highly skilled workers who know how to craft cars, boats, buildings, and artificial limbs in physical prototypes and models. Their jobs will change as electronic models replace their physical efforts. From their perspective, electronic simulations pose the very real threat that their roles will change, be reduced, or perhaps disappear.

There are many other, less dramatic psychological and cultural implications to working in the simultaneous distributed mode. Simultaneous distributed work can be disorienting. Working with people that are unseen, perhaps unknown, who are "out there somewhere" can produce a lot of anxiety in those who favor living and working with people to whom they can physically as well as emotionally relate. Working with faceless stakeholders through the medium of an information object, a design, or document, may be too cold and detached for some. By not being able to physically relate, they may be unable to create, trust, or remain motivated to drive through the hard times in a project.

Trust among stakeholders is essential to the success of any simultaneous effort. Electronic information created, evaluated, revised, and consumed by everyone, is the current that flows through the work system. Mutual trust must pervade the information web; trust that information is accurate and perspectives are consistent with overall goals; trust that early, incomplete, or inelegant information is "enough to go on," that keeping the value-adding process moving is more important than being absolutely sure of accuracy.

Working in parallel with all other functions on a project causes other stresses, among them an urgency not always present in serial work. For example, simultaneous distributed work doesn't allow for slack. The urgency to share new information and react to it in real time imposes a responsibility to communicate and turn around work continuously, not sporadically. This incessant pressure, the stress of continually needing to sort out seemingly limitless information, deciding what's important and what isn't, can wear people down quickly.

Design-driven work processes, which we'll look at in some detail in the next chapter, further wrench our conventional sense of time by having us look at our work in a different time perspective. Since everyone starts designing at Day 1, what used to be "downstream" processes, occurring late in the project, now occur "upstream" early in the project. Manufacturing expectations are addressed at the start of the development cycle, not the end. We worry about customer expectations being met before, not after, we design. Testing for quality is an issue before, not after, the product is physically realized. This shift in time perspective can be destabilizing and threatening at first; people must have help in developing tolerance for a simultaneous perspective.

Finally, as stakeholders work together on a project, they must appreciate and understand the perspectives of the other stakeholders. In the past, people were responsible for their piece of the whole project. They didn't need to know a lot about what "the other guys" did or how others' work related to their own. Now everyone is asked to consider, care about, and understand the needs of the other functions and other component units. People are asked to commit not just to their own piece, but to the ultimate product. We've spoken about the impact of change here, but refrained from offering advice on what to do about it. That is the province of management, to which we'll turn now.

SUMMARY

Simultaneous distributed work comprises the processes through which value is created in capability-based environments. These processes help organizations achieve business goals of cost, time-to-completion, and quality by enabling the simultaneous execution of traditionally serial tasks.

We have characterized simultaneous distributed work in terms of the following concepts and processes:

○ Concurrent task performance.
○ Concurrency management.
○ Electronic information.
○ Universal distributed data access.
○ Communications among stakeholders.
○ Knowledge sharing.
○ Total product quality.
○ Architecture and design.
○ Simulation.
○ Personal and social environments.

Successful work in this environment requires attention to all these elements.

We have gone on to suggest the importance of design, both of product and process. In the next chapter we will look in more detail at several aspects of design and their role in achieving high standards of quality in fast-track, simultaneous development projects.

NOTES

1. But there are barriers to adopting systemic innovation. See Hirotaka Takeuchi and Ikiyiro Nonaka, "The New New Product Development Game," in *Harvard Business Review* (1986). Also, one type of resistance to innovation is peculiar to newer companies: "The biggest problem a new technology-based company faces is getting their second product. Every company has a tendency (especially if there are a lot of engineers and technologists involved) to refine and enhance the existing product, which absorbs all available manpower." (Unattributed quote in Marcene Sonneborn and David Wilemon, "Sustaining Innovativeness in Emerging High-Technology Companies," *IEEE Engineering Management Review* (September 1990): 6.

2. Paul Strassman offers a powerful productivity model that positions the ratio of price to cost as a survival metric; what is most desirable is the longer-term "inequality" by which customer benefit exceeds price, which in turn exceeds cost. This "social" model includes the customer as a stakeholder in the value-adding process, recognizing that benefits to the customer eventually return to the vendor as the opportunity for future business. See *Information Age,* pp. 118–119.

3. The current concern for quality is evidenced in the number of books, articles, advertisements, and awards focusing on this aspect of products and services. For example, see John Hoshula, "The Baldridge Badge of Courage—and Quality," *The New York Times* (October 21, 1990): VI-12. See also "Quality Progress," June 1988; and William Eureka and Nancy Ryan, "The Customer-Driven Company" (Dearborn, MI: ASI Press, 1988).

4. Peter Senge points out that a new dimension of quality leads us beyond customer expectations . . . with products meeting "latent needs" discovered by imagination, not market research, e.g., the Mazda Miata. See "The Leader's New Work," *Sloan Management Review* (Fall 1990): 8

5. Robert A. Cheney, *Computer-aided Acquisition and Logistic Support* (North Hampton, NH: EMCA, 1989).

6. "These Computer 'Printers' Spit Out Molds," *Business Week* (September 10, 1990): 99.

7. Some corporations are beginning to explore the possibilities of simultaneous electronic delivery of key information to both sales and marketing personnel. See Thayer C. Taylor, "How the Game will Change in the 1990s," an interview with Andrew Parsons in *Sales & Marketing Management* (June 1989): 52.

8. Bill Smith, *Motorola, Six-Sigma,* videotape presentation at Digital Equipment Corporation, December 1989.

9. See Don Clausing and John R. Hauser, "The House of Quality." *Harvard Business Review* (May–June 1990).

10. See Christopher Alexander, *Notes on the Synthesis of Form* (Cambridge, MA: Harvard University Press, 1964) for a clear but controversial position on what designers (or architects) should or should not do.

11. Alexander feels that designers are abdicating their responsibilities to fit or link complex elements into the precise form required by the environment. The modern designer, instead of facing the difficult tasks, "preserves his innocence [by relying] more and more on his position as an 'artist,' . . . on catchwords, personal idiom, and intuition—for all these relieve him of some of the burden of decision, and make his cognitive problems manageable." *Notes on the Synthesis of Form,* 10–11.

12. For insights into the value of comprehensive design, see Daniel E. Whitney, "Manufacturing by Design," *Harvard Business Review* (1989).

13. The graphic capabilities of simulation can be illustrated in the process of designing a freeway interchange. The interchange itself can be represented with the attributes of interest to various stakeholders: traffic flow engineers, environmen-

talists and landscapers, pedestrian safety officials, trucking representatives, and road construction engineers. The behavior of the whole interchange "system" under different key parameters is clearly and immediately obvious. See also Alexander, p. 88.

Chapter 12 | Simultaneous Distributed Work: Continuous Design and the Quest for Quality

In characterizing simultaneous distributed work we have mentioned the major role of design. In this chapter we'll look more closely at how the process and scope of continuous design contribute not only to time savings but also to increased quality.

Traditionally, organizations fabricated products and services by learning to perform the work processes, designing the end product, applying processes and resources to implement the design, and reworking whatever didn't meet the expectations of the design, thereby increasing quality. The process was primarily serial, though independent tasks were often done in parallel. Think of any job you might have had; the work might have progressed this way:

1. Learn the work process.

○ Get an education—high school, college, graduate, postgraduate.
○ Join the organization—see how things are done.
○ Get training—learn how to do the process.
○ Apprentice—learn by doing.

2. Design the end product.

○ Get the order, specifications.
○ Design the form, content, and behavior of the product or service.
○ Get the design approved by management.

3. Apply process to resources—find the people, tools, components, and information you need for your processes.
4. Implement the design; build and deliver the product.
5. Rework to meet expectations—repeat steps 2 through 5.

The point of this simplistic summary is that learning the process generally preceded the product. Remember, we're using "product" in the sense of all organizational products, not just what goes to a customer. Once learned, the knowledge was reapplied to succeeding cycles: new projects were done with old knowledge, boosted by whatever learning took place between projects. When the purpose changed but the process didn't, quality suffered. In the best case, knowledge developed and was applied, but at a linear rate that did not keep up with the exponential, discontinuous leaps in capability required in high-performing organizations today.

The problem with this approach is that functional groups and individuals tend to want to do their jobs the way they always have done them. It's probable that they have been told, by training, maintenance, customer services, and documentation that the work has to be done in the traditional way.

It's difficult to get people to innovate, to handle new challenges and to explain that a new project will require different behavior from stakeholder groups. A manufacturer setting out to build a composite fishing rod logically will put in place different processes from those used in manufacturing a bamboo rod. But within the value-adding process of the product group, people tend pretty much to do their pieces as usual. Lead times, reports, marketing efforts, and support plans are based on previous models, usually successes, with slight modifications.

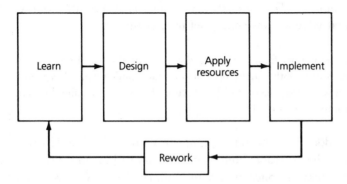

Figure 12-1 Serial Project Cycle

When processes and materials do not meet the standards for the new output desired, defects occur: useless reports, brittle components, people without the appropriate skills. Often, defects are caught and fixed through rework at the end of the process. More enlightened managers ask why the defects occur and fix the processes. Process changes are made and one quality problem disappears.

In other words, work processes are usually modified:

○ Minimally or not at all.
○ In reaction to product defects.

The rate of change in products, services, process technologies, and required work skills, along with the ever-decreasing development cycle, make this kind of inflexible work process unacceptable in simultaneous distributed work. It is not enough to adjust process design in forethought or afterthought; process must evolve continuously, simultaneously with the design of the final product or service. Only through this continuous evolution of both process and product design can the final output be requisite to its quality expectations.

In this chapter we'll look at the roles continuous process and product design have in simultaneous distributed work, and conclude with an example applying the principles to a stakeholder-based project—the development of a university curriculum.

Continuous Design

Early in Laurence Sterne's eighteenth-century novel *The Life and Opinions of Tristram Shandy,* young Tristram laments the "design flaws" that were to cause him grief in later life:

> I wish either my father or my mother, or indeed both of them, as they were in duty both equally bound to it, had minded what they were doing when they begot me . . . I would have made a quite different figure in the world. (1)

Thus does Tristram start spinning the tale of his life. His remarks are founded in the venerable homunculus theory of human development. This belief held that at conception a tiny human being was created who had "designed in" all the physical, intellectual, and social attributes that he or she would carry through life. Once produced, nothing could be done but to let the person behave the way he or she—"the product"—was designed to behave.

Tristram attributes his peculiar adult behavior to certain design defects introduced at the moment of his conception. The problem was that his imminent parents lost their concentration at a critical moment in the design/production process, when his mother asked his father, "Have you not forgot to wind up the clock?" That distraction interrupted the simultaneous design process, with the lifelong implication for the product, Tristram.

Similarly, simultaneous distributed design includes all product, service, or program attributes and determines how the product will behave under various conditions. But design is not merely an early event in the project cycle; rather, it is a continuous process. In continuous design, project stakeholders build and refine the product as data through the duration of the project. All aspects of the product are represented, evaluated, and revised, with the purpose of bringing the representation into conformance with the expectations of all project or program stakeholders: suppliers, builders, and consumers. The essence of the design process is that all stakeholders work together continuously to represent their needs and expectations in the design from start to finish. The banner might read:

Everyone designs; no one is a designer

Designs have multiple perspectives: a house or a computer network may have a physical design, a functional or operational design, even a packaging design. All design aspects respect architectural constraints, increasing the likelihood that the artifact will work. Designer goals are to meet customer expectations far beyond the fundamental architectural constraints.

A visible model of this kind of product development was mentioned briefly in Part I: concurrent engineering. Traditionally, engineers might have finished a design and "thrown it over the wall" to manufacturing people. Now in simultaneous distributed work, the two constituencies—cultures—work together in real time, regardless of their physical location or professional perspectives, so that the product is designed for manufacture as well as function.

In planning a new ballpark for the city of Baltimore, designers decided to emphasize the "park" aspect and developed a product that would hark back to the feel of older, cozier ballfields rather than the more modern, cold, concrete edifices. (The architecture—basepath dimensions, location of stands—remained unchanged.) The project financiers, designers, and city planners studied old baseball fields to get a feeling for the characteristics they wanted in this new ballpark. At one point the designed pitch of the upper deck was deemed too steep for fans' comfort; through a lengthy process the slope was reduced to an acceptable degree, at the cost of removing one entire level of the stands. Because the people responsible for ensuring that there would be enough seats to guarantee profitability were also in on the discussions, other ways to win back the space were found. One planner commented that making the change was "like a Chinese puzzle . . . every time you change one thing it affects three others." With attention to all aspects of design, and input from all stakeholders, any modifications that were made kept the design goal of "feeling like an old-time ballpark" intact. (2)

Another virtue of continuous design is that by constant feedback and change it defuses the problems inherent in trying to integrate a large number of related components into a complex whole system at one time. We all have seen the unhappy spectacle of such attempts in the realms of products, processes, or even organizations. Component work proceeds splendidly on schedule until integration time, when all the interrelationships, cross-dependencies, and conflicts conspire to create havoc: it takes as long to integrate such systems as it does to build the components.

We know that world-class components do not necessarily make world-class systems. Russell Ackoff has used the example of an automobile made by selecting the finest carburetor, engine, and transmission available on the market, each optimized for its own function. But would they work optimally as a system? Probably not. (3) More than once the software industry has attained interoperability among components in complex systems through the use of "translators" and "interfaces" after the fact. The stratagem works for a while, but the Chinese puzzle usually triumphs in the long run, as incompatibilities continue to surface.

When problems occur in integration, the human toll is high. Teams used to working independently are suddenly forced together to find out who left out a function or didn't predict certain side effects of the interactions. Denial, blame, and low morale can seriously and permanently affect an organization. The painstaking ferreting of the problems and reworking of involved components invariably takes place under extreme time pressures; everything is late and getting later.

Furthermore, integration efforts consume precious project resources as

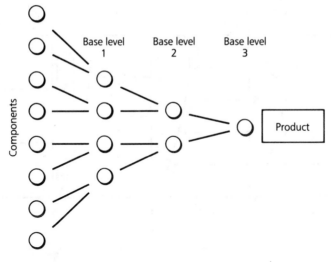

Figure 12-2 Component Integration

development pauses to accomplish the integration. Granted, successful integration provides stakeholders with a feeling of accomplishment, an event in which everything comes together. In the longer view, however, integration is an interruption in the process of building product through design. It is not a triumph but a troublesome barrier that consumes time and energy.

Simultaneous distributed work allows us to move beyond integration to holistically evolve systems of related design aspects. From the earliest stages, all parts are continuously related with one another. The complex product, process, or organization always works as a whole, at first with lower levels of functionality or information, but with the internal relationships being continuously tested and examined. As design evolves to realization, higher levels of expectation are met with no expensive surprises.

The Scope of Design in Simultaneous Distributed Work

The list of "design for's" in the canon of simultaneous distributed work continues to grow: design for manufacturing, design for testability, design for quality, to name a few. The overarching design goal is quality—quality of process and quality of product. All other design considerations help organizations achieve and sustain quality by predictably

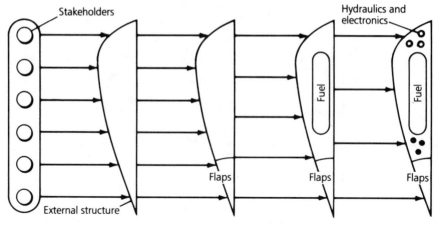

Figure 12-3 Continuous Integration in Aircraft Wing Development

meeting all internal (process) and external (product or service) expectations. As more perspectives on product and process are identified and understood, more "design for's" will emerge. Here we'll look at representative design aspects that have reached some level of recognition in industry:

○ Design for capability.
○ Design for testability.
○ Design for manufacture.
○ Design for simulation.
○ Design for disassembly.

This is not a complete list, but it should carry the message that design is not just part of simultaneous distributed work, but that simultaneous distributed work is largely design.

Design for Capability

In earlier chapters we indicated the key designs for capability: design for communication in networking, design for change in networks. With commitment to these and other capability designs, such as design for training, design for motivation and reward, and design for data access, teams can add value both for the present and the future.

To accomplish this, teams need to work beyond their dual roles as vertical, functional contributors and members of lateral stakeholder communities. The third dimension involves teams in leveraging capability of the networking enterprise as a whole. Like Janus, the double-faced Roman god of gateways, they must simultaneously be seen as project and as pilot; producing valuable output for the market, while at the same time creating, testing, and validating knowledge for application in parallel and future simultaneous distributed work efforts. (4)

Design for Testability

Whatever a group produces, the continuous design process should ensure that it is possible to verify that the output meets the expectations set by the various specifications and held by the various constituencies. The Heisenberg uncertainty principle (5) illustrates the problem. Focused in the domain of subatomic particles, this principle states that one can know either the position or the speed of a particle, but not both. This is because to measure one is to affect the other. The lesson in our physical world is that we must ensure that we can measure or test products without altering them.

Testability is closely related to maintenance. A bad testing design would have you cut a hole in the hood of your car to check the oil, or burn out a flashbulb to see if it works. In fact, automobiles, now have plug-in test points for computer analysis hookups: you don't need to break the valve cover seal to see if the valve cover seal is OK.

Design for testability takes the long view by proactively looking for downstream implications of upstream design decisions.

Design for Manufacture

Concurrent engineering efforts that constitute leading-edge simultaneous distributed work focus on problems with quality at the point of manufacture. The costs incurred by rework and waste because of product defects have become a major threat to organizations' capabilities to compete worldwide.

We can't afford to just discover and fix defects. If we do fix the defects, we can be assured that there are a significant number of latent defects that won't be apparent until the customer uses the product over time. So we stop trying to fix the defects and instead focus on designing processes that will produce, as a goal, zero defects. Again, this means ensuring product quality at every step of our value chain.

The approach taken in the engineering community has been to:

○ Move engineering and manufacturing process designs into parallel.

○ Statistically ensure that product designs reflect manufacturing process requirements and be robust enough to retain high quality, even if manufacturing processes fail to perform as anticipated.

In other words, there are certain tolerances built into manufacturing processes. For example, a process turns out a bearing that varies by .02 mm. If the design of the product calls for a bearing race that allows only .002 mm variation, then it can be statistically shown, according to the past performance of the manufacturing process, how many bad bearings to expect.

The goal is to keep the tolerances at the design level at multiples of the tolerances at the manufacturing process level, equating to a constant of quality. (7)

$$\frac{\text{Tolerances of design (specification limits)}}{\text{Tolerances of manufacture (normal process variants)}} = \text{Constant of quality}$$

Another example extends the design-for-manufacturing model into the domains of delivery and presentation. Consider the life-saving candy machine. Today the most prominent model is the kind that has a digital keyboard for input, a glass display for presentation, and an array of coiled wire dispensing racks for delivery—output. After depositing the coins or bills required, you push the numbers on the keyboard corresponding to your selection, and the wire coiled around the row of selected candy bars begins to rotate (using the Archimedes screw principle) to work your bar out the end of the coil and drop it into the pickup bin.

That's the expectation, anyway. Too often the bar gets to the end of the wire, the wire stops . . . and the bar hangs there, too bulky by a microbe's whisker to fall over. The fix can be unpleasant: kicking, banging, pleas to uninterested cafeteria personnel (not stakeholders), and finally, more money for a new try. Whatever the problem—the candy bar's center of gravity, flexibility, size, shape of the wrapper—a defect has thus thwarted a customer's expectation.

But such defects can be avoided with effective upstream attention. For example, the candy bars and wrappers should be designed with the dispenser in mind. Tolerances in the candy and packaging processes must be made acceptable to the customer—in this case the candy machine, not just the end-consumer. At the same time, the candy machine should deliver its product to its customer predictably. High quality in terms of a candy machine is the right bar clunking into the hopper every time.

For example:

1. Articulate "drop every time" as a machine quality attribute.
2. Design machines to work with wider tolerances in machine manufacturing.
3. Design machines to work with a wider tolerance of bars than are expected from bar manufacturing.
4. Articulate "within machine tolerance expectation" as a quality attribute of bars.
5. Design bars to be within acceptable range even when bar manufacturing produces bars and packages outside the expected size and shape limits.

As a final example of design for manufacturing, or in this case for presentation, we draw from the world of music. Anyone who has attended a baseball game in the United States probably has experienced the futility of trying to sing the latter portions of "The Star-Spangled Banner." The early parts ("O say can you see . . .") are no problem; but when people get to "the rocket's red glare" and "the land of the free," they tend to hit a wall beyond which standard-design vocal chords will not go. The result, of course, is that most people don't even try to sing the National Anthem, and its quality is diminished. Clearly, a composer should design and develop a piece with some sense of the instrument required to perform it. The lesson is: design for performance.

Design for Simulation

We briefly mentioned simulation as a characteristic of simultaneous distributed work. Computer-aided design tools play a key role in the design-driven SDW process. With these tools, all product and process domains in a project can be designed with some predictability of how they will behave in various circumstances. Behavior is the key here, not representation. In simpler times a document could represent, with text and images, concepts, two-dimensional, and even three-dimensional shapes. But with complexity caused by the interactions of large numbers of variables, static representation became inadequate.

Electronic simulations allow design teams to create a world of known dimensions—a world model. They introduce into this model the process or product, piece by piece. By interactively varying key aspects of the product or of the world, they can learn how the product will behave.

The candy bar/dispenser design could be accomplished most quickly through the use of a simulation plotting the statistical probabilities of variants in candy bar against the probability curve of dispenser variation. The simulation would reveal the probability of certain combinations of variants causing the bars to stick. Tolerances then could be adjusted at the design phase that would reduce those probabilities—and customer frustrations.

When considering a major highway intersection, the stakeholders in the project—demographers, public transportation and construction officials, environmentalists, politicians, truckers, and automobile service providers—set about designing an intersection that will meet all their needs for, say, five years. They use data from traffic studies, emissions volumes and effects, materials strength, interstate commerce projects, economic projections, maps, and town plans. They can simulate the world as they expect it will be in five years, then visually display their alternatives: locations, vectors, stacking and sizes of ramps. As they feed the data in, the ramps widen or narrow, seek greater arcs to carry larger volumes. Behavior under different stresses at the various sites can be compared, and decisions made on soundly based and clearly articulated expectations of future behavior.

Organizations, communication links, processes, parts, supply lines, packaging options, documents, complete systems . . . all can be simulated quickly using the common base of product and process information. The simulations are shareable in real time across the network of project stakeholders; we each can see how our bit is affected, feed back our concerns, and watch how the alternatives work.

Simulations in aerospace save millions of dollars yearly. Northrop reports that on the Advanced Tactical Fighter project, solid model representations of design data reduced engineering changes by 70 percent and design time and labor by 30 percent. (8) We have much to learn about the application of simulation techniques to nonengineering and manufacturing tasks. But with the growing availability of simulation tools, from PC animation systems to system-level computer-aided design systems, we will heed the call to

DESIGN EVERYTHING; SIMULATE EVERY DESIGN.

Design for Disassembly

A recent issue of *Business Week* simultaneously carried articles entitled "The Big Brouhaha on the Little Juice Box" and "Built to Last—

Until It's Time to Take Apart." (9) The "big brouhaha" was over the use of aseptic containers, hand-sized boxes that can keep milk and juice fresh on the shelves for months. It seems that the boxes, because they consist of thin layers of paper and metals fused together, are extremely difficult to separate for recycling. This is leading to threats of banning the boxes on environmental grounds.

Ironically, the second article proposes an approach to addressing just such problems. This recounts efforts going on in industry to design products for disassembly, ensuring that when products have completed their useful life-cycle, they can be repaired, or disassembled and separated for recycling.

Design, then, is a life-cycle perspective on products and services, incorporating knowledge from across the entire cultural geography of the stakeholder community. In the next segment we offer a scenario to illustrate the way continuous design in multiple dimensions can be applied, not only in the manufacturing world, but in such environments as the extended educational community.

Simultaneous Design: Developing a University Program

The following fictional account describes how a geographically distributed state university might use SDW techniques to quickly respond to an opportunity, for example, creating a program to develop teachers of gifted and talented public school students. Given relatively fixed resources—faculty, buildings, expense dollars, libraries, and student population—most university constituencies would be affected and need to participate in the design of such a program. Each would make contributions to and have expectations of the program.

The actual design of the program could proceed this way:

1. Proposal from the dean of the education department to the university curriculum committee for a new program to meet the emerging educational need and opportunity. This assumes that the university has designed itself to remove barriers to innovative suggestions, even encouraging or rewarding them. Such a design is not to be assumed in any organization. The proposal and supporting preliminary information, geared contexts of particular constituent groups, should be distributed ahead of the presentation, with feedback time allowed.

The presentation will probably be at a face-to-face meeting involving all stakeholders. The stakeholder list might look like this:

○ University faculty, students, administration, alumni.
○ University computer center, creative arts center, materials acquisition, student events.
○ Prospective students.
○ State Department of Teacher Education.
○ State Division of Gifted and Talented Curricula.
○ State high school guidance offices, principals, teachers.
○ Elementary school teachers.
○ Experts from other universities, consultants.
○ Government agencies (might be grants in the offing if their expectations are met).
○ Regional museums, concert halls, libraries, industrial training facilities.

2. Accomplishing all the steps to approval of the proposal. Again, the steps should be designed to minimize the routine grief normally associated with getting large constituencies to agree on anything. Clear decision-making protocols and open, available communications in all media, issue, and feedback milestones are required.

3. Accepting the basic criteria of the market statement and the realities of any business criteria or constraint: The state will need 2,400 gifted-and-talented teachers by 1995. Only three new teachers the first two years; no new buildings; to be sited at the main campus. Or, it has to be implemented in fourteen months, or rival private schools will get first crack at the market. The federal government may offer $10 million if the university puts the program at a branch in an economically depressed area.

These constraints may be modified, but it's enough to get started.

4. Several face-to-face meetings should be designed to help build a common context around the design effort. The purpose of the effort is not to aggrandize any particular department, win prizes, fill seats, or satisfy alumni. Each stakeholder group, or constituency, or function would be able to express to the other constituencies:

○ What their own perspectives were on the proposal.
○ The impact of this overall purpose on their own goals.
○ What they expect to put into and get out of the program.

Some feedback and even resolution might occur at such face-to-face meetings; more probably, as those involved sensed interactions, dependencies, impacts or cross-purposes with others, they would continue the discussions privately. The results of these private meetings, of the first-order expectations, inputs, outputs, would need to be closely documented and communicated to the other stakeholders:

○ Prepared documents must follow a consistent format and presentation to ensure that the interactions will be visible.
○ Minutes from each meeting should be recorded.
○ "Digested" minutes must be prepared, in a format that puts content into useful categories.

5. A first pass at discussion and resolution of differences should come next. At this point it would be better to involve all stakeholders. Every university has some kind of computer network, most likely a mail and computer conferencing system used by students in informal pursuits, and occasionally by faculty and administration to support policy discussions. The following must be taken into consideration.

○ Time for debate is limited.
○ A record of dialog is desirable.
○ The overall group is distributed across the state, probably the country.
○ The information must be accessible by all (except for private mail messaging) in some coherent way:
    Keywords
    Constituency name
    Issue category or name
    Milestone or deadline date
    Whatever other category the group desires
○ Personal schedules practically guarantee the futility of ad-hoc phone conversations or meetings; asynchronous communication seems warranted.
○ University people are generally good writers and prefer to write.

Given all this, a communication design for electronic mail and computer conferencing would seem particularly suited to support the deliberations.

6. Instead of periodically reviewing, assessing, and approving the complex needs, requirements, and concepts in the growing design, reviewing must be as continuous a process as the designing itself. Again, the protocols for review and approval must be clear, simple, and accessible. Every constituency should feel represented in the concepts and convinced that their expectations for the final product will be met. The faculty must know they will participate, be joined by professionally qualified colleagues, and not have their budgets cut to pay the new cost. Financial support should be forthcoming to pay for the added computer services needed to deliver programs to remote sites. Alumni must be assured that the program will be of a quality that elevates the prestige of the university.

7. As the particulars of the design develop and interrelationships among variables become more complex, the designing group can easily lose the ability to measure the effects that changes in one variable, based on new information, will have on the whole project. At this point it's clear that there needs to be some way to simulate the effects of design changes. This can be done with face-to-face role playing in meetings, with computer-assisted scenario exercises based on game theory, or with fully developed computer modeling that can monitor the behavior of the variables in the design under different conditions. This last alternative, the use of quantified variables and probabilities for certain expected outcomes, has the capability to model organizations, processes, and the design of university curricula.

8. At an expected point in this process, the design will be a curriculum. If the design medium—for example, shared electronic files, with version control and hypertext linking related information—has been designed with publication in mind, then no state change is required between the design and the product. Design has proceeded to product through simulation.

9. Finally, not only the new curriculum design, but the entire process of that design is available to future constituencies faced with the same need, regardless of where they are located on the globe. The product can be shared electronically. Indeed, the deliverable product, a publishable electronic document, can be structured with hypertext links to provide reports, summaries, presentations, or other perspectives on the information quickly and easily.

Given the increasing rate at which demand for people in various disciplines shifts, the education industry will need to supply qualified people more quickly than they have in the past. There will be no time for five-year plans to reform the educational curriculum. The organizational capability for designing new curricula can help universities reach this new level of performance.

What we've just presented is not just an illustration of some aspects of design, but a "design for design," on a project that could be accomplished productively using continuous, simultaneous design techniques.

⌐ SUMMARY

We have looked at the interrelationships between design and quality in several dimensions and can reasonably conclude that product quality is a direct result of attention to all product attributes throughout a continuous design cycle. "Product," as we use it, means all outputs from all stakeholders along every step of the value-adding process. Quality cannot be tacked on at the end of a design or manufacturing cycle; it must be everyone's primary concern, every step of the way.

Continuous, comprehensive design can assure quality in a variety of environments, including consumer products manufacturing, structural engineering, and even educational programs. As we might expect, simultaneous distributed work processes as a whole have been applied most frequently in highly complex, time-sensitive work environments, where management realizes that the likelihood of success with traditional serial processes is remote. We devote the next chapter to just such an effort: the simultaneous distributed development of a complex computer disk storage device.

⌐ NOTES

1. Laurence Sterne, *The Life and Opinions of Tristram Shandy, Gent.* pp. 191–192.
2. Mark Cohen, "Building the Perfect Ballpark," *GQ* (September 1990): 126–128. See also Paul Goldberger, "A Radical Idea," *The New York Times* (November 19, 1989):VIII:39.
3. Ackoff, *Creating the Corporate Future,* p. 18.
4. Jeffrey S. Stamps makes the case for the part/whole unity, or "holon," being essential to all systems, including people and technology networks. See *Holonomy* (Seaside, CA: Intersystems Publications, 1980).
5. See Fritjof Capra, *The Tao of Physics* (New York: Bantam Books, 1984), 43–45.

6. Frederick Reichheld and W. Earl Sasser, Jr., argue convincingly for a second order of zero quality defects. The longer you have a customer, the more profitable the relationship: cost of sales of products and services is higher with new customers than with old. So the cost of losing a customer (a "defection") is significant. And current customers are the first to become aware of product and service quality issues; they know the history. Therefore, achieving zero quality defects not only leverages sales in general, but specifically the more profitable sales to existing customers. "Zero Defections: Quality Comes to Services," *Harvard Business Review* (September–October 1990):107.

7. In recent years the Motorola Corporation has championed a concept known as "Six Sigma," an approach to achieving product quality through statistical measurement of all stages in the design and manufacturing process. The goal is to achieve an operating state in which the allowable variation in outputs is six times the variation (standard deviation, or sigma) of the process itself: hence Six Sigma. This statistical constant will resolve to a product defect rate of about 3.4 defects per opportunity, although some organizations that use the method claim close to zero PPM.

8. Rohan, p. 46; and Scott, pp. 16–21.

9. Bruce Nussbaum, John Templeman; "Built to Last—Until It's Time to Take Apart," *Business Week* (September 17, 1990):102–106; and Gary McWilliams, "The Big Brouhaha on the Little Juice Box," op. cit., 36.

Chapter 13 | Simultaneous Distributed Work in Action

Some organizations, particularly in the high-technology sectors, have already taken initiatives to bring products to market using simultaneous distributed work processes—with impressive results. The case discussed in this chapter has been documented in sufficient detail to enable us to "reverse engineer" the project, illustrating the essentials of SDW. (1)

Background

A leading developer, manufacturer, and supplier of information systems—computer hardware, software, and information services—with facilities distributed worldwide has initiated a project to design, manufacture, and deliver a state-of-the-art computer disk drive.

Company Profile

Enjoying industry leadership in several areas, the company consistently invests to maintain its position as a supplier of integrated networked information systems. Its employees pride themselves on the company's engineering excellence, and this pride provides the foundation of a very strong organizational culture. This culture is reinforced by the successful development and broad market acceptance of several product families and systems upon which the company has built its reputation and current organization.

This company is committed to providing electronic information access to all its people: it operates a true information utility.

The entire organization is electronically linked, and each worker who processes information (just about the entire employee population, to be precise) has access to a network that can provide connectivity to the entire organization worldwide. If one were to rate the company on a percentage scale in terms of network implementation and network use, it would be close to 100 percent in both areas. Data, voice, and image information formats are available to most workers. Connectivity also extends to outside suppliers and customers. The case will illustrate the benefits of this extended network.

The senior managers are organizational innovators. The culture encourages a form of entrepreneurship in which individuals and groups can follow independent directions as long as they observe some basic rules and can make persuasive arguments that show how their efforts will benefit the organization. Frequently, the organization will support several initiatives simultaneously that focus on the same objective with the belief that the best will survive: the "Darwinist School of Management."

Managers place great value on information exchange among the work mechanics, distributed groups that design, contribute to, and participate in work processes. However, the company's large size, its widespread geographical distribution, its focus on leading-edge technologies, and, to some extent, its zeal in preserving the ambience of its organizational culture have all created a stovepipe environment where the open flow of information often hits cultural barriers such as those discussed earlier. Frequently, the company is described as a "nation of tribes." These tribes have every means to communicate with each other, but often do not.

The senior managers are also very aware of the reality of doing business in their highly competitive international market. They must deal with escalating customer expectations and the rapidly changing and increasing complex technologies upon which their products depend. It is becoming increasingly evident to them that the company's work must be accomplished more quickly to meet market demand, protect investments, and maintain leadership.

The managers of one business segment of this complex organization made a deliberate decision to alter their traditional serial development processes and bring a new product to market using concurrent or simultaneous engineering techniques. Their cooperation in reaching—and acting upon—this decision demonstrates how innovative managers can overcome functional boundaries to consider a situation, evaluate assets and alternatives based on mutual goals, arrive at a consensus on their objectives, plan a simultaneous distributed work process, and work together to make it all happen.

Vision and Business Goals

Management in the Disk Drive Business Unit felt the group had an opportunity to attain global leadership by introducing a new generation of products. These products would set price, performance, and reliability standards that competitors would find difficult to exceed or even match in the near future. The new disk drives would not evolve from existing products: they would be innovative, unique, and built from the ground up.

The key to creating this market lead was to get the first product to market within two years, while conventional wisdom and expectations called for a five-year schedule.

In essence, the management vision had placed extraordinary expectations on the traditional business goals: quality, cost, and time-to-market. There was much risk, but success promised the great reward of market leadership if the goals were met.

The Challenge

This company's expertise involved knowing about emerging new technologies and dependent products. The talent was available, but the individuals were not all in the same place, not part of the same group, and not under the control of the same manager.

Basically, the challenge faced by the project leaders was not so much knowing how to start designing and manufacturing the product as designing and implementing the work process. They knew where to go but not how to get there.

The new disk drive required breakthroughs in three areas:

○ The electromechanical configuration and mechanics of the heads that read and write the data to the recording surface.
○ The physical properties of the storage media.
○ The mechanics of the drive system that spins the disk.

These elements required delicate balance and had to be made to critical tolerances. Because the scope of the project and its cost were too great for any single group to handle, a distributed development team was formed, and a simultaneous engineering project was initiated. This "virtual" development team set up networking procedures to bring the required expertise to bear on each segment of the problem in a coordinated and simultaneous effort.

Management was keenly aware of two key project constraints:

○ Time—reducing the project cycle by more than half the traditional time. All aspects of the project—design, development, manufacturing, and support—would have to proceed simultaneously. Only then could worldwide delivery and product support goals be met.

○ Space—resources were distributed worldwide. Collocation of resources was not an option; the company did not have the luxury of moving people around. Key resources were situated in several widely dispersed locations. Forty-two major component suppliers—both internal and external—were scattered, some as far as Europe.

All the players were connected through the corporate network, facilitating the exchange of information and data over the distances and time zones involved. Available to them were several networking applications, such as electronic mail, computer conferencing, electronic note files, and a variety of business analysis and graphics tools.

In addition, the network provided the flexibility to experiment with different organizational models and work processes as the project got under way. The network also provided a medium robust enough to ensure that managers and workers could share knowledge and profit from a common experience base. They could communicate because the network was in place and they had the networking tools.

In short, the solution was simultaneous distributed work; but since no model existed, the project set out to do the work and define the new model in the process.

The Process

Because of the technical innovations in the product, the project required continuous participation from scientific, engineering, manufacturing, logistics, and support disciplines. The success of the undertaking also required the implementation of several new components with minute tolerance specifications, and the integration of computer-directed product support specifications into the design process.

The company has always used the team concept for product development and engineering, and its employees are quite familiar with parallel work processes. They are, after all, engineers. But this project involved taking the concept of parallel work one step further. From the beginning it was understood that to be successful, groups had to break the business-as-usual mold. Parallel work processes had to become simultaneous. The distinction is critical. It was not enough for different groups to be working at the same time, in parallel; the groups had to integrate themselves into one entity at the outset of the project and work in total unison toward the common goal. The basic resource in this activity would be product information in electronic form. Designs, memos, deliberations, and decisions would be developed and shared by all constituencies instantaneously, no matter where they were located.

Resources

Engineering and manufacturing resources located in Europe also became major players in the development process. In the past, these groups were simply builders and distributors of products designed in the United States. Their task with previous products was to adapt the U.S.-designed products for the European market. Their role in this project was to be very different.

Since one of the key objectives for the new product was simultaneous distribution, it was essential that the European groups be part of the joint development team from the beginning. The Europeans adopted team models that fit their particular roles, but were congruent with the U.S. management structures. As in the United States, European engineers were connected to functional specialists and remote coworkers through the worldwide network. Their reliance on electronic communications, in particular electronic mail, grew as the project matured because it allowed people to form and maintain interactive, real-time links with their peers at other facilities. Networking applications also provided a convenient way to overcome the time differences between Europe and the United States, and to cross organizational reporting boundaries to expedite problem solving.

Design Issues

Innumerable questions had to be answered and a common denominator of knowledge agreed upon before the distributed groups could even begin to function as one virtual team. For example, in determining how to measure the fly height (the minute distance between the head and the moving disk), a common standard of measurement had to be defined before the distributed groups could be sure that they were talking about the same thing. Developing the measurement standard meant developing new test equipment. Because the processes and materials were new to the industry, there was no off-the-shelf equipment available. To reach a consensus, it was essential for the distributed groups to be able to share and compare parametric or "raw" data from their independent research to understand the context of each set of design considerations.

The mechanical designers focused on more rapid but stable movement of the head; the disk designers needed more bits-per-inch around a track of information; and the head designers would rather have more tracks-per-inch along the radius. Each team had to understand the interaction of all these factors even as the specialists were breaking new ground in these complex technologies. With a common focus on the end product, engineers constantly negotiated compromises over their competing objectives.

Customer support and service providers participated fully in the design process, and customers benefited in several ways. Customer services and design for serviceability were an integral part of the plan from the beginning. This meant modular design for easy field service: the five basic modules of the product can be removed from units at the customer's location and replaced without tools. This feature exemplifies the principle of design for manufacture.

Another feature facilitating easy support is that the unit can be remotely accessed and diagnosed for preventive maintenance from the company's central service organization. In addition, the team's service engineers designed a small cartridge, which can be plugged into any unit by a field technician. The cartridge automatically makes changes in the unit's microcode. This provides an effective interface to the unit and allows enhancements or upgrades to be made with little impact on the unit's productivity.

A second electronic link to the customer's unit provides access to the company's service organization expert system. This link allows the customer to connect into a service data base, which interprets data in the customer's system error logs. The expert system also polls several monitoring points, processes the readings, and makes recommendations for preventive maintenance if necessary.

All of these features were designed in because of the participation of customers and service groups from the very beginning of the development process. There would simply not have been time enough to build this level of serviceability any other way. The measurable benefits are that the customer's systems' security and reliability are dramatically improved, and there has been a 75 percent reduction in installation problems at customer sites compared to earlier products.

⌐ Communication and Information Sharing

The network provided the means for this continuous exchange of information. The constant interaction built bonds of trust and professional respect among members of these dispersed groups as they became integral members of the same project team. Everyone had to share a common understanding of the objectives, the current status, and the problems, and they had to learn how to work concurrently as cohesive distributed teams.

In the new work model, professionals had to share data even if they were incomplete and not as good as they would be if "we only had a few more days (weeks, months) to work on it." People had to remain convinced that their reputations and credibility would not suffer because, in the interest of sharing early, they released incomplete or erroneous data.

This kind of cooperation was evident when the manufacturing team pointed out that one of the critical components of the product had to be assembled in an automated "clean room" environment to reduce damage from manual assembly and to enhance manufacturing yields by avoiding human contamination during assembly. Directing robots to assemble a complex and delicate component is not an easy task. The manufacturing program manager described the challenge to the product designer thus: "You want the product to be designed is such a way that all the parts can be assembled with one hand in one direction—from the top down. Humans work with two hands at once, and replicating this dexterity in robots generates more than an order of magnitude of difficulty." With all stakeholders simultaneously aware of manufacturing requirements, initial designs accommodated the realities of automated production.

Two of the most important distributed stakeholders that influenced the ultimate success of this product were the outside suppliers and the customers. Interaction with both of these groups was an early consideration of the management team. Traditional arm's-length relationships with these important stakeholders would not be conducive to the design goal of the best possible product or the best support and service.

External suppliers were brought into the development process early on. Electronic gateways with appropriate security extended network connectivity to vendor facilities. This enabled communication between suppliers and the company's development groups for the exchange of data and technical correspondence, graphics, and test simulations.

In this way suppliers could keep pace with the development process and the performance of their parts as the final product evolved. Suppliers were able to synchronize their activities with the distributed teams, make timely changes and adjustments in their own processes, and contribute their expertise as and when required; in other words, they became active extensions of the company's product development community.

This interaction continued into the manufacturing phase as these suppliers became part of the just-in-time and total-quality-control elements of the process. Interactions with suppliers even moved to the shop floor in some cases as electronic communication provided real-time access. Surprises and misunderstandings were reduced as a consequence of having developed mutual respect and good faith among the team players.

The management selected representative customers, who provided direct input into the development of design specifications. Frequently during the program, customers received work and later provided test environments for the product and support systems.

In this complex environment, the virtual teams used all available networking applications at various times. But electronic conferencing was particularly well suited to the complex fabric of interactions, providing participants with a form of electronic bulletin board. In electronic conferencing, participants who may be distributed worldwide belong to one or more discussion groups, each with a different topic. All topic-related documents, queries, answers, and comments are stored in a conference file that is accessible to all participants from their networked terminals and workstations. The conference file provides a continuing record of the discussion on the given subject, and it is accessible to help new members as they "get up to speed" when they join an ongoing work group.

Access to the conference is open, and membership can include individuals from all work groups. The benefit of such an open conference is that individuals belonging to different work groups may recognize potential conflicts of ideas and expectations at the earliest stages of discussion, when compromise is easiest.

Here's how it worked in this company. An engineer would enter the conference and "post" a question for comment. Participants responded, and the responses became a part of the record. Each response prompted new comments or questions as the issue percolated. At some point, consensus was reached and the originator attained the desired solution.

Monitoring the conference files also provides management with real-time indicators of the viability and attitude of the virtual teams. Silence on the conference network is a very loud indicator that something is amiss, that the distributed individuals do not view themselves as part of the team.

Simulation

The interactions of the design and manufacturing teams made it possible for the product to be designed with manufacturing input from the very beginning. Using shared CAD systems to negotiate manufacturing criteria early in the design process, the design team was able to minimize complexity, reduce the number of parts, standardize and simplify fasteners, and design self-fixing parts.

Repeated designing and fine tuning was done without having to build multiple physical prototypes. This process of "virtual prototyping"—electronic simulation of components and their behavior as a system—saved the cost and time of building and testing expensive electromechanical devices. In addition, the electronic prototypes were available to the distributed teams and could be examined, altered, stressed, and otherwise "simulated" using the network and the networking communication tools.

Management

The initiators of this program started by forming a committee of four, representing the four major functional groups that would take joint responsibility for directing the program. This management structure was known internally as the "4 × 4 team." Members were drawn from product engineering, manufacturing, customer service/support, and product management/marketing. The team worked together from the inception through market introduction, and continued their alliance throughout the entire lifecycle of the product. The members shared the responsibility and ownership of the business success of the product.

A decision was made to locate the 4 × 4 team at a single site, to give a jump start, as it were, to the concept of simultaneous development. Each member came to the team as a peer of every other member. Hierarchy and status were deemphasized within the team; the four members were equal partners in managing the project. This team became designated as the "project manager," with responsibility spread over all members. Together, they ensured that all appropriate resources and expertise were brought to bear simultaneously, creating a pool of leadership rather than vesting all responsibility in a single person.

The 4 × 4 team provided a model that facilitated and encouraged cooperation and interaction among the four normally independent groups. The relationships within the project management team were replicated by cloning the 4 × 4 team in the geographically distributed subgroups as the program matured.

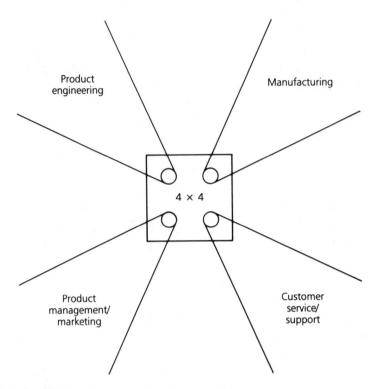

Figure 13-1 The Management Team

The individuals on the project team found that they worked faster, more smoothly, and had fewer unexpected problems. They reported 50 percent lower costs-per-unit of performance (an internal metric that provided a common datum throughout the project), a 50 percent improvement in product reliability, and a 50 percent reduction in time-to-volume-production over previous products at the same project stage.

The creative use of information that expedited the technical process also resulted in benefits to administrative and managerial functions. The 4 × 4 project team used available network applications to keep track of schedules and milestones, and to monitor the project's progress. The subgroups used the network to monitor their individual process and to share information. Managers and engineers, looking at the same data, were able to anticipate and solve problems sooner and so forestall the development of crises.

In addition to schedule information, production metrics such as yields, cycle times, scrap, and rework statistics were compiled from distributed locations. The team had access to market studies and financial analyses prepared by corporate staff groups. The free flow of information helped the collective leadership reduce conflicts, promote more informed decision making, and create a relationship based on trust between the technical and business members of the team. The notion of team ownership was at work.

Results

This was a large and ambitious project. It involved hundreds of people from groups located around the world. Its objective was to probe ahead of existing technology and processes and deliver value to the company. The success of this SDW initiative is evident in these results:

○ 50% improvement in product reliability over previous product.
○ 50% lower cost per megabyte of storage capacity.
○ 45% lower overall project staff requirements.
○ 75% fewer installation problems at customer sites.
○ 50% reduction in manufacturing space.
○ 50% reduction in time-to-volume production.
○ 50% reduction in six-year development cycle.
○ Simultaneous worldwide product availability.

These results validated the risks the company took to gain the advantages it felt were strategic to its business. The company not only developed a world-class product, but simultaneously developed support procedures and work processes that will continue to return value as teams move to the next challenge. The individuals who participated in this project learned to recognize the real value of networks—in teaming with their colleagues to solve problems. Extracting value from the network investment has become a key goal for the company, rather than being concerned only with the network's cost.

SUMMARY

The organization we have just examined built on its base of knowledge and technology to sustain worldwide simultaneous distributed work processes.

The simultaneous distributed work characteristics and goals demonstrated here included:

○ Agreement at all levels on the primary business goals of quality, cost, and time-to-market.

○ Processes that would reduce project cycle time dramatically.

○ Processes for all stakeholder functions—marketing, sales, research, administration, engineering, and manufacturing—to simultaneously contribute design decisions to the developing product. This included dependent as well as independent tasks within the same function, proceeding independently of geographical or organizational boundaries.

Parallel evolution ensured that the resulting product met all stakeholder expectations.

In addition, finance and project management had access to all project data as it developed; with this real-time window into the project they could spot trends, slippages, and patterns that could be managed with redeployment of resources, additional dollars, or whatever it took to keep the project on track.

○ Emphasis on development through electronic design, based on networked stakeholder information sharing.

○ Innovative management to support the project in an environment where people are strained by time compression and by physical, functional, and cultural separation from their coworkers.

NOTES

1. Frank Dubinskas, *Managing Complexity* (Maynard, MA: Digital Equipment Corporation, 1989). The information in this chapter is based on Professor Dubinskas' excellent case study. Copies of the unpublished report are available from Digital Equipment Corporation.

Part IV | Getting Started

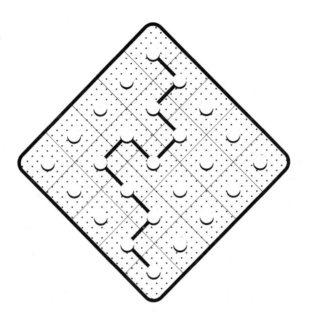

Chapter 14 | Benchmarking the Organization

This final part is addressed to the work mechanics who are ready to respond to the organizational capability and simultaneous distributed work messages. Since each organization is unique, we cannot offer a single handbook or roadmap through the entire process of building the new capabilities. But we can help kick-start efforts by providing guidelines to bring your organization face to face (or node to node) with the opportunities of the simultaneous distributed work environment.

In this chapter we will discuss benchmarking and present a series of questions and comments to help quantify benchmarking in the critical areas of networks and networking. Our goal is to help you develop a perspective on where your organization is in terms of its commitment to, and implementation of, this infrastructure for simultaneous distributed work. Chapter 15 presents a final prelaunch checklist, a set of considerations and questions that need to be addressed to manage the risk prior to launching simultaneous distributed work pilot programs.

The suggestions we offer are intended to stimulate thinking, and can be easily modified to fit the unique status and needs of your organization. Keep in mind that after all the analysis and modeling; after consensus is reached on the status, objectives, and expectations for the capability-based environment; after the design and planning; after the mobilization of leaders and teams; after the assignment of technology resources, what is needed most is continuous commitment by the organization, and more important, by individuals.

Only individuals can decide on form and substance, participate in electronic meetings, know and change the culture of the organization, and have the trust of other individuals needed to try out new methods and technologies that can better serve the needs of the enterprise. Individuals can be trained to be comfortable with the technologies and techniques needed to make simultaneous distributed work a reality. These trained individuals become a cadre who use technology, information, and outside expertise to generate the impetus for continuous evolution of the organization's communication capabilities as the work requirements change. They become the leaders needed to initiate pilot projects that test and refine networking techniques. The success of pilot projects communicates in graphic terms the commitment of the organization. And successful projects provide the most persuasive arguments for continuing the process.

Finally, capability-based environments do not spring from one-shot interventions, regardless of the source of inspiration. Only the ongoing participation of individuals, teams, and groups can provide the energy and innovation to make the successful transition to the new work paradigm.

Benchmarking

The first step requires that the work mechanic engage in major introspection and in gross evaluation of the state of the organization to:

○ Assess the external and internal factors that relate to the work environment and to the capability model.
○ Determine where specific value will accrue from capability processes.
○ Establish whether top management is ready and able to sustain the technology infrastructure and to provide tools, training, and rewards to build the confidence and trust required for the transition to the capability-based environment.

If the payback seems to be there, the work mechanic must decide to take the risk of championing change.

Begin with cataloging what you have to work with: what tools are available, where they are located, and how they are currently being used by workers. In general, extract data points that mark the current ability of the organization's technical and social resources to support capability-based work. Specifically, set the network and networking benchmarks. Identify what is in place that can be used as part of the capability-based environment. Determine what is not yet available, but will be required to begin. For most organizations, establishing a capability base means using, reconfiguring, or adapting what is already there. The option of pushing all the old stuff out the back door to make room for the new is not realistic and probably unnecessary. What is needed is a catalogue of assets and a method to establish the value of these assets to support a capability-based environment. Ultimately, the catalogue will become a foundation for an architecture and will provide design specifications for the capability-based environment.

Key Players

We have used the term *key players* to isolate those individuals who, because of their relationship to the processing, distribution, and direct use of information, share a common interest in the systems and processes that provide the capability base. Benchmarking should be based on information gathered from significant numbers of these stakeholders. This is not a statistical sample; it is a sample of the individuals who are in key areas and whose participation is necessary for success. To some degree, this is also a learning exercise that can begin to elevate awareness as part of the transition process.

There are four distinct groups that must be involved:

○ Information systems and network personnel.
○ Line and staff managers.
○ Knowledge workers on teams.
○ Top managers.

Information Systems and Network Personnel

This group comprises the workers and technicians who labor daily to support the information infrastructure. They process the data, ensure that the network is working, and deal with the adds, moves, and changes that constantly alter the information infrastructure of the organization. They need to understand what is required of their systems and to prepare for the new roles they will play as the services they provide become increasingly the center of the organization's activities and work processes. They are also the group most sensitive to what the installed technical resources really can do. Their pragmatic knowledge will balance the expectations of those whose perspectives are more strategic.

Line and Staff Managers

This group includes the line and staff managers concerned about improving the performance of work groups. These people understand the business goals and the real ability of the organization to deliver. They are also sensitive to compressing time and managing change, information, access and distributed resources. They also understand the risk and pain associated with the adjustments they find themselves making. These are the individuals who most need clear visions and organizing perspectives to help them plan and deliver value.

Knowledge Workers on Teams

Individuals who already understand these concepts and perhaps have had some experience as managers or members of successful teams form this group. Their views will have a system perspective that can reflect the mission of the entire enterprise. This is also the group that will provide the champions needed to take the risk and provide the energy for new pilot programs, and will have the interest to document results and spread the word.

Top Management

Finally, the groups being consulted must include top management, the level responsible for providing vision and resources. These are the individuals who must be ready to make the necessary commitments and ensure that a reward and recognition policy will reinforce the efforts of the champions and team workers. In large organizations, it will be necessary to target management representatives from within the boundaries of a specific work process to avoid modulating data with the political baggage that is always a part of "life at the top." One way is to define the value chain in very specific terms: as a product, a process, a service, a division or group, or any other segmentation where the input, value-adding process, and output can be bounded. This will identify the management segment that has vested interest in what capability-based operations can deliver.

The Benchmarking Process

The benchmarking process we will offer focuses on the sum of investments, policies, experiences, and commitments as regards technical resources (networks), human resources (networking), and management resources (commitment).

The format will be to pose questions, the answers to which will help you evaluate the organization's network and networking position and commitment in respect to the key network/networking attributes we cited in earlier chapters:

- ○ Connectivity/interoperability.
- ○ Manageability.
- ○ Performance.

These attributes, which can be shared across technological and cultural spaces, allow network managers, human resources personnel, and process designers—all work mechanics—to communicate about capability-based work using common references. For this reason we treat network and networking serially in the following model. It helps to keep these relationships linked in our minds. At the end of the exercise, when we combine the relative scores, the juxtaposition will add insight to the analysis.

The process is simple. Identify the individuals for the survey from the four groups listed earlier. Make sure that they will represent the entire enterprise, or at least the subset of the organization expected to play an active role in the transition to capability-based activities. Decide if the surveys are to be made using direct interviews or printed forms. (Interviews will provide the best results, but additional care must be taken to ensure that the interviewers are fully briefed on the process. The best number of interviewers is one.)

We suggest a very subjective data-organizing format: a continuum scaled for 0% to 100%. The interviewer estimates the proper position of scores based on the respondent's replies and his or her own estimate of intangibles such as the interviewee's confidence, personal experience, commitment, and perhaps even passion. Convert these results into a plot on the continuum.

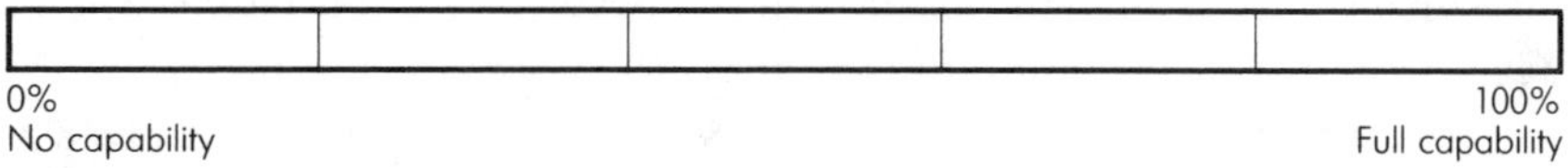

0%
No capability

100%
Full capability

Figure 14-1   Capability Scale

When the entire series is completed for each respondent, average the plots and generate an integrated scale that will represent the organization's relative position vis-à-vis networks, networking, and commitment. Cumulatively, these scales will present a comprehensive picture of where the organization is on the spectrum of capability, and where investments are needed to achieve higher levels of organizational capability. We have included commentary with the questions on pages 215–231 to stimulate your thinking and help the process of building a customized guide for your organization and situation. There are no right answers, but the process will produce a fairly clear snapshot of present position, capability, and attitude in critical dimensions.

It is highly unlikely that you will find your organizational network at either end of the scale. Most organizations are already in the capability stream. The goal isn't to have "some" capability, but to have capability requisite to support new work challenges. Only work mechanics know what that level is, and what rate of growth it must sustain. The downside to being out on the track instead of at the starting gate is that the existing network and networking inventory will probably need to be changed to meet the criteria of enterprise-wide connectivity, interoperability, manageability, and performance. This is not the best of all possible worlds, where the telecommunications manager would have the time to carefully design and install the proper network topology and transmission media, and identify preferred routing paths for wires and cables.

Networking, too, is a preexisting state. And, being socially and culturally based, local networking practices often are difficult to adapt to enterprise needs. People gravitate to the most comfortable methods for communicating; with whom, by what methods, and under what circumstances. A small group that likes to "go to the mat" in face-to-face confrontations to hash out decisions may find it stultifying, at first, to be just another set of stakeholders in a relatively formal electronic deliberation. Just as existing technology can become a barrier to interoperability, so can existing networking commitments hinder the development of networking at the level of the capability-based environment.

Here, too, effort must be extended to fix current position, decide where investment in the "human system" would have the highest payback, and begin to design an evolution to the capability-based organization.

Measuring commitment is an intuitive process, but a fair measure can be extrapolated for the data compiled on networks and networking. We suggest that a third continuum be developed after the network and networking analyses are completed. There is a direct correlation between what is physically in place and practiced and the organization's response to the capability concept. For example, an organization that is heavily invested in network technology clearly has set a high value on electronic information. But if the same organization is not as progressive in supporting networking-based work processes, one can assume that management has not yet focused on using its technology investment as a direct tool in its value-generating activities.

Commitment necessary for an effective capability-based environment is often driven by much larger issues. For example, today globalization is a high-visibility organizational goal. But to effectively operate in the global marketplace, management must put in place several practices and policies that provide excellent indications of the commitments we are interested in. The following questions, designed to measure risk associated with global enterprise operations, demonstrate this synergy.

○ How well has the organization measured market and competitive requirements relevant to its products and competition? How are these data compiled? How are real-time changes and developments received, processed, and distributed to stakeholders throughout the organization?

○ Does the organization have the flexibility to accommodate the rapid pace of change in the world market? Are the information systems that support manufacturing, distribution, customer support, and other critical activities responsive enough not to cause barriers to these activities?

○ Are essential human, physical, technological, and market support assets accessible throughout the extended enterprise—including suppliers, trading partners, dealers, and local support specialists? How are these distributed resources connected to the organization and to each other? Have they been trained to function as virtual teams and still ensure product and customer support quality? Have global, regional, and local management options been determined for all important functions?

○ Have all nonvalue-adding activities, functions, and resources that represent added cost to the customer been cut? Does information flow effectively after streamlining?

○ Has the organization created a culture equal to the demands of the global market? Does this new culture ensure constant improvements, proactive responses to constant change, and performance and quality gains reflected by increased value to the customer? Can the information system ensure that all members of the extended enterprise are aware of the visions and goals that the culture needs to support, and can the system provide metrics that managers can use? Will the culture support distributed decision making, risk management, and resource development?

Globalization is a useful example because it clearly defines what may be an obvious business strategy for growing organizations. But a clear view of high-level business objectives may mask the capability condition needed to be successful.

Enterprise Globalization Strategy Commitment

0%   100%
No capability   Full capability

Enterprise Commitment to Global Integrated Information Network

0%   100%
No capability   Full capability

For this environment both position markers had best be high on the scales.

In plotting the organization's position relative to commitment, the real value will come from the discussion and thought processes that will determine where the position mark should be placed. Keep track of the issues and how they were resolved. What issues generated the most heated discussions? What groups took which positions? What were the persuasive arguments that resulted in compromise? Although this is hardly a scientific process, when the mark is placed on the continuum, it won't be far off target.

Benchmarking Networks, Networking, and Commitment

Now we begin the process of benchmarking the actual capability of the organization's information infrastructure. The process is the same, but be diligent in ensuring that the sample draws from each of the key player groups. The size of the sample is less important than that it fully reflects these constituencies.

Connectivity/Interoperability in the Network Context

0%   100%
No capability   Full capability

1. What percentage of the workers in your enterprise have a direct connection to information support systems? To the telephone system? To the data system?

(*Direct* means from the person's workplace, whether this is a desktop, a position on the assembly line, home, or any other location from which the person contributes directly to the work processes of your organization. Whether workers make use of their access is not relevant here; we are establishing capabilities at this point. In large organizations it may be useful to organize this data by groups, locations, or functions to make additional judgments about capability. For now, we are interested in the general condition of the enterprise and its potential for information exchange among workers.)

0%   100%
No capability   Full capability

2. To what extent is access to information flexible?

(Do adds, moves, and changes cause operational difficulties, excessive costs, or service compromises? Is there expansion capacity in the information distribution plant? Are interconnections among various systems possible and practical, or is network flexibility constrained by proprietary protocols? Do records clearly indicate what's out there? Has management approved plans that exceed or put a strain on current network capabilities?)

0%   100%
No capability   Full capability

3. To what extent is the network architecture flexible?

(Look at the integration of network subsystems: LANs interconnecting to a backbone WAN, networks from different vendors, voice integration into digital backbones. Look at the ratio of leased and private network systems and resources, and determine what outside services are in use to support the network.)

0%   100%
No capability   Full capability

4. Does the network management system provide the data and information needed to maintain the level of service the users need?

(Network management information should include performance data for all network segments; fault and trouble alarms and alerts; fault isolation and identification; notification tables that include names, addresses, physical and logical locations, software versions and patches, vendor contacts, and any other information that will expedite service restoration. Operating procedures, network operations training programs, automated diagnostic and support tools, and centralized and distributed management options are also good indicators of a company's network management capability.)

0%   100%
No capability   Full capability

5. How automated are the network operating systems?

(Features such as automatic rerouting are available, and can ensure critical connectivity even during periods of unusual activity or trouble. Networks that automate the process of building and maintaining address tables cope more efficiently with growth and change than networks that have to be manually reconfigured every time a new node is added.)

0%   100%
No capability   Full capability

6. What is the integration status of voice and data?

(Many of today's work processes interface simultaneously with these information media, and the trend will continue. Has the organization taken a position on the Integrated Services Digital Network as an integration strategy? Are there computer-integrated telephony applications in use or in development?)

0%   100%
No capability   Full capability

7. Does the network conform to standards?

(Determine if network segments can interoperate using accepted standards. If work processes are distributed globally, check that internationally approved standards are in place. Is conformance to standards directed in procurement policies? Where there are nonstandard compliant network segments, determine what the ratio is for interoperability.)

0%   100%
No capability   Full capability

8. Is there a program to integrate all network resources?

(Is there an approved architecture for an enterprise network? Is such an architecture in the process of being developed? Look into the status of voice/data integration. Is the backbone, wide area segment being used to integrate various telecommunications media?)

0%   100%
No capability   Full capability

9. Are there any unnecessary state changes in the current communication flow?

(Look for instances of information being reentered into different network segments, and ask why. See if there is duplication of effort or if paper copies are in general use. Do many tasks end with a physical prototype, a printed document, or a final report? How much of any given work process stays electronic?)

0%   100%
No capability   Full capability

10. Is the flow of information through various network segments automated, or does it require human intervention?

(In automated environments, check to see what level of effort is required to maintain address algorithms. How are users involved in routing traffic? Is there a security problem? If so, what is being done to resolve it? What monitoring is available to check traffic flow and identify potential problems?)

0%   100%
No capability   Full capability

11. Can temporary leased, dial-up, or microwave be used for urgent, temporary, or experimental requirements?

(Many options for using low-cost, high-bandwidth systems are ideal for short-term requirements. These options are also useful as a strategy to bypass more expensive options, or to avoid excessive cost such as construction in urban areas. Look into portable microwave systems to back up or restore critical WAN links.)

0%   100%
No capability   Full capability

12. Can requirements be more cost-effectively supported by a public network, a value-added carrier, or a public packet network? Is flexibility the dominant requirement? Is a private packet network providing virtual rather than physical connections a more practical solution?

(The packet-switched data network (PSDN) principle is simple: unless a network resource is in use at a specific time, it should be available for use. With packet switching, user data and the accompanying control information needed to ensure delivery to the correct destination node are formed into discrete entities or packets. The nodes of the PSDN dynamically interleave the packets of many users and route the packets to their destinations, ensuring that messages arrive at their proper destinations in the proper sequences. Once data are received at a destination node of the network, the software on that node must interpret the data and reassemble the packets into a comprehensible message. Public PSDNs compute charges based on volume of data transferred rather than on distance or connect time. This creates an economical option for WAN applications with medium traffic volumes between widely dispersed locations. Private PSDNs can be used effectively to support large numbers of dispersed users who use the network randomly, such as in an electronic mail application.)

0%
No capability

100%
Full capability

Overall Network Connectivity/Interoperability

(Remember, this is a synthesis of all the individual scores from all respondents in the survey. It represents the organization's position in support of the connectivity/interoperability network attribute required for capability-based work. Later, this and the other summarizing continuums for the other network and networking attributes will be blended into an overall network/network presentation.)

0%
No capability

100%
Full capability

Connectivity/Interoperability in the Networking Context

1. How do major work processes flow through the organization?

(Look at the distribution of work and how it is passed from group to group. In a simultaneous distributed work environment, these interface points should not require state changes; data and information should remain digital as long as they will be communicated or distributed.)

0%
No capability

100%
Full capability

2. How does the organization communicate between locations?

(Look at where the work is done—locally, in different buildings, or in different countries. Then see how individuals communicate between these locations. Are there recognized problems—language or cultural barriers—with communications between locations? What media do workers use: face-to-face meetings, telephone, data, fax, or electronic memos, for example? Have any communication gaps been identified?)

0%
No capability

100%
Full capability

3. Are there any enterprise information distribution and sharing applications in use or in development?

(Look for applications and services such as shared compound document editing, hypertext, electronic mail, computer conferencing, corporate videotex, or other applications that support the simultaneous distribution of information. Is audio-, computer-, or video-teleconferencing used in support of work processes such as training programs, customer services, and engineering development?)

0%
No capability

100%
Full capability

4. What are considered to be the most important communication assets?

(Segment these observations by interest groups. What does senior management believe are the most important, and why? The technical staff, the workers, and the suppliers may have different views.)

0%
No capability

100%
Full capability

5. Are there plans that describe goals and objectives that are dependent on networking?

(Look for clearly stated and approved programs and the degree to which their success is dependent on simultaneous distributed work processes and electronic information exchange. Determine if these plans are widely distributed and clearly understood throughout the organization. Check to see if these plans include rewards and incentives that will encourage their acceptance.)

0%
No capability

100%
Full capability

6. Do all members of simultaneous distributed work teams have access to compatible communication systems?

(Check if compatibility and interoperability of communication systems is a prerequisite for forming teams. Check with working teams to ensure that their devices can communicate with one another. Do workers know what is available? Are they trained?)

0%   100%
No capability   Full capability

7. Has management established and supported a recognition and reward program to encourage innovation and creativity in network-supported teamwork?

(If a program exists, is it well publicized? Are there success stories?)

0%   100%
No capability   Full capability

8. Are there network systems in use to support work processes that extend beyond the boundaries of the organization?

(Look for work processes that involve customers, suppliers, collaborators, or government agencies. Are there any technical problems that constrain the organization from going beyond its boundaries? Has anyone identified possible benefits for expanded activities with customers and outside suppliers and vendors? If so, what are they doing about it?)

0%   100%
No capability   Full capability

9. Has management set networking performance goals for the enterprise?

(What is the general awareness of these goals? Are they coupled with incentives and/or penalties? Is there any activity in pursuit of these goals— pilot projects, sponsored research, or the use of consultants, for example?)

0%   100%
No capability   Full capability

10. Is there any new pressure for networking?

(Has the organization acquired new resources or formed new partnerships? Has there been a shift in market expectations and demands? Are customers demanding more attention? Are there new government directives? Has another sector of the industry made a breakthrough in products, processes, or position? Is there more aggressive management attention to cost control and productivity? Do workers have different expectations or require new tools? Is the organization feeling pressure to globalize operations?)

0%   100%
No capability   Full capability

11. What is the ratio of electronic to face-to-face meetings?

(See if there is any management policy on meeting format. Look into the use of electronic meeting facilities. Check if critique forms are used in electronic meeting facilities, check the distribution of these forms to see to what management level they reach and what action is taken on recommendations. Look at training for meeting facilitators. Check expenses for third-party teleconference productions. Check on the frequency with which pilot groups use electronic meeting facilities, who attends, who participates, and what issues are covered by the agenda.)

0%   100%
No capability   Full capability

Manageability in the Network Context

1. How large is the enterprise's investment in network management?

(Look at budgets, numbers of individuals on the technical staff and their training, and commitment to internal versus outside operations support. Look at the titles and positions of the senior network managers and the roles they play in the overall management of the enterprise. Is there any effort to convert network resources from cost to revenue by reselling excess capacity or offering technical services to customers? To what extent is the network budget under management pressure?)

0%   100%
No capability   Full capability

2. Is there top management involvement in network planning?

(Is there a strategic planning process that links the network into the goals and objectives of the enterprise? What is the review and approval process for these plans? Who approves the budget? Does the organization use outside consultants in developing its strategic plans? Who has the final word?)

0%
No capability

100%
Full capability

3. How is the network management group organized?

(Is the network managed by a well-organized team? Does this team use a formal operations facility that can access, monitor, and control all segments, or is network management a loose confederation of individuals performing extra duties?)

0%
No capability

100%
Full capability

4. Have formal support agreements been negotiated with outside service and facilities providers?

(Look for contracts and service-level agreements that are used by the operations staff to expedite service restoration activity. Is there a fault escalation and notification plan in place? Are there specialists on duty whenever and wherever the workers depend on network access?)

0%
No capability

100%
Full capability

5. Do the network managers have the tools for predicting potential trouble spots in the network?

(Look for monitoring tool such as LAN traffic monitors, graphic generators for producing electronic topology maps, voice traffic monitors, simulation tools to predict future trends, traffic logs, and wide area dynamic routing monitors. Check that the network operations staff knows how to use these devices and that records are being maintained.)

```
|        |        |        |        |        |
```
0%   100%
No capability   Full capability

6. How are network costs accounted for?

(Look for artificial segmentation between communications media, between groups who interact on a regular basis, and between locations. Check the basis used for recovering cost. Is it based on use, or simply apportioned over the entire organization? Is top management involved in the recovery of cost? Who is responsible for cost recovery?)

```
|        |        |        |        |        |
```
0%   100%
No capability   Full capability

7. Are there dedicated network resources that provide a platform for various distributed applications, such as an enterprise-wide electronic mail system, computer conferencing, and other network applications essential to the capability-based environment?

```
|        |        |        |        |        |
```
0%   100%
No capability   Full capability

8. What commitment is there to ensuring that the network resources are reliable?

(Check work processes designed around distributed teams, which might be located anywhere in the world; determine if there is a twenty-four-hour network management day. Determine if the network manager has efficient and effective control over the entire network, including the segments that are dedicated to special applications within the organization. Check if there are tools and staff necessary to rapidly isolate and diagnose faults and troubles in all the network segments, including those that use public telecommunications facilities.)

```
|        |        |        |        |        |
```
0%   100%
No capability   Full capability

9. Are all new requirements combined with other active or projected requirements that might justify a broad-band integrated link or an investment in a high-capacity fiber optic link?

(Growth happens, and it is always more cost effective to anticipate requirements than to pay for crash projects. In the capability-based environment, available bandwidth is like money in the bank.)

0%
No capability

100%
Full capability

10. Will new initiatives trigger the need for major reconfiguration analysis of the entire enterprise network?

(Because some network segments tends to be more stable, reconfiguration opportunities may be overlooked.)

0%
No capability

100%
Full capability

Overall Network Manageability

0%
No capability

100%
Full capability

Manageability in the Networking Context

1. Is someone clearly in charge?

(This applies to any identifiable segment of activity: the organization as a whole, a work group, or a team. See if there is someone who accepts the responsibility to ensure that everyone in the group understands the goals, processes, measurement metrics, and schedules.)

0%
No capability

100%
Full capability

2. Is there a formal chart or diagram that reflects direct and distributed reporting and communication structures?

(Even though a distributed simultaneous work organization is flexible and in a state of constant change and adjustment, the interaction among teams and groups must be deliberate. Look for indications of planning and processes to maintain the intergroup communications links.)

0%   100%
No capability   Full capability

3. Are there rewards given for group, team, and individual excellence?

(Look for a program designed to encourage individuals to perform as participants in distributed teaming. Is there training in place to help workers understand and become comfortable with this environment? Look at the kinds of activities that are rewarded. Do these activities support group and teamwork? Who makes the rewards, and do these individuals reinforce top-level management commitment?)

0%   100%
No capability   Full capability

4. Are responsibility and/or authority distributed?

(Check if the leaders of distributed teams share the same understanding of how the management of the work process operates. Is there a mechanism to ensure that changes in any part of the distributed work process are communicated and coordinated by all leaders? How are leaders held accountable for their team's deliverables and their performance within the extended group?)

0%   100%
No capability   Full capability

5. Is there a procedure allowing leaders to interact as peers?

(Look for regular teleconferences where the operation of the process is discussed. Is the "circuit rider" technique in operation, whereby an individual visits all distributed locations involved in a distributed project—or even a major teleconference—to make sure that all participants understand the objectives and are prepared to contribute? Look at reports and their distribution. Do meeting schedules correspond to the schedule and milestones of the work process?)

0%
No capability

100%
Full capability

6. Do the leaders feel that the group is effective in meeting group goals?

(Check if leaders of teams within distributed groups are more focused on team goals than the goals of the extended group. Do they recommend rewards for team efforts or individual excellence? Do they ensure that all workers are familiar with the group goals, problems, and status?)

0%
No capability

100%
Full capability

7. Are the leaders familiar and comfortable with the network as the tool that helps them manage the simultaneous distributed work processes?

(Determine how much of the work process is electronic and makes use of the network. How active are the leaders in providing the network managers with new requirements or comments on current network performance? Have they included network requirements in their initial process planning? Do they experiment with new ideas and techniques that use the network? Have the leaders considered which communications links and/or services are most critical to their success?)

0%
No capability

100%
Full capability

8. To what extent does the organization experiment with simultaneous distributed work?

(Look at internal programs to see how much they penetrate the organization and how many distinct work processes are linked together. Check on any extended experiments involving outside organizations such as competitors, collaborators, consulting groups, associations, or universities and government groups. Look into records of experiments to see how widely they are distributed. Check if senior management is involved in these experiments.)

0%   100%
No capability   Full capability

Overall Networking Manageability Position

0%   100%
No capability   Full capability

Performance in the Network Context

1. Have performance metrics for each network, network segment, and communication medium been established?

(Check if performance metrics are included in daily operations logs. Look for test equipment on hand and in use for measuring performance. Look for performance trend analysis over time and indications that these data are used in planning and budgeting. Review contingency plans for restoration and recovery. Check customer service records for performance-related comments.)

0%   100%
No capability   Full capability

2. Are user inputs used in network operations, design, and modification activities?

(Consider how user input is obtained, processed, and followed up. Look at training opportunities for users, and what the level of user participation is in the organization. Check for user-expectation setting activity.)

0%   100%
No capability   Full capability

3. Is performance a specific and detailed parameter in the network selection process?

(Look at past and current vendor requests and proposals for performance specifications.)

0%   100%
No capability   Full capability

4. Are selections for network resources made on the basis of approved industry standards?

0%   100%
No capability   Full capability

5. Is network integration planning focused on maintaining performance standards for the enterprise network?

(Look for compromises in planning strategies that will affect performance. Review planning designs to see if integration introduces performance bottlenecks or weak links into the network system.)

0%   100%
No capability   Full capability

6. Are performance metrics used to determine the most efficient use of telecommunication resources?

(Check for documented cost savings using broadband services to integrate voice, data, and image media. Look for bypass technologies, microwave radio links, fiber-optic distribution plants, "T" Carrier backbone segments, and the use of special tariffs from network suppliers that avoid high-cost leased services.)

0%   100%
No capability   Full capability

Overall Network Performance Position

0%   100%
No capability   Full capability

Performance in the Networking Context

1. Is the information exchange between workers and teams electronic?

(Select several distinct work processes or tasks and do a detailed analysis of the communication links required. Note how communications are effected, electronically or otherwise. One exciting innovation in this area is described by Charles Savage in *Fifth Generation Management*. (1) The concept is known as Netmapping and is an exercise in which the conventional pyramid-style organizational chart is replaced by a circular model. Peer-to-peer relationships that exist among groups are then drawn. Because of the geometry of the circular model, linking the relationships creates an interesting representation of the required network topology. As the number of links grow among various groups, the network manager can extrapolate bandwidth and connectivity requirements. Software will soon be available to automatically generate circular "maps" to identify relationships and communication requirements for distributed organizational planning.)

0%   100%
No capability   Full capability

2. Are workers aware of how the network impacts their work?

(Select a sample and have workers describe how they do their jobs. Note how often they make a direct reference to electronic communication.)

0%   100%
No capability   Full capability

3. Is electronic communication considered in the planning and design of new work processes?

(Look for formal references to task and processes dependent on the availability of the network. Look for references to distributed segments of the work processes and how communication will be conducted.)

0%   100%
No capability   Full capability

4. Are user expectations in line with network capabilities?

(Look for indications of missed opportunities, noncommunication, lack of awareness, or hostility in users' comments about the network and its effect on their work and their relationships.)

0%   100%
No capability   Full capability

5. Does management reward workers for their networking skills and innovations?

(Check project logs for reference to rewards based on networking. Look for recognition awards. Look for any formal criteria for promotion or incentive rewards based on networking activity.)

0%   100%
No capability   Full capability

Overall Networking Performance Position

0%   100%
No capability   Full capability

By now you have a portfolio of individual charts indicating relative scores for each of the network/networking attributes. You should try to normalize these "scores" using whatever benchmarks are appropriate. Often, it may be possible to use the results of an internal experiment or pilot project as a baseline. Instinct, intuition, or input from an outside consultant can be used. The idea is to establish a comfort level for whatever process is used, and to use consistent standards for evaluating your data.

To fix a relative position for your organization's network and networking position, simply combine the individual network and networking scores and fix these values on two new scales. An exact fix is not required; what's needed is a sense of the relationship between degrees of network and networking capabilities.

SUMMARY

Do not be surprised if there is a wide spread between the two positions—network and networking. Many organizations are completely wired, with each worker having access to information through multiple media.

Systems are compatible, and little or no conversion of information in digital form to other presentation media is required to allow work to flow electronically through the entire work process. The network continuum of such organizations would be close to—or at—100 percent.

But these same organizations may be composed of functional islands— "stovepiped"—so that there is little or no cross-functional or stakeholder networking. Tasks are completed in work groups that are essentially isolated from the other players in the process. Groups pass along blocks of completed work serially from one station to the next, where it is recast into the form preferred by that group; then work is further processed, completed, and passed along again. The networking quotient in this kind of environment is extremely low relative to the network capability.

The opposite is also possible. Some organizations have limited technological network resources but have reached a very sophisticated level of networking. Start-up companies, focused as they are on specific and well-defined objectives, often work as a highly integrated team, primarily face to face or with low-level technologies such as the telephone, fax, and LAN mail. But they rely heavily on networking techniques during their early stages. Most start-up entrepreneurs would contend that these networking times were their most productive periods, when everyone knew one another, knew the goal, and was committed to working with the team to achieve success.

Finally, there is an interesting relationship in the relative distance between the network and the networking lines. This distance is a reflection of the culture of the organization: how sensitive the organization is to technology, work processes, and the tools that enable simultaneous distributed work to exist and develop. Again, setting this distance parameter is also a subjective exercise, but the intuition will come more easily after the individual network and networking exercises are completed.

All these "fixes" must be dynamic. They are not permanent conditions, and the challenge is to move them into relative positions that are advantageous for the organization and the work processes upon which the value-added chain is dependent. These relative positions will be different for all organizations, and finding the right combination becomes the responsibility of top management. For effective simultaneous distributed work, however, the gap between the network and networking capabilities must be bridged.

NOTES

1. Charles M. Savage, *Fifth Generation Management* (Bedford, MA: Digital Press, 1990).

Chapter 15 | Managing Risk

This is where the rubber hits the road, and unless significant effort is committed to understanding and neutralizing risk, the probability of failure is too high. In Chapter 10 we discussed augmentation pilots as a way of reducing risk, guiding investment, ensuring that technology and human systems concerns would evolve in balance, and providing a built-in mechanism for spreading learning—capability—through the larger community. Such piloting certainly is an appropriate vehicle for this capability-building endeavor. The questions that follow will help identify high-risk areas. If the answers are not intuitively obvious, it may be useful to include these questions in the survey of key personnel. This is also a way of developing priorities for actions to manage unacceptable risks.

- Do the available network resources/proposed systems solutions conform to approved standards? Is there an acceptable reason why not?
- How easy will it be to grow, modify, and move segments of these systems?
- Is vendor support available in every location where this technology is installed?
- Is the network compatible with the information formats in current use? Are the communication and information presentation formats required for the pilot project in capability-based work compatible with the installed network resources?
- Is there complementary technology available that will provide the options to use the existing wiring and transmission facilities, or those that offer better cost performance?
- Do the network vendors have an investment strategy that will support growth, flexibility, and performance needs over time?
- Will the life-cycle costs of the system inhibit the growth of the capability-based environment?

○ Is help and adequate support available to ensure availability of the systems?

○ Are all network elements manageable as segments of the total enterprise support system? Do all segments interconnect through a WAN configuration?
(When considering the WAN aspect of the enterprise network, a key element is cost-effective options for integrating multivendor network segments.)

○ Are network segments based on approved or reliable standards?

○ Is the network able to communicate over private or public transmission facilities?

○ Are all network segments easy to change, operate, control, and manage?

○ Are network segments easy to use? (Users should not have to be retrained as the network adapts to new technologies or configurations. The network should appear as part of a seamless information utility to the user.)

○ Are there measures of reliable connectivity and interoperability among work groups using information processing systems from different vendors? (Networks must deliver performance metrics that demonstrate value on an enterprise-wide scale. Look for examples of special software required to interoperate between dissimilar network segments. Check the distribution of support personnel dedicated to interoperability management. Check complaints from users, and service calls to outside vendors for indications of unbalanced activity.)

○ Does the network have artificial limits? (Check if there are outstanding requirements that exist pending new network construction. Look into communication that moves off network: special delivery mail, Federal Express, Telex.)

○ Are new network segments transparent to network users? Will any additional access codes, signaling, or addressing be required to complete a connection because of these additions or modifications? (Look for situations where different vendors are involved, or where nonstandard or proprietary protocols are proposed. Ask qualified vendors if they have experience integrating with the existing protocols in your network.)

○ Will network operations need to develop or procure any new software to interface required network segments into the enterprise system? Where will this effort come from, and will it have to be modified if any other part of the network is changed? (If this situation is indicated, use a life-cycle approach to determine the full cost of the investment. Studies indicate that approximately 60 percent of network ownership costs are contained in the activities and staffs required to provide life-cycle support.)

○ How will new network segments be supported? By whom? How and when can outside support agents be reached to resolve problems? Are there any additional costs associated with the level of support required? (Remember, the capability-based environment needs a twenty-four-hour network day.)

○ Has the business case been completed? Does the business allow sufficient time to amortize the installation and activation cost of this service? (Check whether the requirement has been reviewed by individuals who are responsible for the strategic direction of the enterprise.)

○ Have all stakeholder groups been informed of any other network options that might support their requirement? (Frequently, requirements can be effectively supported with alternative communication solutions: for example, audio or enhanced audio/image conferencing as an alternative to a dedicated full-motion video link.)

○ Will additional training be required for users and support staff?

○ Are any segments of the enterprise network provided by foreign carriers or service suppliers? (Increasingly, foreign network segments have become a fact of life. Where this occurs additional planning is required, and more emphasis must be placed on monitoring and control issues.)

○ Have equipment and service vendors been included in the risk assessment? (Vendors must share the organization's strategic visions and strategies; vendors must demonstrate that their own investment direction will support network system growth and flexibility over time. Network managers must ensure that selected vendors and suppliers are committed and capable of providing worldwide life-cycle service support. Nothing less will do.)

○ Network managers can test a vendor's commitment using the same criteria they apply to their internal decision process. For example, vendors can be asked to reply to questions such as:

Does the proposed investment enhance our connectivity capabilities or make significant improvements in the network's ability to move information regardless of the transmission media in use?

Does the proposed solution improve system integrity and provide easier and more logical integration based on standards compliance? Does it deliver better information throughput, better accuracy, better security, quicker fault isolation, and problem diagnosis?

Will network users find the solution simple, easier to use and comprehend? How are you prepared to ensure user acceptance?

Managing Networking Risk

Networking, for all the reasons discussed in the chapter on networking, frequently strains people's established work styles and comfort zones. Very often what is required for effective networking places individuals in positions that conflict with the very attributes and skills they believe are the foundation of their personal success. For example, the senior executive who achieves consistent results because of the force of his personality in face-to-face meetings may find the lack of visual cues during electronic teleconferences completely destabilizing.

At the heart of the networking adaptation process is the notion of organizational commitment to the capability-based environment. The following questions address risks and barriers to effective networking capability.

O Is the organization committed to the use of electronic information access to improve work processes?
(Look for clear positions articulated by top management indicating why and how the organization must adapt to meet critical objectives and goals. Check for relationships between value-generating work and the information-based capability-based environment, and for synergy between the electronic network and networking applications that unify the enterprise. See if that management has selected pilot projects and that champions have been identified, trained, and given the responsibility and authority needed to demonstrate simultaneous distributed work processes and techniques. Check that test programs have been provided with the means to communicate effectively.

Check that rewards and metrics have been identified and well communicated to all participants and observers.)

○ Is there an approved plan for transition to organizational networking?
(Look for a formal, well-distributed document. Ensure that the plan specifies a design architecture for the network and the work processes. See if an architect has been appointed, someone who has overall responsibility to make decisions and to adjudicate compromises about the communication and information support systems. Ensure that the architecture addresses system growth and change, protects investments, and stimulates networking innovations.)

○ Is the networking design based on customer and user inputs?
(Ensure that all specified goals and objectives have roots in the requirements of customers and the needs of the workers. Examine how these inputs were compiled, and question third-party inputs from vested vendors and industry observers.)

○ Is the organization committed to proactive rather than reactive action?
(Look for references to time and quality management in planning documents and project specifications. Look at the wording and emphasis in vision and goal statements. Check existing work processes for lack of communications media integration in the use of distributed teams, and for the availability of electronic work support applications.)

○ Are there formal training programs for workers dedicated to applications, techniques, and technological resources?
(Look at the training programs for new employees, entry-level management programs, and at special programs for projects and program managers, and determine if the content is appropriate for working in or managing simultaneous distributed work. Look for firsthand experience by the instructors, or if recognized simultaneous distributed work champions are used to clarify and motivate. See if there is senior-level management involvement.)

○ Is there a formal process to reward successful experiments?
(Check how often individuals, teams, or groups are recognized publicly for leadership or participation in a simultaneous distributed work effort. Check on what form the recognition takes: praise, money, or promotion. See how far the recognition extends: groupwide, enterprisewide, or industrywide. Check to see if successful in-

dividuals or teams are encouraged to continue refining their skills and spread their expertise.)

○ To what extent are the key players organized?
(Use an expanded definition of key players: the technology providers and system architects, network managers, and information processing staffs; the organization mission planners, senior business managers, and functional process managers; the simultaneous distributed work community, leaders, workers, customers, suppliers, and collaborators. Determine to what extent key players interact on the design and operation of work processes. Check on the procedure used to approve and implement recommendation of this group. Look at the budget for indications of coordination or disproportionate influence.)

SUMMARY

The realities of the current network environment comprise multiple vendors' products and services, dissimilar operating protocols, conflicting or incomplete standards, insufficient technical support resources, high operating costs, high risks of catastrophic failures, connectivity limits caused by rigid architectures, and restricted growth potential. These make it difficult if not impossible to limit choice to historically preferred solutions.

Risk can best be managed through continuous interaction among stakeholders to make sure that requirements and capabilities are mutually understood. All must understand the capabilities of the network and the factors that limit growth and expansion of services. Clarity at this stage will ensure that both providers and users have accurately set expectations. It is very easy for network professionals to become obsessed with their technologies; conversely, network users become complacent with favorite and comfortable applications. Everyone involved becomes defensive and protective, perhaps even a bit paranoid about change. Experimentation and creativity become associated with risk, and the conventional wisdom is to avoid risk. To avoid stalemate, both sides must stay focused on the evolutionary objectives of the capability-based environment.

Epilogue | Futurework: A Predictive Fantasy

GYREX INTERNATIONAL PROFITS UP
. . . Again! Rey tells why.

—*World Companies Weekly,* July 26, 1995

Recently in Nice, our senior business analyst, Gale Sanders, interviewed Marcel Rey, CEO of Gyrex International. Gyrex is a leading producer of componentry for transportation products and services that we use daily. Gyrex had just announced increased earnings for the third consecutive year. Given the struggles of Gyrex's competitors and leaders in related industries, we thought we'd get the inside word—or some of it at least—on how Gyrex remains consistently profitable.

wcw: Marcel, you've done it—and you've done it again. You've managed to successfully gain market share in a maturing market, while cutting operating expenses substantially. How do you do it?

MR: Well, of course I won't tell you all our secrets. . . . In fact, I won't tell you any secrets, just some obvious truths that we've been paying attention to for the past few years. The simplest truth, of course, is produce faster, better, and cheaper . . .

wcw: . . . and the world beats a path to your door, eh? Everyone knows that, Marcel. But *how* do you work that way, given the rising costs of doing business, time pressures, red-hot worldwide competition . . . all that exponential change we've been hearing about; do you ignore it?

MR: Well, you can't ignore it, but to use your words, you can manage it. What we've done is design our work systems to reflect the realities of our environment, taken advantage of state-of-the-market technology and work methodologies, and always, *always* kept an eye on what we're going to do next—that's how you deal with change.

WCW: Any specifics? As far as we can tell, for example, your engineering, manufacturing, marketing, and sales costs went down, while your research investment stayed pretty flat. Yet you generate the same, even higher, revenues. I know that means you work smarter, but how?

MR: OK, but specific innovations won't make sense until I give some background.

Let's start at the beginning. About five years ago we were experiencing some very difficult times. We had more or less reached the end of what we referred to as our capability pool. Everywhere I turned I heard the same reason, or excuse, for why things were not working out as planned: we need more time, more resources, more tools. On the other hand, we have always invested heavily in technology, automated systems, and applications, all of which were justified on the basis of saving time, resources, and improving the quality of our tools. Most, if not all, of our work processes were based on the exchange of information and, in our case, most of our information was in electronic form. Of course, almost all our management activity was based on passing through paper documents, on endless face-to-face meetings, and on moving people and work through various stages step by step. You know the drill.

Clearly, it was time for us to stop and reconsider the realities of our environment; and that too was pretty clear—the world wanted affordable, higher-quality products, sooner. And markets were fickle; demand shifted in weeks and months, not just years.

The processes we depended on to create our products and services had become more and more complex. The skilled and creative people who solved our problems and supported our customers were stretched to their limit. We decided to find out where we were and to reexamine our goals and plans.

It soon became apparent that we had drifted away from our original vision and burdened ourselves with a great deal of technical, administrative, and bureaucratic overhead. For us, the solution was rather obvious: face the emperor, clothed or not, and figure out what goes, what stays, and what needs to be added or modified.

To get started we created a "change agency," a distributed team chartered to develop a plan that would move us to a new level of capability. We formed the team using individuals who had one dominant virtue: all had succeeded in a project or task that overcame the constraints of our own organization. The concept was to gain objectivity by having representation from a lot of different constituencies. Everyone has a point of view, no one is impartial. But put all these views together and you get what does approximate objectivity.

The team made some insightful observations, did some analysis, and concluded that if we expected to grow and prosper in the global business environment of the nineties, we had no choice but to change. They provided us with a plan, and they demonstrated to me and my senior staff how we had to manage, lead, and demonstrate our total commitment to this process.

Our strategy was to focus on managing time, working effectively in our distributed environment, and measuring every effort we made against new quality standards for our products and services. A big change was to model workflow on simultaneous rather than serial work processes. And I don't mean just sales and marketing or engineering and manufacturing working in parallel; I mean that we looked at every task that produced value in our company and figured out how to perform it simultaneously with other dependent and independent tasks.

WCW: Well, that makes sense in reducing time-to-market; how does that help quality?

MR: Think about it. We do very complex work at Gyrex; the number of interdependencies in tasks and products is enormous. When we do simultaneous work, we sort of force people to watch those interdependencies, those unexpected interactions in real time, not just at intervals when output is integrated.

Here's an example. One of the last stages in developing a stabilizer foil—one of our most complex assemblies—has been to document the installation procedure in various environments. And since you needed both the environment (say, the latest GMX hydrofoil platform) and the component, or product, that task had two major dependencies: it couldn't be done until both environment and stabilizer were, well, stable.

Our customers won't except "dependent" delivery dates for products—they don't care about our dependencies, only about our meeting their expectations for receiving the product. Nor will they fall for the ploy of "here's the stabilizer, installation instructions will follow." Our customers have a business to run too.

So what we've done is put technical writers in place at the very start of the project. They connect electronically, across a network, with our engineering development sites and the companies that manufacture the environments—the vehicles upon which our stabilizers are mounted. Writers, usually situated within a documentation group because they work on multiple projects at once, start the installation documentation at the same time we start designing the product. The documentation, product, and host environment engineering develop simultaneously, the details of each visible to the other groups—no stovepipes, as we call organizational information walls.

WCW: I can see how that saves time, in theory; but you are a worldwide company. Your expertise is scattered across the globe. Corporate finance and marketing, I know, are here in Nice, with engineering and manufacturing done elsewhere in Europe, the United States, and the Far East. How can you sustain the close working relationships you need?

MR: That's where we take advantage of both technology and human work processes. We've become a fully networked company; our data and information are electronic and we move them between people and processes without having to constrain our activities because of time or space differences. We spend a lot of time encouraging communication between people, advocating the teaming paradigm. The thing is, a lot of what we needed was readily available—in networks, in applications, in books, and in people's heads. We just needed our agency to put it together.

In fact, we think it's *better* to work distributed. Now we can instantaneously access knowledge wherever it is, and we can change our resource configuration according to economic, social, or political pressures: labor costs in country X too high, shift load to country Y; best research going on in country Z, bring country Z's universities into the programs, electronically.

WCW: So why doesn't everyone work this way? What's the knothole? Why should Gyrex be riding along on this wave of simultaneous distributed work while a lot of other companies struggle?

MR: First of all, others are working this way. Aerospace, high technology— they opened the door a few years back, and quite a few of us have tried to push it open a bit further. Now it's up to other manufacturing enterprises, hospitals, banks, publishers—and makers of stabilizer platforms. The second point is that this doesn't just happen. Simultaneous distributed work must be designed, and indeed it succeeds because it emphasizes design at all levels of work. You need to take the time to survey what's out there and design the process that fits the needs of your enterprise. We started this five years ago; only in the past couple of years have the results started to be so visible, so predictable, and so good!

WCW: You mentioned universities; are those ties with the academic or educational establishment the reason your company so consistently leads the field with innovation?

MR: Partially. Actually, we try to focus on learning rather than education. As I suggested earlier, we simultaneously address the future as we deal with present projects. We know that in changing environments the next successful product will be different—as will the process needed to create it. So we're always running pilots within our present programs and projects. We pilot and prototype new technologies and work methods as well as product components. We always build our knowledge base, and we keep that knowledge available through designed internal knowledge access systems. We design in the capability base to do future as well as present work. In changing environments the investment makes sense.

Remember, building knowledge is everybody's job—learning and sharing knowledge is as much work as designing a widget or doing budgets. We don't depend on academics alone to build our knowledge base.

WCW: That sounds great, but isn't there resistance to some of these processes? How do people feel about working so closely with "other functions"? How anxious are they to give up their own creativity and accept someone else's innovations? You know—Not Invented Here?

MR: There are so-called cultural problems, but we address them with as much care as we give to the technical side. For example, we have meeting architectures as well as computing architectures: we design an infrastructure to make it easy for people to communicate with each other, face to face or electronically. We've figured out what forms of communication— e-mail, video broadcasts, neutral site meetings—are most appropriate for different information-sharing needs. We train people within our organizations to use and facilitate all these communications events.

So, yes, it does take time for people to adapt to working under the stresses of time compression, constant close interaction with individuals from other functions (cultures), and constant innovation, but we're learning. In fact, we have processes in place for making innovation available to everyone in the enterprise in a nonthreatening way. We make it easy to participate in cross-functional pilots that continuously innovate in both the technological and methods domains. These communities help defuse the competitive "us-and-them" cultural attitude that creates such barriers to information sharing.

WCW: A final question. Does a project ever fail? If so, what do you do?

MR: I have two answers to that. In one sense we fail a lot, because in our model we pilot, prototype, and simulate all aspects of a project—both process and product components—and such pilots work on the principle of learning from failure. Take the installation guide we spoke about earlier: the first few versions were pretty vague and frustrating—downright wrong in some cases. But as more data came in, the document grew from some facts and a lot of guesses to a valid version that reflected the needs and expectations of all the stakeholders. In a way that's "design by failure."

Unplanned failure is different, and occasionally we do that. But we've learned from these failures, too. For example, in most cases we fail—that is, we fall short of expectations for time-to-market, cost, and quality expectations—not because we don't know enough about the product, but because we haven't paid enough attention to project needs—resources, design, communication. What we do when we fail is learn—build capability for the next time. You don't punish failure, you learn from it, building capability for the future.

WCW: Thank you, Marcel. We expect many more great years from Gyrex.

The gateway to competitiveness in the 1990s that Rey referred to is opening wider as more and more organizations push through to capability. We hope that this book has suggested reasons and methods for this transformation to capability; that it has strengthened your appreciation of the value of getting all the heads together, even if they are apart, to do complex work.

Finally, we hope that reading this book will help you contribute to your organization's understanding that success in our new reality depends on developing excellence in our tool systems and human systems, our networks and networking.

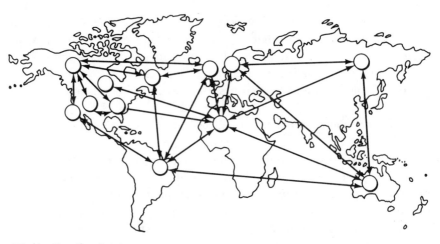

Working Together Apart

References

Ackoff, Russell L. *Creating the Corporate Future: Plan or Be Planned For*. New York: John Wiley, 1981.

Alexander, Christopher. *Notes on the Synthesis of Form*. Cambridge, MA: Harvard University Press, 1964.

Allen, Thomas J. *Managing the Flow of Technology: Technology Transfer and the Dissemination of Technological Information Within the R&D Organization*. Cambridge, MA: MIT Press, 1977.

Angel Heart. An Alan Parker Film, a Winkast-Union Production, 1987.

Argyris, Chris. *Organization and Innovation*. Homewood, IL: R.D. Irwin, 1965.

Argyris, Chris, and Schön, Donald A. *Organizational Learning: A Theory of Action Perspective*. Reading, MA: Addison-Wesley, 1978.

Barber, Paul. *Applied Cognitive Psychology: An Information Processing Framework*. London: Routledge, Chapman & Hall, 1988.

Bartlett, Chris, and Ghoshal, Sumantra. *Managing Across Borders: The Transnational Solution*. Boston: Harvard Business School Press, 1989.

Bloomfield, Leonard. *Language*. Chicago: University of Chicago Press, 1984.

Brooks, Frederick P., Jr. *The Mythical Man Month: Essays on Software Engineering*. Reading, MA: Addison-Wesley, 1975.

Campbell, Jeremy. *Grammatical Man: Information, Entropy, Language and Life*. New York: Simon & Schuster, 1982.

Capra, Fritjof. *The Tao of Physics: An Exploration of the Parallels Between Modern Physics and Eastern Mysticism*. New York: Bantam Books, 1984.

Caswell, Stephen A. *E-Mail*. Toronto: Gage Educational Publishing, 1988.

Cheney, Robert A. *Computer-aided Acquisition and Logistic Support: A Revolutionary Evolution*. North Hampton, NH: EMCA, 1989.

Chisholm, Donald. *Coordination Without Hierarchy: Informal Structures in Multiorganizational Systems*. Berkeley, CA: University of California Press, 1988.

Clausing, Don, and Hauser, John R. "The House of Quality." *Harvard Business Review* (May–June 1988).

Cohen, Allan R., and Bradford, David L. *Influence Without Authority*. New York: John Wiley, 1990.

Cohen, Mark. "Building the Perfect Ballpark." *GQ* (September 1990): 126–128.

Cowan, Robert. *Teleconferencing: Maximizing Human Potential*. Reston, VA: Reston, 1984.

247

Cranch, Edmund T. "Fire Safety," Excerpts from a Presentation at Dartmouth College published by John and Suzette Mcleod, editors of "Simulation in the Service of Society." *Simulation* (December 1989): 305.

Cross, K. Patricia. *Accent on Learning.* San Francisco: Jossey-Bass, 1976.

Davis, Stanley M. *Future Perfect.* Reading, MA: Addison-Wesley, 1988.

De Bono, Edward. *Lateral Thinking: Creativity Step by Step.* New York: Harper & Row, 1970.

Deutsch, Claudia H. "Business Meetings by Keyboard." *The New York Times* (October 21, 1990): IV:25.

Dickens, Charles. *A Tale of Two Cities.* New York: New American Library, 1980.

Diva. A film by Jean-Jacques Beineix, produced by Les Filmes Galaxies and Greenwich Films, 1981.

Drucker, Peter F. *The Frontiers of Management.* New York: Harper & Row, 1986.

Dubinskas, Frank A. *Managing Complexity: Cooperation and Integration in the RA 90 Project.* Unpublished report. Maynard, MA: Digital Equipment Corporation, 1989.

Engelbart, Douglas C., "A Conceptual Framework for the Augmentation of Man's Intellect." In Greif, pp. 35–65.

———. "Authorship Provisions in AUGMENT." In Greif, pp. 107–126.

Engelbart, Douglas C., and Lehtman, Harvey. "Working Together." *BYTE Magazine* (December 1988): 245–252.

Eureka, William, and Ryan, Nancy. *The Customer-Driven Company.* Dearborn, MI: ASI Press, 1988.

Galer, Graham. *Computer Conferencing in a Multinational Company.* Report delivered at the American Association for the Advancement of Science 1990 Annual Meeting.

Glegg, Gordon L. *The Design of Design.* London: Cambridge University Press, 1971.

Goldberger, Paul. "A Radical Idea: Baseball as It Used to Be." *The New York Times* (November 19, 1989): VIII:39.

Greif, Irene, ed. *Computer Supported Cooperative Work: A Book of Readings.* San Mateo, CA: Morgan Kaufmann, 1988.

Guterl, Fred V. "Goodbye Old Matrix." *Business Month* (February 1989): 32–38.

Hoshula, John. "The Baldridge Badge of Courage—and Quality," *The New York Times* (October 21, 1990): VI:12.

Houghton, James R. "The Age of Hierarchy Is Over." *The New York Times* (September 24, 1989): VI:3.

Hout, Thomas M., and Mark F. Blaxill. "Make Decisions Like a Fighter Pilot." *The New York Times* (November 15, 1987): III:3.

Johansen, Robert. *Teleconferencing and Beyond: Communication in the Office of the Future.* New York: McGraw-Hill, 1984.

————. *Groupware: Computer Support for Business Teams*. New York: The Free Press, 1988.

————. "Groupware and Collaborative Systems: A Big Picture View." Report prepared for Globecom '89, IEEE Global Communications Conference, Dallas, November 27–30, 1989.

Kesey, Ken. *One Flew Over the Cuckoo's Nest*. New York: Penguin, 1976.

King, Robert. *Better Designs in Half the Time: Implementing QFD Quality Function Deployment in America*. Methuen, MA: GOAL/QPC, 1988.

Kogut, Bruce. "Designing Global Strategies: Comparative and Competitive Value-Added Chains." *Sloan Management Review* (Summer 1985): 15–28.

Kraut, Robert, and Egido, Carmen. "Patterns of Contact and Communication in Scientific Research Collaboration." In *Proceedings of the Conference on Computer-Supported Cooperative Work, 1988*. New York: ACM, 1988.

Lakoff, George. *Women, Fire, and Dangerous Things: What Categories Reveal About the Mind*. Chicago: University of Chicago Press, 1987.

Lipnack, Jessica, and Stamps, Jeffrey. *How Groups Think* (unpublished.) West Newton, MA: The Networking Institute, 1988.

Machlis, Sharon, "Three Shortcuts to Better Design." *Design News* (November 11, 1990): 89–91.

McCullough, David C. *The Path Between the Seas: The Creation of the Panama Canal, 1870–1914*. New York: Simon & Schuster, 1977.

McLuhan, Marshall. *Understanding Media: The Extensions of Man*. New York: New American Library, 1964.

McWilliams, Gary. "The Big Brouhaha on the Little Juice Box." *Business Week*, (September 17, 1990): 36.

Meyer, N. Dean, and Boone, Mary. *The Information Edge*. New York: McGraw-Hill, 1987.

Moran, Robert T., and Harris, Phillip R. *Managing Cultural Synergy*. International Management Productivity Series, Vol. 2. Houston: Gulf, 1982.

Morgan, Len. "New Age Airbus." *Flying* (May 1990): 42–45.

Neilson, Jacob. *Hypertext and Hypermedia*. San Diego, CA: Academic Press, 1990.

Nelson, Theodore H. *Literary Machines: The Report on, and of, Project Xanadu Concerning Word Processing, Electronic Publishing, Hypertext, Thinkertoys, Tomorrow's Intellectual Revolution, and Certain Other Topics Including Knowledge, Education and Freedom*. Ann Arbor, MI: XOC, 1981.

Nussbaum, Bruce, and Templeman, John. "Built to Last—Until It's Time to Take Apart." *Business Week* (September 17, 1990): 102–106.

Odiorne, George. The *Change Resisters: How They Prevent Progress and What Managers Can Do About Them*. Englewood Cliffs, NJ: Prentice-Hall, 1981.

Parker, Lorne A., and Olgren, Christine H. (eds.). *Teleconferencing and Interactive Media*. University of Wisconsin Extension Center for Interactive Studies, 1980.

Pascale, Richard Tanner. *Managing on the Edge*. New York: Simon & Schuster, 1990.

Pava, Calvin, *Managing New Office Technology: An Organizational Strategy*. New York: The Free Press, 1983.

Petroski, Henry. *To Engineer Is Human: The Role of Failure in Successful Design*. New York: St. Martin's Press, 1982.

Porter, Michael. *The Competitive Advantage of Nations*. New York: The Free Press, 1990.

Porter, Robert. *The Practical Guide to Joint Ventures & Corporate Alliances*. Quoted in *IEEE Engineering Management Review* (September 1990.)

Postman, Neil. *Conscientious Objections: Stirring Up Trouble About Language, Technology, and Education*. New York: Knopf, 1988.

Quarterman, John S. *The Matrix: Computer Networks and Conferencing Systems*. Bedford, MA: Digital Press, 1990.

Reddy, W. Brendan, and Jamison, Kaleel (eds.). *Team Building*. Alexandria, VA: NTL Institute for Applied Behavioral Science, 1988.

Reichheld, Frederick, and Sasser, W. Earl, Jr. "Zero Defections: Quality Comes to Services." *Harvard Business Review* (September–October 1990).

Robbins, Harvey. *Turf Wars: Moving from Competition to Collaboration*. Glenview, IL: Scott Foresman, 1990.

Rohan, Thomas J. "Designer/Builder Teamwork Pays Off." *Industry Week* (October 7, 1989): 45–46.

Sabbagh, Karl. *Skyscraper*. New York: Viking, 1990.

Savage, Charles. *Fifth Generation Management: Integrating Enterprises Through Human Networking*. Bedford, MA: Digital Press, 1990.

Schein, Edgar H. *Organizational Culture and Leadership*. San Francisco: Jossey-Bass, 1985.

Schrage, Michael. *Shared Minds: The New Technologies of Collaboration*. New York: Random House, 1990.

Schwartzman, Helen B. *The Meeting: Gatherings in Organizations and Communities*. New York: Plenum, 1989.

Scott, William B. "YF-23A Previews Design Features of Future Fighters." *Aviation Week & Space Technology* (July 2, 1990): 16–21.

Senge, Peter M. *The Fifth Discipline: The Art & Practice of the Learning Organization*. New York: Doubleday, 1990.

———. "The Leader's New Work: Building Learning Organizations." *Sloan Management Review* (Fall 1990).

Shneiderman, Ben. *Software Psychology: Human Factors in Computer and Information Systems*. Cambridge, MA: Winthrop, 1980.

Shuster, David H. *Teaming for Quality Improvement*. Englewood Cliffs, NJ: Prentice-Hall, 1990.

Smith, Bill. *Motorola Six-Sigma*. Videotape presented at Digital Equipment Corporation, December 1989.

Smith, John B., and Weiss, Stephen F. (guest ed.). *Communications of the ACM*, Vol. 31, No. 7 (July 1988).

Sonneborn, Marcene, and Wilemon, David. "Sustaining Innovativeness in Emerging High-Technology Companies." *IEEE Engineering Management Review* (September 1990): 6.

Stamps, Jeffrey S. *Holonomy: A Human Systems Theory.* Seaside, CA: Intersystems Publications, 1980.

Sterne, Laurence. Great Books of the Western World, Vol. 36, (Mortimer J. Adler, ed.). *The Life and Opinions of Tristram Shandy, Gent.* Chicago: 1955.

Strassman, Paul. *Information Payoff: The Transformation of Work in the Electronic Age.* New York: The Free Press, 1985.

Takeuchi, Hirotaka, and Nonaka, Ikiyiro. "The New New Product Development Game." *Harvard Business Review* (1986).

Taylor, Thayer C. "How the Game will Change in the 1990s," an interview with Andrew Parsons in *Sales & Marketing Management* (June 1989): 52.

"These Computer 'Printers' Spit Out Molds." *Business Week* (September 10, 1990): 99.

Treacy, Michael E., *The Costs of Network Ownership.* Index Group, Inc., Five Cambridge Center, Cambridge, MA 02142.

Ulrich, Jim. "Fast-Track Design of a Complex Motherboard." *High Performance Systems* (December 1989): 79–84.

Vallée, Jacques. *Messengers of Deception.* Reading, MA: Addison-Wesley, 1979.

Welter, Theresa. "The Genesis of Product Design." *Industry Week* (October 16, 1989): 16–22.

———. "How to Build and Operate a Product Design Team." *Industry Week* (April 16, 1990): 35–58.

Whitney, Daniel E., "Manufacturing by Design." *Harvard Business Review* (1989).

Winner, Robert I, Pennell, James P., et al. *The Role of Concurrent Engineering in Weapons System Acquisition.* Alexandria, VA: Institute for Defense Analysis (December 1988).

Worth, Sol, and Adair, John. "Navaho Filmmakers," *American Anthropologist,* Vol. 72, No. 1 (1970): 9–34.

Zuboff, Shoshana. *In the Age of the Smart Machine: The Future of Work and Power.* New York: Basic Books, 1988.

Index

253